LIBERATION OF MUSLIM WOMEN

LIBERATION OF MUSLIM WOMEN

NASEEM AHMAD

PUBLICATIONS

KALPAZ PUBLICATIONS

DELHI-110 052

Liberation of Muslim Women
(Religion, Women)

ISBN: 81-7835-070-X

Published in 2001 in India by
Kalpaz Publications
C-30 Satyawati Nagar
Phase-III Ashok Vihar
Delhi-1100 52

Lesser Typesetting : Com Biz Online, Delhi-110 002

Printed At: Mehra Offset Press

Contents

Preface

Contradictory to the common belief, women enjoy a special status and protected rights in Islam. In fact, Islamic law (Shariat) provides with an iron cover around them against all sorts of exploitation and safeguards them from being instrumental in the hands of men. Needless to say that most of our societies, including societies in the Muslim World are practically male-dominated.

There is a wave of women's lib all over the world and the Islamic (or Muslim) world is not far behind. Be that Egypt, Turkey. Indonesia, Malaysia or Pakistan, there one notices the fair sex taking part in all activities and contributing its mite to the national cause in all walks of life. Moreover, there are strong women-lib movements in all these countries. Even in Iran—which is considered to be a closed society—now women are even members of legislatures, not to talk of their role in education, media, and other spheres.

The fundamental motive behind scribing these pages, that follow, has been to correct a wrong belief and remove a misconception - which have fortunately been widely accepted — that Islam does not entitle women to all rights, legal, human and moral — at par with man. Truely speaking, according to the book, Islam bestows all these rights on women — even right to property and right to seek divorce.

Although it's not possible to cover all the aspects of this vast subject, in a volume of a few hundred pages, yet I have tried to study the whole issue in the right earnest and present it in a proper perspective, in order to make the whole matter, as transparent, as possible.

I don't claim this frail book of mine would cause a sea change in society here, still I'll thank God and feel contented, if the readers may have an access to a right line of thinking, regarding the issue. Even, if that much happens, I'll take it as the success of the endeavour, encouraging me to go ahead with my academic pursuit.

Naseem Ahmad

Shahjehanabad
(Delhi)
May, 2001

Introduction

Because of the pressure of many forces every country of the Moslem East, as we have seen, shows some trend of change in the relationship between religion and life. The control of Islam as an ironclad system of rules and traditions is giving way to a more individual interpretation of religion. Since this new spirit of religious liberalism deeply affects the life of women, one constantly feels the desire to know the personal attitude of Moslem women toward their religion, and their share in determining the new religious thought in Islam.

The older generation as a whole in every country tends to be conservative in all religions but this is especially true of Islam. This unquestioning adherence to the literal interpretation of the teaching of their religion is especially characteristic of women in the middle and lower levels of society, regardless of age, and also of the village women of Asia. This great majority of Moslem women, who have remained untouched by Western influence, have been little conscious of any changes in Islam, and have themselves undergone no change in their religious outlook. In fact, they constitute very often a distinct deterrent to change, opposing any deviation from established social customs, which are in their minds identified with religious sanctions. It is very often the orthodox wife or mother who maintains the rigid conservatism of the home, however lax men may become in their observance of religious customs outside the home.

The full meaning of Islam for the devoted Moslem woman is difficult for a mere outsider to understand. This is one veil of Moslem life which the Western observer cannot lift. Accustomed to a different form of religious experience, one from the West may easily draw a false conclusion regarding the relationship of Moslem women to their religion. The small number of women in the mosques in most countries -Turkey is an exception-which offers a striking contrast cc to the usual predominance of women in churches in the West, might be interpreted as a lack of worship of Moslem women, if one did not know that it is not the public prayers in the mosque but her private prayers at home which have primary significance for the Moslem woman. In her home the orthodox women will pray, with her face turned toward Mecca, five times daily in the name of the Prophet to the one God, and will cherish the devout hope as a constant follower of Mohammed, that she may make the pilgrimage to the Holy City.

The keynote of the Moslem woman's religion is complete acquiescence to fate; to protest against a lack of privileges is quite foreign to her nature. Islam may have deprived her of privileges but not of responsibilities. Her primary obligation is to accept as the will of Allah, whatever is written on her forehead" as her fate. This spirit of fatalism has insured the undisturbed control of Islam over the destiny of Moslem women through the centuries. Today, although the great majority of Moslem women have remained unchanged in their personal attitude toward their religion, a small minority of women has begun to question the relationship between the accepted teaching of Islam and the demands of their modern world. Education inevitably is undermining the characteristic attitude of fatalism toward religion and life. One begins to find in the different parts of the Islamic world Moslem women expressing an independent opinion of the interpretation of Islam, in order to bring religion into accord with modern needs.

Modern Muslim Women V/s Islamic Institution

In speaking of purdah in a public address, Lady Abdul Qadir, one of the outstanding Moslem leaders of India, said: "Purdah, as observed among certain classes of Indian Mohammedans, is far beyond anything enjoined by Islam -and requires modification according to the needs of the day and the rapidly changing times."' Another interesting illustration of the modern approach to Islam by a Moslem woman in India is the aggressive challenge to the Ulemas, the authorities of Islam, made by Begum Habibullah, an enlightened Moslem leader in Lucknow in a newspaper article, in which she showed that the Koran does not teach educational inequality and segregation of women.

Indian women are deeply imbued with religion, but their religious devotion today does not cloud the vision of the educated minority, nor even of a larger number, so that they cannot discriminate between religious and social questions. The widespread testimony against child-marriage gathered from Indian women of all classes by the Age of ass came as a great surprise Consent Commission, doubtless to many in India and eleswhere who had not realized that there is a. Growing spirit of religious freedom among Indian women. The All-India Women's Conference, representing as it does the inter-communal effort of women leaders to release social reform from the bonds of religious tradition, has repeatedly given utterance to the new religious liberalism. In India, more than in any other country of the East, women have been impelled to protest individually and collectively against social handicaps. The active promotion and support of the Child Marriage Act, and the repeated resolutions against polygamy passed by the All-India Women's Conference, are exerting a powerful force toward the freedom of Hindu and Moslem women from these and other social customs, hitherto regarded as determined by religious sanctions.

The fact that women have challenged the inviolability of these sanctions is perhaps no less important than the social reforms themselves. Some Indian leaders are especially concerned to keep their endorsement of social advance in harmony with religious teaching. In the discussion on polygamy at a recent 'All-India Conference, one of the Moslem delegates explained that she favoured the abolition of polygamy, but she wished to call attention to the fact that "it was permitted by their religion only in case of strictest necessity arising, as for example, in the event of there being no issue from the first marriage.

Muslim Women V/s Islam in Islamic Countries

Syria offers an interesting example of an interpretation of the social teachings of the Koran, made by a young Druse girl, Nazira Zein-el-Din, in her book, As-Sufur-Weel-Hijab (Unveiling and Veiling), which evoked much comment. This book was translated into several languages, widely circulated, and brought the author a trunkful of clippings from all over the world. The Islamic teaching concerning the veil was discussed also in an oratorical contest at the American University of Beirut by Madame Ihsan Shakir El-Kousy, to whom reference has already been made. In her address, which received the second prize, she showed that the Koran does not prescribe the veil. Thus incidentally she justified her own presence unveiled in a large university.

These two examples, however, are not typical of the women of either Syria or Egypt as a whole ' but less so of Syria. There is very little evidence of any analysis of Islam and very little articulate expression on religion by women in Syria: a very small minority of Egyptian women is actively interested in the relation of religion to reform. The attitude of Madame Sharawi Pasha, to whom reference has already been made as the outstanding Moslem woman leader in Egypt, shows general conformity to the prevailing policy in Egypt as regards the promotion of social advance. She has carefully based her demands for social reform on the spirit of the Koran and has not promoted reforms which do not have Islamic sanction. For example her claims for equality of education for girls have been based on the teaching of the Koran. She has urged a law prohibiting polygamy. Reference has been made in an earlier chapter to her very effective protest against polygamy in a public lecture at the American University in Cairo last year. But while protesting against polygamy she recognizes the exceptions for polygamy which are granted by the Koran (adultery, childlessness and incompatibility). One has the feeling that this policy of maintaining a careful balance between Islamic teaching and social reform, which is followed by Madame Sharawi and the Feminist Union, is dictated more by political expediency than by religious conservatism.

Among the women of Palestine no deviation from the conventional attitude toward Islam is evident. Moslem women simply reflect the prevailing religious conservatism. However, the interesting feature in the situation, to which reference has already been made in another connection, is that Moslem women pay the price for this conservatism, of which the veil is the symbol, willingly and with a sense of pride; since by retaining the characteristic Islamic c-customs they feel that they have a certain distinction in contrast to the Zionist community. It is worth recalling the incident showing the counter-influence of Arab national feeling in reference to the veil, when the, group of Arab women unveiled made a protest against Zionism. But as already explained, the veils were later resumed when the habitual spirit of conservatism reasserted itself. The great majority of Moslem women in Palestine, as elsewhere, are not aware of the new conflicting currents of thought.

The attitude of women in Iran and Iraq toward religion, as toward social advance, is one of passive acquiescence. Changes in Turkey have aroused much interest in both countries, and the Turkish method of drastic social and religious reforms has been little questioned in reference to its having an adverse effect on religion. The women of Iraq and 1ran have been primarily interested in the achievement of Turkey. Very often in Iraq I heard the statement: "We need a Kamal Ataturk." In Iran the hope was frequently expressed at the time of my visit several years ago, that the Shah would follow Kamal Ataturk's example and issue an order to remove the chaddur. In Iran as elsewhere it was erroneously believed that unveiling in Turkey had been made compulsory. This hope has now been realized and, it is interesting to note, that the definite regulations against the chaddur have not apparently caused a widespread religious shock among the women of Iran. Even the conservatives are accepting the new freedom, I have been told, as they accepted the former social restrictions, in an attitude of acquiescence.

In marked contrast to the attitude of women in Iraq and Iran toward Turkey, Moslem women in India have repeatedly asked me with deep solicitude whether Turkey had cast aside Islam. "Have Turkish women lost their religion?" Was the question that came alike from the student group and from conservative older women. The new freedom of Turkish women, if secured at the sacrifice of religion, would seem to Moslem women in India to have cost too high a price.

In Turkey women have regarded religious changes together with all other changes, as merely a natural part of the general transformation taking place in Turkish life. There has been remarkably little analysis of the new situation in reference to the effect on religion. During the first crucial years of change the conservatives retained the veil, which older women doubtless associated with religion. But by this time the veil has, I believe, for the great majority lost any religious significance it may have had. However, recent municipal legislation of Adana and some other cities, has doubtless brought a shock to those who still have the feeling of the relationship between the veil and Islam. But they will probably accept the enforced change philosophically, as did a conservative Turkish woman in Adana, whose comment on the new regulation was: "Well, the sin will be charged against those who issued such an order and not against us, because they are forcing us to do this against our wills." This idea that unveiling is an actual sin, is probably held by very few Turkish women today.

The viewpoint of these orthodox Turkish women can scarcely fail to be affected unconsciously by the modern atmosphere, which has become steadily more natural, even in the smaller towns of the Interior. The new type of preaching of the hodjah has also had its effect. As a simple Turkish woman in Talas told me several years ago, "They tell us different things about religion today. The hodjahs formerly taught that women must always be veiled and their voice never heard in public. But they say now that these things are not religion." Thus the most orthodox women have been steadily exposed to the new idea, that social customs are not necessarily identified with religion.

The educated Turkish woman has adopted such new ideas as a logical part of the modernization of Turkish life. Before the recent period of reform this educated minority was already progressive in religious thinking for, as has already been mentioned in the discussion of Turkish education, the social-religious revolution in Turkey was preceded by a gradual period of preparation. Today due to many forces there is said to be a decline in the formal practices of Islam. "Many people no longer pray five times a day. Everyone is too busy," was the comment of a young Turkish business woman. A young teacher explained why comparatively few young people go to the mosques. "We must make our worship more modern to suit our modern clothes and customs. Praying without shoes and with many genuflections was a good thing in the Prophet's day but does not suit our present kind of life."

Although the Private prayers of the formal type are still continued by many Moslem women in the homes and to a lesser extent in the mosque, as has always been the case among women, the turning away from the ritualistic worship by the younger generation is undoubtedly a marked present-day tendency. However, this should not, as has been said before, be interpreted merely as a trend toward irreligion, but perhaps it may indicate the genuine urge for a reform in worship, so that it may be something more than a prescribed ceremonial. "We are beginning to recognize the difference between essentials and nonessentials," a thoughtful Turkish woman said. "The religious forms and social restrictions are not suitable today. These can be changed without destroying our fundamental belief."

Another Turkish leader, talking with a Moslem woman from Jerusalem, who had expressed the belief that Turkey had sacrificed Islam, said, "We have separated religion from externals and made it personal. Religion is not a matter of clothes-the veil and the fez. It is not based on form but feeling. The repudiation of Islamic formalism therefore does not mean giving up Islam. The women of Palestine may be more outwardly religious in the orthodox sense of Islam but not necessarily more truly religious in the inner meaning of the term than are the women of Turkey."

In regard to this transfer of emphasis from the external to the more individual idea of religion, a young Turkish woman student in Istanbul University expressed the opinion that there is need now for a more positive interpretation of religion. "Most of the younger Turkish girls will grow up with very little idea of Islam," she said, "since nothing positive has taken the place of the old forms, which have lost their appeal, and since very little attention these days is paid to religion." The need for a more definite constructive idea of religion is probably not as yet generally recognized by the younger generation in Turkey, which associates religion merely with a peaceful existence of quiet contemplation in the shade of mosque walls and not with an intensely active modern life.

However, a number of thoughtful Turkish leaders, both men and women, but perhaps especially women, are beginning to realize the need of a new relationship between religion and life. It is, I believe, not too much to expect that Turkish women, who have gained so much from the social and religious reforms in Turkey, may now make some special contribution to the rethinking of religious values. Their voice, and the voice of Moslem women in other countries, which have been so little heard in shaping religious thought in the past, may help to answer the crucial question in the East today, as to whether the present spirit of religious liberalism in the Moslem world will mean the disintegration of Islam or the beginning of a new era of more vital faith.

1
Islamic Social Order

Political themes, either related to leadership, political parties or social control, are essential aspects at communal rituals in Islamic Iran, along with ethical themes on justice, equality, power and empowerment. A ritual symbol may stand for many things at the same time. By this he means that one must consider the informant's explanation of the socio-structural implication of the treatment and usage of ritual objects in performance, as well as the spatial and hierarchical positioning of ritual objects independent of exegesis and usage. At the women's Quranic meetings, the female preacher often went into great detail to clarify the complexity of various issues and examples. She played an important role, not only in teaching women the correct performance of prayers and Islamic rules, but also in teaching how to understand surrounding political events.

The degrees of political involvement and political rhetoric of preachers were distinguished both symbolically and through actual request. This can be deduced from the distinctive personal, social, and political views expressed in the context of sermons and the participant definition. It was not unusual to find that a ritual was performed and interpreted by different preachers in a slightly different manner, depending on the political and educational background of the preachers.

A woman volunteer started distributing *mohr* (the clay of *Karbela)* to each participant, and as the reading approached the verses requiring the performance of the two units of *sajdeh,* we laid our foreheads on the assumed clay of Karbala, and repeated the verse read by the preacher loudly. The preacher asked those who were menstruating to leave the meeting and stay outside where they could not hear the sound of the verses. This created an unpleasant situation for those women who were obliged to leave the room, and some preferred to leave the meeting altogether.

There are explicit differences in the flexibility of a preacher's interpretations and views regarding women's act of purity and veiling. First it is a matter of social and ritual obedience, and secondly it is a matter of ritual in its cognitive sense, and not a problem of a social nature. In several meetings it became clear that the *hezbullahi* preacher was distinguished by the participants as one who made repetitive and restrictive references to women's rigid veiling and conventional behaviour. This was contrasted by the modesty of the politically neutral preacher (*bi-taraf*), who took a more moderate view.

Some meetings were conservative, as judged by factors such as the number of women wearing head-scarves under their *chador*, the content of the Quranic commentary given by the female preacher, and the repetitive offering of the blessing (*salvat*) to Imam Khomeini; and his successor, and president Rafsanjani. The negative term *monafeqin,* which means conspiracy, is a strong multivocal symbol conveying various messages and contrasting attributes concerning a series of illegitimate social and political divisions. *Monafeqin* may refer not only simply to good and evil, but also to state political norms, such as the Iranian case of women who are poorly veiled, as well as to any act of political resistance.

Ideological Content of Quranic Commentary

The preacher Zaki usually stopped reciting after every short verse *(ayeh)* to offer a commentary. She was one of the preachers who thought it better not to continue before ensuring that the participants had a proper understanding of what was being read. She translated the Quranic meaning into a daily context, thereby making its realisation more practical for the participants, who were from various social categories (the majority being housewives and young schoolgirls). The preacher maintained that the kind of suppressions one could experience varied, and convincingly demonstrated this point by the use of metaphors. The reality of one's experience of 'suppression' was open to interpretation.

According to the preacher Zaki Islamic suppression may be related both to the lack of juridical teachings concerning the rights of men and women and to being a good Muslim in practical terms according to legitimate Islamic codes. Public lessons on juridical matters were often brief, and in response to complicated questions the preachers might postpone answering to make further inquiries from a more learned religious person, such as a male or female *mujtahed*. The metaphor of suppression continued on another level in another Quranic meeting a few days later. This time it was raised by the preacher Mostafi, who defined suppression as acts of political tyranny, and as something that could be harmful to the whole Muslim community.

The *rowzeh* participants were familiar with the name of Salman Rushdie 94 and the Islamic state's political fight against him. He was understood to have committed an act of blasphemy by denying the existence of God and the legitimacy of Muhammad as his Prophet. The preacher Mostafi wishing him a misfortune *(nefrin),* and punishment by hanging. Some of the attendants supported her statement by saying *amen.* The metaphorical references of suppression and the model of corrupt leadership were two on-going political themes in mass media. They were phrased according to the Islamic state dominant political view.

However, on one occasion it was clear that the preacher lacked accurate knowledge of the international political situation, but was familiar with the Islamic state's political rhetoric. For example, on one occasion the preacher Mostafi referred to the both CIA (American Intelligence Service) and KGB (Soviet Intelligence Service) as the American secret service without anybody making any attempt to correct her. This did not prevent her from conveying the desired political message to her listeners, as she accused these international agencies of 'suppression', in their attempts to undermine the Iranian Revolution and its Islamic virtue.

A suppressor of poorly-veiled women The identities of 'poorly-veiled' and 'non-veiled' (bi-hejab) despite their wearing Islamic suits (manto), have emerged in conservative political slogans, condemning the degree of immodesty among women. Posters covering streets walls, with slogans such as 'death to *bi-hejab* and *bad-hejab',* attach a negative label to women who neglect to veil themselves fully.

'Poorly-veiled' is a negative term applied to those whose appearance and social manner may be defined as fashionable, tempting and provocative; i.e. to those wearing colourful scarves, light colours, fashionable styles, make-up, transparent stockings, etc. This is considered a political act of *monafeqin,* and is generally applied on those who are believed to oppose and destroy Islamic values, instead invoking perversion. The negative image of a poorly-veiled woman as a suppressor of the Islamic community has developed through religious speeches. This is further illustrated by the case of a widow who arranged the votive meeting of *anam,* in order to mark the annual remembrance ceremony for her husband. Close and distant relatives, as well as friends and local women, gathered for the meeting.

The female preacher Mostafi frequently paused to interpret Quranic recitations, and whenever she came to the term *monafeqin* (conspirators), she explained it in terms of external and internal enemies of Islam. She also included women who wore thin stockings together with Islamic suits, for being 'provocative' and modem in style. Furthermore, she accused women who failed to dress properly of weakening the ideology of the revolution, and repeatedly saluted the martyrs *(shohada)* and prisoners of war *(asiran)* with the verse of *salvat.* She unexpectedly addressed the married daughter of the house, a university lecturer who was serving tea to the attendants, asking her to stop serving to allow the audience to concentrate on the sermon.

After the ceremony some participants believed the preacher had become cross with her on account of the way she was dressed. The initiator of the *rowzeh* complained that she was very disappointed, and that the memorial ceremony for her husband had been used for political ends, which was an insult to his memory. She regretted not having invited another female preacher whom she knew herself, rather than this one who had been recommended by her religiously 'orthodox' sister.

An another example of being an Islamic

conspirator, the preacher Zaki cited shopkeepers, who would hoard goods *(ahtekar)* and sell things at inflated prices. Economic gains at the expense of those Muslim customers who are in a financially difficult situation was considered an unmeritful act during their fife of permanent economic well-being. Such undertakings were categorised as illegitimate (*haram*), because the aim was solely to accumulate capital.

Despite hoarding being described in official terms as acts of immorality and corruption, businessmen increasingly adopted it as a new avenue for economic success. These Islamic lessons not only suggest the moral identity of authority at the level of family, community and state, but the way they can be corrupted and distract communal social order. Disagreement was expressed among attendants in private religious meetings either as defenders or against the preacher. Although women seemed reluctant to counter the Islamic state policy directly, they often did so metaphorically. They often felt more free to express themselves outside the religious meetings when talking to a friend, to me, or to relatives.

Once, in the month of Ramazan in 1989, and during a regular lesson concerning the performance of prayer, an older participant interrupted the preacher Mostafi and asked the following question: 'I wonder how it can be an act of *halal* (permission) to perform the prayers of *namaz* on the floor of a house, which has been a forcefully confiscated property (*qasbi*)?' This was not simply a ritual question, but had numerous connotations for participants, who could clearly explain the political issue the questioner had in mind. This created a funny situation, and some smiled slightly at the preacher who could not give a proper answer, and thus postponed it in order to make further inquires. On another occasion, also at a meeting held by preacher

Mostafi, and following the month of Ramazan, a participant expressed her disagreement on the ethical lesson concerning a Muslim duty, saying: 'I wonder how it can be a sinful act to ask why the price of potatoes has increased so rapidly?' The preacher had repeatedly said that in order not to disturb the ongoing operation of the Islamic state, we should avoid any kind of criticism.

A politically reserved attitude, and a symbolic mode of expression, are more common than ever before in Iranian everyday culture, due to the social and political burden. Thus, in the meeting of rowzeh, some of the preachers, either as a matter of personal loyalty to the state, or as a way of avoiding politically sensitive issues, may fail to answer 'improper' questions, and cut them short with a *salvat.* The contradiction between the actual political economy of Islamic states and Quranic notion of *zulm* gives a false representation of ideal religious values. Some middle-class and educated participants were more sensitive to speaking up, and expressing such a distortion.

The political opposition between questioner and preacher could be stated metaphorically. In response to the direct and critical political questions, which a preacher could accept as reasonable, she may excuse herself from answering by giving the impression of not being bothered with such issues. She might request her listeners to recite a *salvat so* to avoid answering the question before inviting the participants to continue the ritual of reading the Quranic verse for the day or before resuming her *tafsir.*

The political overtone of the male preacher at the mosque was even more direct, and covered broader political and social matters to a larger audience. Some considered that the political link to rituals would reduce the 'true' value of Islam. For this reason some hosts were reluctant to listen to or invite, any preacher.

The Quranic term of *efrat-va-tafrit* (too much and too little), is often used by disappointed religious participants, such as Narges, about situations where local events overlap political and religious commitments. Political intrusion is frequently given as the reason for the loss of one's former religious belief, and the loss of sacred traditional religious symbols in general. Nezhat, a regular religious participant at private meetings, felt disturbed by the political overload in everyday religious activities. She found the regular Quranic recording from our neighbouring mosque loudspeaker disturbing and tiresome. She telephoned anonymously, asking the authorities to turn down the volume of the loudspeaker because she had a sick relative at home.

The connection between the ethical conduct of women's daily behaviour and the entire order of nature was often an element in the Islamic speeches of the preacher. The negative publicity given to unveiled women in the religious arena by male and female preachers was often the cause of public ideological conflict. In an anthropological study of a Muslim community in Tunisia, the rain ritual at the time of drought is described as an act of penance and a rite of reconciliation by which the members of the community are 'purified' and reincorporated.

In the context of the urban Shirazi, misfortunes or natural disorder are not only defined as a basis for community solidarity, but also as a metaphor for disagreement and political hostility between social categories, e.g. between the Islamic conservatism and the more liberal middle-class Muslim believers. In day-to-day social situations ideological differences have become aspects of individuals' social identities, frequently leading to conflict, and in extreme cases to public violence such as in 1989. The concept of *mosibat* or *bala* denotes misfortune as a result of too much sin. Sin is destructive to individual wellbeing and is believed to create social and ecological disorder, with drought as a consequence.

The idea is that God is angered by ingratitude, arrogance, immoral behaviour, and particularly by non-veiling. Heavy rain and drought are both believed to be caused by social disaster *(bala),* bringing negative consequences to the whole community. In March 1989, in daily Ramazan lessons, the preacher Zaki raised the unveiling question as usual. This time an attendant supported her view and defined it as a cause of a recent natural misfortune. Reproduction of Islamic order in ongoing political, social, and economic life has produced a new form of cultural complexity which is acted out in various social arenas such as religious meetings.

Women's Prayer Lessons

In addition to the reciting of the Qur'an and its commentary, there is also reading from the book of *Tawzih al-Masa'il"* (clarifying ritual problems) and the giving of prayer instructions at the religious meetings. The *Tawzih al-Masa'il,* in Persian, is the kind of book which may be found in the home of a student in a Quranic class. The women's lessons of prayers *(mas'aleh-go'i) is* central to each Quranic meeting, and is often performed by a leader of the Quranic seminaries or a preacher.

The preacher will spend approximately 15 minutes out of the 2-4 hour meeting on instructions. The instructions are most often performed in the beginning, but sometimes also at the end. The female preacher, her assistant, or the religiously 'learned' give the instructions to the participants. Some of the participants use the free minutes in the middle or at the end of the *rowzeh* meeting to put their personal questions to the preacher, being ashamed to speak about some family and sexual matters in the presence of others.

The preacher, or ritual expert, referred a question to the local male preacher, or postponed her answer, as she herself was in doubt about the correct answer. The lessons concerning the performance of prayers deal with questions closely related to the women's need to carry out the ritual as it is generally prescribed, particularly in the month of Ramazan. The dominant themes are the fast, the purification for prayers, alternative and compensation prayers, alms, and various forms of ablution (such as for death, *namaz-e mayet*).

The other themes are compensation for prayers neglected or not performed for physical reasons such as menstruation, of *sigheh, of mahram* and non-mahram, of *zakat* (religious tax), of abortion, and of illegitimate property. The lessons of prayers are largely concerned with ethical and personal matters. The question of the prayers and the matters which could lead to its break, e.g. praying in a house, or touching objects classified as unlawful property, were dominant themes in the religious lessons. The lesson of prayers is not simply about giving and taking. More importantly it provides an atmosphere for the preacher, ritual experts and audience to expound the prayers and the interpersonal norms of Islam, as well as its theology and sociology, in an informal manner.

Ablution

In course of the lessons on ritual purity and impurity (*najes* and *taher), obligatory* prayers *(vajeb),* merciful acts (mostahab), and illegitimate objects or acts *(haram),* the preacher would often go into detail about the social, sexual and psychological problems women might experience. The aim was to instruct and correct their rituals of prayer. The female preacher often went into great detail to clarify the complexity of questions, by reading to the participants from the book of *Tawzih al-Masa'il,* as well as quoting stories, telling a relevant narrative, and citing examples from day-to-day social and political life. The extent of an individual's sin and religious debt is emphasised in social and psychological terms with reference to whether the act could be considered intentional or unintentional. These are two central Islamic juridical concepts that determine performing a correct religious duty.

The quality of an individual's ritual is evaluated in terms of impure and pure objects, and permitted and forbidden acts. Unintentional neglect of obligatory prayers is not considered the fault of person and is thought to be excused by God. For example, failure to comply with the ritual prayer is said to be acceptable if the reason is humanitarian, such as saving a child.

Menstruation, pregnancy and childbirth are considered arbitrary and natural causes, and are thus considered as legitimate reasons for not performing ritual prayers, but the women are still expected to undertake some form of compensation prayers at another time. This debt of prayers may be performed during one's lifetime, or they can remain a personal duty of another family member after a person's death. These are ritual services that may be purchased, that is, a spiritual man is paid to perform prayers on behalf of a dead relative. The living are obliged to perform the neglected ritual in the form of a substitute prayer, or in the form of fasting, when they have recovered.

When water is not available for performing ablution it may be replaced by earth and sand. Dust is substituted for water to allow flexibility and continuity in the praying ritual. In this case the prayer performed is incomplete, or so-called 'half performed', and is made in a sitting position. This also applies for very sick people who remain in bed. Such alternatives are not considered appropriate for a healthy person, but are most common among people who travel a lot and who therefore are unable to perform their prayer in the prescribed form. The religious meetings often place a high priority on women's debt to God and after-life. For example, women who fast are advised not to submit to their husband's sexual demands. Sexual abstinence signifies a purity of one's obligatory prayers over the sexual desires of the husband.

Very often the subject concerning the ritual ethic is raised as an important condition to its performance. For example, the act of praying is said not to gain full merit if the worshipper refrains from wearing 'pure' and proper clothing, or if the ritual is not performed on a lawfully owned property. The interpretation of correct prayers does not ignore the present lifestyle and economic situation. For example, once a question was raised as to how one could perform the ritual of daily prayer on the airplane, or while travelling from one town to another.

Another example concerns the intentional or unintentional act of consuming food when this is prohibited. The former state applies when one is tempted to eat in secrecy, forgetting that God is a witness; the latter applies when one's health is threatened and requires the breaking of the fast. Those guilty of ignoring such a moral issue and ignoring God as witness not only lose merit, but also perform sin.

In fact, some particularly orthodox women may practise the ritual of fasting to an extent where they begin to suffer physically, and the doctor may suggest that they should avoid fasting. This is considered by the young and more liberal middle-class as 'madness', and by elderly women as a 'true' personal faith. These women believe that fasting reflects the value of hardship. The ideal is that the harder the prayers, the more merit win be gained. Furthermore, fasting to the point of physical suffering is considered as an act of *haram* by the ritual experts.

For religiously oriented women, achievement for after-life depends upon properly performed rituals, and the sanctioning of behaviour considered immoral. For religious companion it is better to enter the world of after-life with 'full hands' (a metaphor for sets of meritorious acts which gave her confidence and reduce the fear of death), rather than to be materially well-off in one's lifetime. Generally, women have more knowledge about the ritual instructions for prayers, as well as about visiting shrines and alms-giving, than the average male. This is largely due to a more regular attendance by women at ritual occasions concerning the family.

Political views were not only expressed in the Quranic language of *hezbullahi* preachers, nor only in the atmosphere of the religious meetings, but were also brought into internal political metaphors, such as in communal religious and poetic songs, and chanting.

Performance of *Salvat*

In salutations to the Prophet Muhammad and his family *(alla-homa-sale-'ala-mohanwd va aleh mohamad),* the Quranic reader not only asks for her own merit, but also for the merit of her parents, or for the happiness of her dead mother's soul and those of other recently dead relatives. Men are seldom the recipients of salutations at women's religious meetings, unless recognised as being highly religious learned, dead or war martyrs. Salutation signifies the women's position with strength and faith, and the reader is honoured as a mediator through whom a salutation is offered to the Prophet Muhammad and his family. The arrival of the preacher, for example, is often highlighted by the offering of a *salvat,* which may be initiated by loyal followers, who then expect others to join in on the chanting of the welcome chant. Any disorder, such as whispering or signs of disagreement among the women, and any interruption to the reading of the Qur'an, may induce a participant to request a *salvat.* The average participant views the recitation of the blessing verses as an instrument to gain merit.

Preachers and hostesses receive most of the salutations: the former for her religious performance, and the latter because she sponsored the rituals. Salutations may be addressed to the preacher herself, to her mother's soul, or occasionally to her husband. The mother-daughter relation, which is identified with the transmission of religious and ritual knowledge, is very often honoured by offering a salutation to the daughter, and to the soul of her dead or absent mother. Offering salutions to a martyr, or to the mothers or sisters of martyrs, are also important, as the latter represent new and prestigious categories within Islam.

In a particular case a woman expressed her emotion by showing her neighbour her hands, on which her hair stood at end, thus expressing her feeling of excitement. Often one of the women would offer a rousing salutation, which was then taken up by the others, even though the story was known to them. Some also whispered 'God is great' *(allaho-akbar)* to one another in their excitement. At the end of text the preacher Zaki raised her hand, and wished that the mothers of the sons that had disappeared, or had been taken prisoners of war, would soon be reunited with them as the holy Jacob and his son Joseph had been reunited.

The image of a miracle, and the wish for the return of prisoners of war, raised the voices of the audience in *salvat.* The ability to work miracles is considered a personal quality of the Prophet. However, a person with a given religious status of *nazr-kardeh* (having been chosen by a holy prophet or holy Imam); or a spiritual person who displays the notion of holliness; or who claims to be able to mediate between worldly reality and spiritual life, or to have met the Prophet or someone of his blessed lineage can claim to have the ability to perform miracles.

Shirazi middle-class women may perform both religious and social visits at a religious house. Such social and religious visits represent important aspects of the free social movement of women, and are taken more seriously by women than by men. Meanwhile, the secular visit of kinfolk is based on mutual visits and gift exchanges according to the type of social relation, age, family events and kin ties. The religious visit to a mosque or a shrine in another town, or even to Mecca, is performed individually or in groups.

In contemporary Islamic Iran the religious practices of *ziarat* involve different aspects. Although we agree with Tapper that the above two visiting patterns are an effective way of gaining social mobility among Muslim women, the religious or sacred journey is not limited to traditional or lower-class Iranian women.

Carol Delaney opposes the view that the pilgrimage is merely a spiritual experience and suggests that 'sacred' and 'secular' are two aspects of a single event, and are integrated into the social domains. She also opposes the view that Muslim behaviour in the form of 'sacred' and 'secular' are two different phenomena. There are many social situations in which a woman may feel motivated to initiate a vow at a mosque or at a nearby shrine. Women may not only vow to make a pilgrimage, but may also vow to stay there for one or more nights.

Women coming from rural areas, are often with their husbands or other family members as part of their vow of making on ziarat. In large shrines, such as the tomb of Imam Khomeini in the Behesht-e Zahra cemetery south of Tehran, the shrine of Imam Reza in the city of Mashhad, or in the Astaneh in the city of Shiraz, there are often places to rest and cook. Urban Shirazi women often travel in twos or threes—for example two sisters, a mother and a daughter, an aunt and a niece, two neighbours, or two fellow religious participants. Two or three who have known each other for years as Quranic students may also travel together.

The holy places, such as the main shrine or the Astaneh, are the kinds of religious places a Shirazi woman on particularly holy nights may stay the night alone, or with other female friends. Sometimes their husbands sit separately in the male section, particularly at the time of *ahya* (all-night watch and praying), or during the month of fasting when religious activity increases both for men and women.

Some women come alone and stay in the shrine the whole night; for example village women, or those who seek to use the shrine as a place of refuge from their restrictive husbands and family problems. This use of the public religious places as a free arena for women contrasts strongly with the highly constrained social mobility of women in secular places where sitting alone in a restaurant, or walking in a park, give rise to the stigmatised identity of being an available woman. This means that the acts of women in the religious sphere can be considered supportive: that is, women can stay away from home, make friends, and move freely, without being constrained by the sanctions that surround them in the secular social spheres.

Many wish to travel to distant shrines where, according to local women, the likelihood of a vow being fulfilled is greater. It is also believed that the longer and harder the *ziarat is,* the more pious it is, and the greater the likelihood of the vow's fulfilment. The degree of difficulty is measured against the hardships experienced by the Imam Husain and his followers in the city of Karbala. The longer the distance travelled, the higher the prestige, and the greater is the relatives' expectations that she will return with presents. Women may go on pilgrimage individually. Nezhat made her first *hajj* journey in the company of her first Qura'ic teacher thirty years ago. Her second journey was from London where her son was living at the time.

Half of the way she was guided by her secular sister-in-law, and the rest she managed by contacting one of the Iranian pilgrimage agencies in Mecca. For a journey to the holy city of Mashhad, married women are more likely to persuade their husbands to join them, or ask their concession for travelling alone. Even in the orthodox and strongly segregated families, in which husband and wife seldom travel together on secular holidays, the husband may make a concession and travel with his wife, or pay for her expenses.

A wife planning a religious journey in the company of other women may be away from her household for some time. She will therefore make sure that a close female relative, such as an older daughter, her own sister, or a sister of her husband, can take over her responsibilities in her absence. The pleasure of these journeys can be summarised in the following three points: (1) performing religious duties, (2) bringing merit to the family; and (3) creating an alternative social network. Thus, travelling to the city of Mashhad to visit the shrine of Imam Reza is a journey for women's friends and their family.

The Ritual of Returning from Pilgrimage

A pilgrim expects to receive a special welcome on her return, and may herself bring some small gifts from the holy town to distribute among family and friends. Already the first day after her return she may receive visitors. On her return she will be referred to as a woman of higher religious experience.

The *ziarat* or *hajj* gifts are usually simple items valued for their 'goodness', such as a prayer stone symbolising the clay of Karbala, a prayer rug, prayer beads, or fabrics for sewing clothes. Embarking on a pilgrimage, both within and outside one's place of residence, has become very popular among middle-class and business families, especially to destinations such as *ziarat* and *hajj*. These have increasingly become the focal point for Islamic cultural innovation and the Islamic policy of nation-building. Such journeys are now being organised by travel agencies on a large scale, and the programmes may also include visits to new shrines.

Through modem technology, and in the context of the new political economy, the journey to Mecca has been reduced from several months to two or three weeks. Before a restriction was put on Iranian pilgrimages to Mecca in 1987,[82] an increasing number of well-to-do women of various ages travelled in small groups, led either by female preachers, male spiritual leaders, or semi-government agencies. Today, as the number of pilgrims has increased considerably due to the use of modem transportation, the state arranges pilgrimages to Mecca twice a year. Due to the political changes after the revolution, travelling to other Muslim countries on pilgrimages has increased. Going on a pilgrimage provides the people with a new political and social alternative.

Meanwhile, the Islamic Iran encourages Islamic journeys of large scale while dismissing some of the customary rituals of visiting holy trees and the like as an incorrect practice of Islam.. For example, a local house believed to be spiritually efficacious was closed by the local Islamic guards following the Iranian revolution in order to prevent the blessing of a tree and its mediation. This practice was perceived by the revolutionary regime as a kind of animism, and thus contrary to the Islamic belief in God as a single entity.

The house was a place where female visitors came from near and far to cook a meal in the yard and to tie a piece of fabric as a sign of a vow. The tree was known among the traditional Muslim-oriented women in Shiraz as a blessing tree that produced miracles and mediated one's wishes. Such visits were common among lower middle-class urban women. In contrast, it is possible to travel cheaply to a country such as Syria. Such journeys have been facilitated by both Islamic state and semi-private travel agencies, and must be booked at least one year in advance due to the large number of applicants. The official state policy of purifying Islam from 'popular' and 'false' elements has affected some of the customary practices. Popular Islamic practice has been encouraged more towards the public religious places and mosques, where rituals of worship are in the charge of learned preachers and state authorities.

Some aspects and forms of rituals are distinctively practised by different socio-economic categories. This can be defined in terms of ritual economy, since certain practices such as pilgrimage and distribution of big communal meal on holy days, are more accessible to the better-off than to the poor. Consider, for example, the cases of two religious companions, Shazdeh and Nezhat. The former believed it better to buy a place for *hajj* this year, rather than to wait for years in the hope that her name might come up in the ordinary waiting list. It cost her three times the normal price. However, since the Iranian revolution of 1979, a new form of identity associated with participation In religious fora has emerged, so religious gatherings and sacred journeys have become a new type of enterprise and social involvement where various categories intermingle. This offers women of different social and class backgrounds an alternative opportunity to meet. The policy of the Iranian state plays an important role in discouraging people from travelling to formerly popular destinations such as Europe, in favour of the less expensive neighbouring countries.

In Islamic Iran women of different social and class categories carry out religion in different form, endowing it with particular meaning. For example, pilgrimages to Mashhad or Syria are a more common kind of religious activity among members of the middle class and entrepreneurial families, and working women, than the expensive journeys to Mecca. Such religious events (whether initiated by oneself or another), have multiple meanings for the participants, who not only share events of happiness and sadness, but also have a chance to initiate their own vows and fulfil their own duties.

2
Family Management in Islam

The importance of the large-scale ideological and economic factors in the everyday life situation of the individual, and the way in which this ideology has opened up the possibility of divergent adaptations and a new household economy. Moreover, the burden that economic changes place on adult males (who still are the main providers in most families), as well as career married women, has increased. This has complicated and intensified the tradition of child-rearing, cooking, washing, cleaning the house, taking care of the family and social networks, as well as the time spent on purchasing goods and supervising children after school. The large-scale economic reforms, and the new household economy, have affected the life of family members in different ways. The form and the rituals of household activities in everyday life are central themes in the following section.

The economic crises of the Islamic state and the new ideological demands have incurred cumulative and overlapping perspectives. This has left a narrow range of options for young and ambitious couples, forcing them to seek opportunities outside the home country, as exemplified by Mahry's extended family. Marriage and higher education has traditionally served as a passage for social and economic independence, although it has often been the case that newly-weds stay in the house of the wife's or husband's father for a while, before establishing an independent household. For ten years Halimeh, a 44-year-old female school teacher, shared a residence with her sister-in-law before she and her husband could save enough money to buy one of the two-room flats offered to school employees.

Marriage has always been an economic security for the wife, and the husband is traditionally responsible for the economic security of the family. The reality of the current socio-economic situation for the average lower- and middle-class category, is such that extra economic support is necessary, either from the wife—particularly in the case of young married couples—or from parents.

A young family's economic independence and higher social status, such as in the case of Mahry and her siblings, depends upon occupation and further education. Mahry and her family had less chance of obtaining higher education because of the increased number of applicants,"' and also because of new Islamic ideological criteria for the selection of religiously active candidates. A new mode of adaptation, and a new economic niche, has emerged for family members who are able to take on additional roles.

As a result of constant price increases on household goods, the consequences of these economic niches have affected males and females differently. Managing the household economy is difficult in lower- and middle-class families, even when the breadwinner (often the man), has previous work experience, or higher education. Families are dependent on a single income from employment in the public sector, such as teacher or office work jobs.

Grown-up children, despite their higher education, are economically dependent on their parents, who returned home from abroad during the Iranian revolution in 1978. This dependency may be permanent for some, thus placing a burden on the parents. In post-revolutionary Iran, large numbers of urban middle- and higher-class Iranians left home.

Two distinctive, significant and completely new household structures emerged in post-revolutionary Iran. These were: (a) the extended household composed of parents and married children who shared a residence, and (b) the households consisting of elderly couples who remained in Iran, while their children left home and took permanent residence abroad. The former household composition is common among families where a majority of the members stayed in Iran, and only a few moved abroad. The latter household composition consisted of elderly couples who voluntarily lived alone at home, visiting their children only once in a while abroad. These are often better-off couples, contrasting dramatically with the lower- and middle-class extended household, where parents accommodate a married daughter or son and their families.

To maintain the economy of daily life many young educated men started a business of their own, or with another male relatives. The inevitable solution for lower- and middle-class families was to have two members of the family in employment. Alternatively the breadwinner of the family would take two jobs, one in the official sector and another in the private sector. In the case of Mahry, close and distant male relatives were employed as civil servants, teachers, low-ranking army officers, social health personnel, etc. Due to the high cost of living they worked in their spare time as independent taxi drivers, as salesmen buying and selling land, as dealers in foreign currencies or rationed goods, or as shop assistants. In comparison women were either housewives or, as is the case among a few middle-aged women, they were employed as nursery teachers, computer assistants, students, social health workers or, like Mahry, they worked with sewing and embroidery.

Most of the young families in the community, either rented rooms that cost them half of their salary as state employees, or they shared a residence with their parents or a close relative in order to save money. Many were also dependent on others for economic support, directly or indirectly, in the form of cash, household subsistence, and goods. Such socio-economic insecurity, along with the poor educational opportunities for themselves and the problems facing their children, as well as the general political harassment, has led many of these middle-class families to join the flow of migrants of the 1980s.

Household work is not only a distinctive personalised domain, but is also a part of the larger economic and post-revolutionary ideological development, as well as being a locus of change. Domestic work in post-revolutionary Iran involved a series of new tasks and more intensive work schedules for women.

Adaptability of household members to changing conditions depended on the availability of facilities and resources. A married woman explained that due to the intensive work schedule and, for example, the lack of communal facilities, she had to do the laundry at night when water was more easily available, and the shopping before sunrise so as to be able to prepare the midday meal for the family. This example illustrates how the mode of work among women mainly concerned with 'domestic' tasks has intensified due to broader political and economic conditions. One could hardly escape the daily observation of lower- and middle-class women (often mothers), accompanied by small children, waiting impatiently for several hours in queues, in order to purchase hygienic supplies of milk, foods, and other 'domestic' items, at a more reasonable price than in the open market. Commonly they were worried about the daily household routines; for example, one waiting in such a queue told how worried she was at being delayed in preparing the noon meal for her husband and children coming home from work and school.

Foreign goods, such as electrical appliances, were very expensive and considered as luxury items by lower middle-class families. Moreover, these items provided a new form of enterprise for well-off families. Being able to sell foreign goods in the home market greatly boosted the income of such well-off families. The extended household has to some extent solved the problem of married children who are not able to establish an independent household without economic support from their parents.

High prices of household equipment and house rent made it impossible for young families with average economic means to establish an economically independent household. However, such an intensive relation and extended household dependency has increased family conflicts dramatically, particularly in already controversial relationships such as between daughter-in-law and mother-in-law.

Career options are limited for young members of lower-class families. Petty trading seems to be an acceptable strategy for boys. Wheeler-dealers, and street vendors, are two forms of economic activity adopted by recent school-leavers. *Bazar-e azad* activity has opened a series of channels through which household items rationed by the state flow into the black market. Such enterprises, and the extra income earned, are often considered insecure, illegal, not quite respectable and even immoral. Middlemen, such as wheeler-dealers, after spending long hours in queues, buying goods such as cigarettes and eggs from the co-operatives shops, and then selling them at black-market prices. This type of occupation may serve as a source of income for young and middle-aged male members of low-income families. For families with low incomes, daily petty trading is not a permanent enterprise.

Self-employment yields more income than a low-paid permanent job. Establishing a business requires both economic and social capital, without which it is difficult to obtain goods to sell, or to rent a shop. When renting a shop a deposit is paid. The price has increased with inflation from around 50 thousand tomans in 1979 to an average of one million tomans in 1990. This means that it is virtually impossible to establish a permanent business. It also means that large profits can be made from letting shops, houses, flats and rooms. Those who have parents with a large capital may set up a small business.

While the father is still alive, they will be allowed to enter the family business as part of their eventual inheritance. The street-corner traders sell items such as dollars, cigarettes, rationed foods, and stockings. *Dast-forosh is* an enterprise open to even those with little capital, and is often a second source of income for individuals such as a grown-up son, or a head of a household. Any form of self-employment to supplement the limited household income, is justified on the grounds that multiple sources of income are necessary. Since a single-income job in the public sector cannot meet all of the household's real expenditures, the idea of a second job has become widely accepted.

Resourceful entrepreneurs will be able to provide for family consumption, as well as accumulate considerable wealth. In contrast, permanent business activities are generally open only to better-off middle-class merchants and craftsmen, and other traditionally independent producers and distributors. These are often co-operative family businesses jointly owned by close male relatives, such as a father and his sons, brothers, cousins and in-laws. This contrasts with the petty trader who sets up his business independently. Recently, because of restrictions, male shopkeepers are forbidden to sell female lingerie, or to open female hair-dressing salons.

As a consequence, female shopkeepers and co-partnership with a female relative has increased. The open market makes non-rationed items available to the public, such as electrical appliances, clothing, and domestic goods, as well as scarce medicines. The scarcity and long queues have forced many people to purchase items in the black market.

The rise in prices of local commodities may be explained by: (a) the government extra export policy for earning foreign currencies; (b) the rise in the exchange rate for dollars; and (c) the two devaluations of the rial. Devaluation of Iranian currency has been of particular importance for the family household economy, since family incomes are in the form of rials. Subsequently they are the hardest hit by inflation, exchange rates, and the black market policy of the state.

Broad structural and economical changes, such as the rationing system for the distribution of goods, has encouraged the development of a new transactional pseudo-occupation niche. Some of these new enterprises are considered immoral, in terms of their transactional and insecure nature. Self-employment and free-enterprise activities are considered to offer greater opportunities for meeting the daily increases of expenditures. Government employees, who are particularly well educated, and with fixed low wages, have become very disappointed with the monthly income of their permanent jobs. It is not adequate to cover their household expenses, such as rent. The difference in the earnings of these well-qualified government employees, and those whose main source of income is selling dollars in the black market, has marginalised the former category both socially and economically.

Wages for average civil servants and employees in official sectors, such as education, have remained relatively the same as they were before the revolution. According to a study by Behdad, in 1980 there had been an increase in the official minimum wage and a change in the rate of income tax to 12 per cent.

Most workers were affected by the new law stipulating minimum wages, the exception being urban workers in large firms. It must be keep in mind that family economic viability in post-revolutionary Iran is a problem for most government employees, hence the interest in free business and double waged jobs.

The most profitable enterprises involve trading in foreign currencies and goods, such as dollars, pounds, gold, household items and land, and money lending. Thus, the families that had invested capital in such commodities as land, houses, cars, gold, shops, etc. prior to the outbreak of the war between Iran and Iraq in 1980 are now in position. Expansion of the black market has an advantageous further benefited those who have access to foreign currencies, imported goods, and are able to travel abroad frequently.

Land Transaction

Land ownership has always been an important source of local identity and power in Iran. After the revolution, long-term investment in land has more than ever become an important form of capital, as well as a strategy for rapidly accumulating wealth. The dramatic rise in land prices since 1980 has applied even to the purchase of the isolated land outside the city limit, which is not even supplied with electricity and water.

An example of rapid social mobility through land ownership is the case of an educated civil engineer. He qualified in England in the 1970s. He and his family returned to Iran shortly after the Iranian revolution in 1980. He started to work for his former employer, where he had previously been employed in a junior position. Due to his high foreign qualification he was soon offered jobs in different cities, including one in a province where he received high wages due to the difficult geographical conditions. Shortly after he returned home from England he bought a piece of land at a low price. The land was on the nonresidential periphery of a town without electricity and water supplies. It cost him 60 tomans per square metre in 1980. However, inflation increased its value to 5,000/6,000 tomans per square metre in 1989.

In the long term ownership of land is highly beneficial, the rapid increase in value making it a secure investment. The demand for land has particularly increased as a result of demographic changes. These can be explained as follows: (a) rapid population growth; (b) the continuous migration from small towns and nearby villages to large towns. The rapid expansion of towns toward the city limits increased the value of cheap and isolated land from 20-60 tomans per square metre in 1979, to 6,000 tomans per square metre in 1989-90. Such land could not, however, be used for building a house until it had been included within the town's official boundaries.

The profit from land ownership was greater than from the ownership of fruit gardens, the latter providing only a small annual income for urban middle-class and business families. This was the common enterprise that led to the serious destruction of the famous orchard land in Shiraz. The grape and apple farms changed into building sites, thereby bringing a high profit to their owners. It would be interesting to evaluate the impact on agricultural production.

Land confiscated during the revolution has been sold cheap to religio-politically privileged community members, such as war veterans, employees of the Islamic institution for rehabilitation, and to families of martyrs or hostages. In recent years government supporters have been favoured for the redistribution of economic and social opportunities, such as obtaining employment, education, rationed goods and land. Special allocations have been given as the rewards for their support. Thus, economic advancement has been possible not only for those who have accumulated capital under the former regime, but also for those who have gained high status as first-class citizens in the Islamic regime, whatever their class background may have been.

Gifts of gold signify sets of kinship relations and are part of large chains of acts distinguishing close relatives, high-ranking guests and close friends. The value of gold is both an objective and a subjective cultural phenomenon, and concerns the relations between people on various levels. Gold has always been associated with prestige and high status and is often exchanged as valuable gifts among Iranians. There is a strong tendency for women to own some gold, receiving and giving in accordance with expectations. The saving and management roles women play within the family in this context is considered to be related to their orientation toward the future. Gold functions for women both as prestigious ornaments, and as a status symbol. Gifts of gold signify a 'proper' bride and provide capital for the family and her husband.

While purchasing land has remained the principal investment and economic transaction for men, gold has played a similar role for women. The constant rise in the value of gold, along with inflation, has meant that its importance not only as solid capital, but also as a status symbol, has grown.

The common strategy is to buy as many articles of gold as possible when the prices are low, and then sell or exchange these items when the prices have gone up. Accumulation of gold is considered a wise policy, both from the point of view of the individual and the family

Gold is a significant gift requested by the bride. The amount to be received is often agreed upon at the time of engagement. Gold jewellery, or a number of gold coins, may be agreed upon as being a part of, or the entire *mahryeh*. The increasing tendency among middle-class brides to have *mahryeh* in gold coins than rials is because gold is more stable in price and more likely to rise in value than fall. The quantity of gold received as wedding presents depends on how wealthy the relatives are, and the number of guests. Such gifts may also be given on other significant occasions, such as at the birth of a child, during the first pregnancy, upon obtaining a higher degree, or on the Iranian New Year in March.

The young married women were considered inexperienced, and were constantly advised by their mothers and sisters about future relations with their husbands and their families. Planning a secure future, the mothers advising their daughters to buy gold instead of toys and decorative items, and to be concerned about the future. Such issues have become important lessons given by mothers to their married daughters. The importance of the gift of gold as capital is revealed at times of family crises. It is increasingly common for married women to give their savings to their desperate husbands to start a business or purchase property. Such a form of economic support brings extra recognition and respectability for the wife. The husband is often willing in return to register part, or whole, of the purchased property in her name.

On one occasion Farideh, a 30-year-old married housewife, proudly exclaimed how she sold all of her wedding jewellery and the children's gold to give tomans to her husband, so he could purchase a piece of land that was especially offered to him at his place of work. Her husband in return registered the land in her name. Another situation in which a woman's gold reserves may be vitally important to the whole family is exemplified by Mahtab, an elderly mother with a family of ten, who was forced to seek shelter in Shiraz during the Iraqi bombardment of Abadan in 1981. The only property they could bring with them was her gold (one kilogram). Soon she decided to sell it, despite the market rate being low, because she considered it was important to provide the necessary clothing and accommodation for her daughters, and to protect the family. The only thing she had been reluctant to sell was a ring that had once belonged to her mother.

A third example is that of a 55-year-old woman, who sold all of her gold jewellery and borrowed money from her oldest daughter, in order to visit two of her children living in Norway. To her the value of the visit was worth more than her gold. She thought, what would be the use of saving when she might never again have the chance to see her children and grandchildren?

The distance, and the high cost of the journey, signified the importance of the visit and, and as she put it, 'it may be the only chance in my lifetime'. She had to insist on the importance of such a visit since her old husband thought that it was more important to take care of the house, and was thus reluctant to give her any financial support. Finally she alone provided the money for her journey to visit her children. She frequently talked about this as an event to gain respect.

A fourth example is that of a couple educated abroad, who had recently returned home and needed to pay for the transport of their household goods from Germany to Iran. The wife, Shahla, decided to sell her own gold, as well as her daughter's, to pay the required sum. She considered the household items to be of equal value to the gold since these were enormously expensive and scarce in Iran. Her mother, Mahtab, proudly returned to this case, telling others how her daughter managed her family fife, thus presenting her daughter as a good wife to a good husband.

Contributions to the family economy in times of crises will allow the wife to emphasise her honourable identity and enable her to negotiate with her husband. The latter may, as noted, often agree to reward his supportive wife by registering some property in her name.

Some women insist on keeping some of the gifts of gold received through their own lineage by transferring it to their daughters or daughters-in-law, or to their mother's lineage (sister's daughter). Such a form of gold exchange signifies sets of kinship relations in which the wife competes with the husband's for support. Thus women often adopt far-sighted perspectives on the value of gold, a view that their husbands may not necessarily share, but from which they often benefit.

Inflation and Dowry

Dowry consist of household goods that the bride will bring to her husband's house. *Mahr is* a sum of money or valuable items such as gold and land that the husband pledges to pay the bride upon marriage. This amount will be written as a legal document for the bride's security, and may become a legal debt upon the bride's request. These two forms of payment play important roles in the dynamics of the marital relation, giving a woman a high degree of security and also a deterrent for a divorce.

It is generally assumed that the larger the dowry (i.e. consisting of kitchen utensils, carpets, bedroom furniture, etc.), the greater is the respect shown to the daughter and, thus, the greater is the prestige gained in the eyes of the husband's female relatives. Due to the open market prices of dowry items people purchase presents through the newly established Islamic state marriage institution, which offers a few items for those newly wed. These might include items such as a stove, a machine-made carpet, and an oil heater. Two or three items were sold to each newly married couple in 1989.

The better the daughter's education, job and appearance, the less pressure is placed on the parents to provide an expensive dowry. This point of view was expressed by at least ten of the working women, aged between 30-45, including 4 teachers (1 nursery, 2 school, 1 university), 3 hairdressers, 1 social worker, 1 accountant, 1 office worker. Of these two had resigned, one of whom was Narges, a 40-year-old woman and former accountant, the other being a teacher who had several times taken leave to avoid the political stress associated with her working conditions.

Working women have often purchased household goods either through the co-operative institution where they worked, or when such goods were available at a special price. Six of them had been working before marriage. As part of their dowry they brought these goods to their husband's house without putting economic pressure on their parents. The average parent, with several marriageable children, may find themselves in serious economic difficulties, unable to provide a dowry for their daughters. However, some parents, in order to reduce these expectations, will give a little dowry to the daughter and in return agree for a simple wedding party and a smaller gift of gold.

In order to reduce the expenses of the groom a one-day celebration for the two phases of the wedding is the most usual form of marriage. The first phase of the wedding party starts with the *aqad* ceremony, in which the Muslim marriage contract will be written. At that time the close relatives of the bride and the groom are invited, and a warm meal will be served at the expense of the bride's family. In the afternoon the second phase of the celebration, known as the wedding party, will be held. Then dinner will be served to a large number of guests, including distant relatives, friends and close neighbours. This part will be held at the expense of the groom. The wedding marks a recognition of the Muslim marriage contract. It is seldom the case that a bride moves to live with her husband before the second phase of the marriage celebration.

Devaluation of the rial brought a series of dramatic changes to families and the household economy. The reduced value of rials provided grounds for parents of brides to request higher *mahr,* to guarantee more security for women at the time of divorce. The average *mahr* requested by the bride's family increased from a few hundred thousands before the revolution, to 3 million for the average middle-class family in 1989, and to 10 million in 1994. Knowing the existence of such a threat causes the girl's family to request a higher amount of mahr.

In the past, the *mahr* was so low that initiating a divorce today has been easy for some husbands, being only a matter of paying an insignificant amount of cash to the wife. The predicament of a woman facing divorce due to low *mahr,* can be illustrated in the case of Narges. In 1970, when she married, her *mahr* was 100,000 tomans; (a high sum at that time). When she divorced in 1989 the average *mahr* was 3-5 million tomans; among the better educated and well-off families. Her husband thought it was an easy matter simply to give her the total amount of 100,000 tomans in cash, thus fulfilling the sole legal condition for a restricted third-degree divorce. For the husband this equalled the price of a pair of car tyres.

The high amount of *mahr* today makes it impossible for husbands to pay it to their wives in case of divorce. However, to women the sum is more a matter of status, providing them with more power and ability to negotiate with the husband in case of divorce. Family insecurity and the increasing number of divorces on one hand, and the continuous devaluation of rials on the other, induces parents to increase their demands of *mahr,* thus hoping to guarantee greater security for their daughters in marriage.

3
Girls' Education

Education in Islamic Perspective

In dealing with women's education from the Islamic perspective, it is recognised that wider issues pertaining to a modern Islamic curriculum have not been addressed. The latter is, indeed, a crucial issue, but our concern here has been one of the key questions of principle that should surely guide current attempts to formulate an authentically Islamic education system, namely the approach to women's education in such a system.

Long as the education system is governed by the spirit of Islam throughout, there will be a harmony between these two modes of social activity, permitting women to express themselves in accordance with their natural dispositions, and to be given the respect and honour which is so central to the real social message of Islam.

Knowledge and education are highly emphasised in Islam. Both are integral parts of the Islamic religion. Islam encourages its followers to enlighten themselves with the knowledge of their religion as well as other branches of knowledge. It holds the person who seeks knowledge in high esteem and has exalted his position) In reality, the entire aim of the Divine revelation and the sending of prophets to humankind has been stressed in the Quran as the communication of knowledge. The Book says: 'The Prophet recites unto people God's revelation; causes them to grow and imparts to them knowledge, and wisdom'. The Divine desires every believer to be well educated in religion, to possess wisdom and broad intellectual knowledge.

The purpose of raising a prophet in a nation is to teach and to impart knowledge. The Quran is full of verses which praise learned people, encourage original thinking and personal investigation and denounce unimaginative imitation. It also emphasises the importance of the study of nature and its laws. According to the Quran, learning is an unending process and the entire universe is made subservient, to man, the agent of God, who has to abide by the truth and not by narrow notions of hereditary customs and beliefs. The verses in the Quran which enjoin people to learn and observe nature outnumber all those related to prayer, fasting, and pilgrimage put together.

In the *Hadith* literature, knowledge is highly appreciated and encouraged also. The Prophet Muhammad always emphasised the importance of knowledge to his followers and encouraged them to seek it. Learned people are regarded as the inheritors of the prophetic wisdom. In this connection, the following *Hadiths* can be quoted: 'The prophets leave knowledge as their inheritance. The learned ones inherit this great fortune'. 'Search for knowledge though it be in China'.

Studies were conducted in the Mosques, circles of discussion *(halaqat)* were set up; and teachers were simultaneously students learning from their superiors and, in their turn, teaching their own students. Education was considered a matter of religious duty--a manifestation of the Muslim's submission to the will of Allah and an act of piety which could lead to a deeper knowledge of the Creator—the One. Hence we find that all members of society participated in that process. Since education was free of charge, opportunities were available to everybody, rich or poor alike. The Prophet said 'Treat equally poor and rich students who sit before you for the acquisition of knowledge'. Gifted students were helped and highly encouraged to continue their education, so that they would be able to fulfil their aspirations.

Moreover, the seeking of knowledge was not circumscribed by age limitations; the Prophet said 'Seek knowledge from the cradle to the grave'. Therefore, we find that the companions of the Prophet sought knowledge even when they were at an advanced age. Also, there was considerable academic freedom; in the classes, the students were entitled to ask questions and to discuss themes with the teacher—indeed, their reputation depended heavily on their success in such sessions of debate and discussion.

Initially, the learning process of the Muslims started with the Prophet who himself used to teach his companions the principles of Islam. When he migrated to Medina, he immediately started the process of eradicating illiteracy. His mosque also served as a centre for Muslim learning. He was so interested in this matter that, soon after the victory of Badr, he instructed each of the Meccan captives, who were literate, to teach ten Muslims how to read and write as a condition for their release. He also sent teachers and missionaries to different parts of Arabia so that they could teach the newly converted Muslims the principles of Islam. He also set up circles of learned men to study and teach the Quran. Later, mosques were set up in every locality and since then have remained as the essential location for educational activities among the Muslims. The Prophet's example as a teacher constituted a sacred precedent for his followers. Hence they considered it their duty to set up mosques and schools in their domain. In the course of time, the simple pattern of the Prophet's school developed into a comprehensive and coherent educational system, fully integrated into the social and economic way of life. This educational system was based on moral and spiritual qualities. It recognised no separation between sacred and secular. Indeed it 'breathed in a universe of sacred presence'.

Whatever was known contained a profoundly religious feature, not only because the object cf every type of knowledge is created by God, but also because the intelligence by which man knows is in itself a Divine gift. The education system therefore dealt with the whole being of the person whom it sought to educate. Its aim was not only the training of the mind but also the entire personality of the student. The teacher in this system was the transmitter of knowledge as well as the trainer of souls. Even the term 'teacher' in itself gained the meaning of trainer. It was embodied with ethical connotations which in the modern world have almost disappeared from the process of teaching and the transmission of knowledge, especially at the higher levels of education.

The Islamic educational system neither separated the training of the mind from that of the soul, nor regarded the transmission of knowledge or its possession to be legitimate without the possession of proper moral and spiritual principles. Indeed, the acquisition of knowledge without these principles was regarded as very dangerous both to individuals and society.

However, despite the fact that the Islamic

educational system encompassed the whole life of traditional Muslims, certain distinct phases can be discerned. The first stage started at home where both parents acted as teachers in matters such as religion, language, culture and social customs. This period was followed by the Quranic schools *(al-Kuttab)* corresponding to elementary school. The aims of these schools were to enable the child to read and write the Quran, and to master the language as well as learn other subjects such as proverbs, poetry and, later, arithmetic. These schools formed the preparatory stage for higher studies where the students could then attend the *Madrasah.*

The *Madrasah* often incorporated the *Jamiah* which can be said to correspond at one and the same time, to secondary school as well as to college and university education. The activities of these *Madrasahs* were divided into two parts. The religious or the transmitted sciences, and the intellectual sciences. The religious sciences included the study of the Quran, the *Hadith,* linguistics and theology and they dominated the educational activity of most *Madrasahs.* The intellectual sciences included the study of logic, mathematics, and the natural sciences, as well as philosophy. These divisions of the sciences were reflected in the curriculum of the *Madrasahs* and were taught alongside each other. These *Madrasahs* enjoyed a high position in society and, in the course of time, they developed into fully fledged educational institutions performing an important role throughout the Muslim world, such as the *Qayrawan* in Morocco and *al-Azhar* in Egypt. Later on, we find the development of a university system with several campuses such as *al Nizamiyyah* and *al-Mustansiriyah* in Baghdad and *al-Nuriyyah* in Damascus.

In addition to the *Madrasahs* where theoretical learning was conducted, there were a number of observatories and hospitals. Some of them acted independently as institutions of scientific learning and experimentation, others were appended to the colleges. Al-Mamun's famous *Shamsiyyah* observatory was a most remarkable example. It was followed in many other cities. Moreover, these higher institutions continually provided society with its intellectual elite, and socio-political thinkers.

Education of Women

There is no priority for men over women in relation to the right to education. Both are equally encouraged to acquire education, as already shown, 'from the cradle to the grave'. Indeed all the Quranic verses which relate to education and which advocate the acquisition of knowledge were directed to both men and women alike. In accordance with the all-embracing concept of *Tawhid*— Oneness—when Islam elevated women physically by abolishing female infanticide, it could not overlook the need for their mental and spiritual elevation. By contrast, Islam would view the neglect of these dimensions as virtually tantamount to murdering their personality. The Quran says: 'They are losers who besottedly have slain their children by keeping them in ignorance'. Neither the Quran nor the sayings of the Prophet prohibit or prevent women from seeking knowledge and having an education.

Prophet was the forerunner in this regard, in declaring that seeking knowledge is obligatory upon every Muslim man and woman. By making such a statement, the Prophet opened all the avenues of knowledge for men and women alike. So, like her male counterpart, each woman is under a moral and religious obligation to seek knowledge, develop her intellect, broaden her outlook, cultivate her talents and then utilise her potential to the benefit of her soul and of her society. The interest of the Prophet in female education was manifest in the fact that he himself used to teach the women along with the men; he also instructed his followers to educate not only their women but their slave girls as well. The following *Hadith* puts it thus: a man who educates his slave girl, frees her and then marries her, this man will have a double reward. The wives of the Prophet, especially Aisha, not only taught women, they taught men also and many of the Prophet's companions and followers learned the Quran, *Hadith* and Islamic jurisprudence from Aisha.

There was no limitation placed on women's education. Women were allowed to learn all the branches of science. She was free to choose any field of knowledge which interested her. Nonetheless, it is important to stress that, because Islam recognised that women are in principle wives and mothers, they should also place special emphasis on seeking knowledge in those branches which could help them in those particular spheres. In accordance with the dictates of the Quran and the *Hadith* encouraging women to develop all aspects of their personality, it was believed that an educated Muslim woman should not only radiate her moral qualities in the environment of her home, but she should also have an active role in the broad fields of social, economic and political development.

The Quran, in particular, commands men and women to perform their prayers, pay their poor-tax and enjoin good and forbid evil in all forms: social, economic and political. This means that both have an equal duty to accomplish these tasks. In order to do so, they must have equal access to educational opportunities. For how can a woman uphold good social and economic policies or disapprove them if she is intellectually not equipped for the task? Following the injunctions of the Quran and the Sunnah concerning female education, early Muslim women seized this opportunity and laboured to equip themselves in all branches of the knowledge of their time. They attended classes with men, they participated in all cultural activities side by side with them and managed to win their encouragement and respect. 18 Early Islamic history is replete with examples of Muslim women who showed a remarkable ability to compete, with men and excelled them on many occasions.

Religious studies was the favourite subject for women in early Islam, and a considerable number of Muslim women managed to become notable figures among traditionists and jurists. On top of the list was Aisha, the wife of the Prophet. She was a renowned scholar of her time. Her foresight and advice in the affairs of the Islamic community were regarded as highly important by the early Islamic rulers. She was credited with thousands of traditions received directly from the Prophet and is to the present day considered a great authority on Islamic Jurisprudence. Another famous name in this subject was Nafisah, a descendant of Alı who was a prominent jurist and the ologian. It is mentioned that Al-Shafi, the founder of one of the schools of *Fiqh* used to attend her lessons and public lectures. Shuhda as well was a renowned name in the subject of tradition, especially *Hadith,* which is a branch of Muslim science which was thought to be exclusively for men.

Muslim women proved their ability to master in Literature and achieved a high reputation among their contemporaries. In the forefront was al-Khansa, the greatest poetess of her day. Her poetry has survived into the present period. She was admired by the Prophet himself when he said that her poetry was unsurpassed. In addition one could mention Qatilah who composed a famous elegy on the death of her brother which, again, was praised by the Prophet.

The humanitarian duties were performed by women

in all the battles fought in Islam. It was a custom that Muslim women accompanied the troops, so that they could bandage the wounded, fetch the water, transport the casualties back to Medina and instil courage in the men whose spirits were flagging. It is said that when the Muslim troops were preparing to conquer Khaiber, Umayyah bint Qays-al-Ghaffariyyah, with a group of women, asked to be allowed to accompany the army. The Prophet granted them his permission and they performed their duties well.

In addition, Muslim women attained a high status as medical scholars such as Zainab of the Bani Awd tribe who was a prominent physician and an expert oculist. Umm al-Hasan bint al-Qadi Abi Jafar al-Tanjali was a renowned woman of broad knowledge in different subjects, and was especially famous as a doctor.

Muslim women proved to be good warriors and they fought side by side with men. They achieved a considerable degree of success, and on occasion played very important military roles. In this respect mention should be made of Nusaiba, the wife of Zaid Ibn Asim, who took part in the famous battle of 'Ohud'. In that battle she fought vigorously and in the critical time when the Prophet was left alone she fought alongside him and wounded 11 persons with her sword. In the same battle, Nusaiba hint Kab al-Mazinia headed the Prophet's army against the enemy forces and at a crucial moment managed to minimise the losses of the Muslim army.

In addition, Muslim women also proved their ability to play a constructive role in other activities of the community. For example, they were involved in the political issues of the time and their opinions in political affairs were highly respected. They often took part in the process of choosing the Caliph." They also enjoyed full freedom to express their ideas and were encouraged to participate in the social life of the community. Public life was like a stage where both men and women were actively involved. In the early period of Islam women used to discuss and debate with the Prophet" and his companions and even protect their fights if they were breached. It is said that during the time of the second Caliph Omar, a woman expressed her disagreement with him publicly in matters relating to the women's dowry and managed to correct him.

The Quran encourages women to speak their minds and not to be silent; nonetheless we see today some fundamentalists propagating the unfounded slogan that the voice of woman is *A'wrah* (private parts to be covered up) and therefore arguing that it is in her best interest to keep quiet. For how can a woman learn and grow intellectually if she is not allowed to speak and communicate with others? How can she widen her understanding of things around her and speak forcefully and impressively if she is prevented from debating with others publicly?

On the contrary, Islam granted woman the right to hold a job and to involve herself actively in trade and commerce. She is entitled to work outside her home and earn a living. During the early Islamic period women often helped men in their outdoor work and were allowed to move about freely among men. Asma, the daughter of the first Caliph Abu-Bakr, used to help her husband in his field work. The Prophet himself praised women who worked hard and well; he also encouraged women, including his wives and daughters, to engage themselves in gainful work. He used to say 'The most blessed earning is that which a person gains from his own labour'.

Women in early Islam even held formal posts of authority in the community such as al-Shafa bint

Abdullah who was appointed by the second Caliph Omar as superintendent of markets in Medina many times. Hence, women can work as teachers, doctors, lawyers; they can work as employers or senior managers and they can work as Judges. It must be stressed that up until the present time and in most Muslim countries with the exception of Tunisia and Malaysia, the position of Judge is still regarded as a male domain. Women in these countries have traditionally been prevented from assuming this position.

The ban has no legal foundation in either the scripture or the Sunnah. On the contrary, Aisha, the wife of the Prophet, was the forerunner in undertaking the position. She acted as a Judge during the era of the first three Caliphs. Also, Abu Hanifa, the founder of one of the schools of law states that a woman might become a Judge and consider all matters except the ones that are under the penal code. Jarir al-Tabari, the famous commentator on the Quran, gives women the right to be appointed as Judge without any conditions. However, despite the fact that the external work of the woman was allowed and respected, a house- wife, unable to work due to domestic responsibilities, did not feel that her contribution was less honourable and less fruitful.

The high status granted to women by the Quranic reforms which prevailed during the early Islamic period did not last long. Firstly, certain pre-Islamic customs reappeared, especially during the Abbasid period; secondly, various social attitudes infiltrated Islamic culture from conquered peoples, and were assimilated as norms and then identified with Islam.

The status of Muslim women started to deteriorate. This was accelerated by catastrophic historical events such as the Mongol and Turkish invasions and the ensuing decline of the Islamic civilisation. The ambience generated by these conditions served to undermine the position of Muslim women who became less and less part of social life in general. They were neglected and treated as sex objects, assumed heavy veiling and were confined to their small circle of womenfolk with no contact outside their homes; they were prevented from participating in the public life of the community and excluded from public worship in the mosque. But the worst deprivation of all was the denial of their right to receive education. It was believed that basic awareness of the religious rites and memorising part of the Quran was sufficient for women.

While girls were welcome to all religious instruction especially in the lower grades, they were prevented from having further knowledge and education. In fact the opposition to female education reached its peak when condemnation was voiced against teaching women the art of writing: 'He the teacher must not instruct any woman or female slave in the arts of writing, for thereby would accrue to them only an increase of depravity'. Thus their role in society centred mainly on preparing them to be good and obedient wives and mothers. Later, when modern education became available, women were denied access to it and only schools for boys were initially developed. Female education was constrained by inherited social customs.

Education for women came to be viewed as being of secondary importance to keeping the home and the family. 'A woman's mission is to be a good wife and a compassionate mother... an ignorant rural woman is better for the nation than one thousand female Lawyers or attorney generals'. Female education was viewed as a threat to the traditional customs and the way of life of these societies. Indeed, educated women were feared and mistrusted as they could communicate potentially destructive or innovative ideas. Educated women were considered to be obtrusive and assertive. They did not appeal to men who expected them to serve them obediently. In addition, leaving home to go to school was in contrast with the idea of women segregation. The Islamic ideal of women's education and intellectual development was thus distorted, confused and actively opposed. The result was a disaster.

The illiteracy of Muslim women reached a peak and became a widespread phenomenon in the world of Islam. Consequently, women throughout the Muslim world became ignorant not only of outside affairs, but also of their legal rights in terms of marriage, divorce and inheritance. Very often due to their ignorance of these rights, they were cheated, deceived and misled. This rendered Muslim women unable to claim and defend the rights guaranteed them by Islam. This situation continued up to recent times, until efforts were made to improve female education in different parts of the Muslim world. However, despite these efforts and the rapid progress which has been achieved in the past four to five decades, the opportunities for women's education in the Muslim world, especially in the Middle East, still lag far behind those for men. Nothing substantial has been achieved, despite the fact that all Muslim countries have encouraged the spread of female education, stated that their aim is to try and raise the educational level of women, and proclaimed their intention to attain universal literacy. The accomplishment of these goals seems very far off.

The Influence of Modern Education on Muslim Women

The gap between female and male literacy rates in several places is increasing and the overall level of illiteracy is extremely high. The Islamic world, especially the Arab world, is amongst the areas in the world which has the highest rate of illiteracy amongst women, the lowest level of schooling for girls and the smallest number of women in paid employment. In 1991, the illiteracy rate among females in Afghanistan was 86 per cent, in Pakistan 78 per cent, in Egypt 66 per cent and in Iran 56 per cent. Although women's literacy varies enormously from country to country and also from area to area in any particular country, women in the Arab world are still a small minority among the student population. In every country the rate of male literacy is much higher than female literacy. Even in those countries which have initiated some reforms, there are still considerable disparities between male and female literacy, as well as major discrepancies between the type of female education offered and the socio-economic needs of the various Arab countries. This has been caused by many factors such as: family attitudes toward female education which still prevail, especially in the rural areas, where the majority of the Muslim population lives; and the high female drop out rate due to the inequality between urban and rural education.

But the most important factor so far has been the historical interpretation of the jurists. This has taken the shape of a clear deviation from genuine Islamic principles by its strong opposition to female education. This factor is still very strong in Muslim society, particularly Arab society, and it influences government policy on education options and opportunities for women. Saudi Arabia presents a clear example where Islam has been used to first deny and then discourage women's education.

In Saudi Arabia, a highly selective and narrow interpretation of Islam have bad a restrictive impact upon the lives of women. Traditionally, religion has been used as an excuse to justify the seclusion of women from the *educational process*. The rigid influence of the conservative theologians has played a critical role in suffocating female education for several decades through maintaining that girls should be prevented from all state primary and secondary schools.

The extremists argued that education of women would create immorality through corrupting their thinking and diverting their attention away from their essential role as good wives and mothers. They also voiced their fear that the outcome of the conflict of values brought about by such an educational transformation would result in discontent and instability both in the home as well as in society. It was under such pressure that public education for women in the Kingdom did not start until 1960.

Female education was introduced in Saudi Arabia in 1960, when the former King Faisal took the decision to set up schools for girls. Initially, the attempt *met* with strong opposition from the extremists who demonstrated their disagreement by gathering at the gates of the schools, expressing their displeasure with the new schools and with those who registered their daughters in them. National Guards had to be called to restore order. The opposition continued, unabated, until the government made two essential concessions: first, the government pledged that female education would be in line with Saudi customs, especially that of rigid segregation.

Secondly, it set up a special body called the 'General Presidency for Girls' Education' to be responsible for girls' education. As a gesture of its commitment to preserve Saudi customs, the government placed this body under the control of the Saudi religious authorities who, since then, continue to supervise the education of girls in the Kingdom.

With this compromise, opposition to female

education was finally mitigated and schools for girls were eventually established. The idea of schools for girls seems now to be accepted and the number of, females enrolled in the educational process is increasing every year. However, despite the fact that female education in Saudi Arabia is becoming popular, and the statistics show that significant gains have been accomplished, equal opportunity between men and women is still far from being reached. This is even more the case in respect of female education in the rural areas, which is an elusive goal yet to be attained.

In fact the policy of female education in Saudi Arabia has been founded on limited bases, aimed more at discouraging than promoting the learning process; this process neither satisfies the needs of Saudi women nor corresponds to the socio-economic requirements of the country. In the elementary schools, for example, girls mostly learn those courses which are assumed to be suitable for them in their traditional role in Saudi society. These courses emphasise mainly the Arabic language, home economics, child caring and religious instruction.

Although the elementary schools have been set up almost everywhere in the Kingdom, the proportion of female drop out after this primary level is still very high, and is a cause of great concern. As the level of education increases, the opportunity for girls to advance or progress become fewer. This is due to the fact that not all levels of knowledge and education available are at the location where the girls happen to be living, and also because in Saudi society women are not allowed to live alone in a residential campus. Hence it is difficult for them to move close to the educational institutions. Secondary schools, for instance, are not available everywhere in the country, neither are colleges.

Vocational education too has been extremely limited

except for nursing schools and tailoring centres. As regard university education, the situation is no better. The universities in Saudi Arabia are mainly for males, although some of them have branches in their departments for females. In these branches there is strict segregation of the sexes in classes and all teachers are female. Sometimes, due to the lack of suitable female teachers, the learning process is accomplished through the use of closed-circuit television. This enables male professors to lecture and answer female questions, without coming into contact with them.

Educational Awakening in Iraq

In speaking of the remarkable general progress of education in Iraq several years ago one of the officials in the Ministry of Education summed up the great contrast between the present development and that under the Turkish regime. "Very little was done for girls. The Central Girls' School in Baghdad which was established for the daughters of Turkish officials was like a foreign school, and did not benefit the girls of Baghdad. There were practically no foreign governesses, even in the better Baghdad families, such as you would have found in Istanbul or Cairo. Some few sent their daughters to the Catholic convent for a smattering of French and embroidery, but education for girls in the real sense did not begin until after the Mandate. At first it developed slowly, but now is going with a rush." What is meant by a rush is evident from the fact that elementary schools are crowded in towns like Baghdad, Mosul and Basra, and each year brings an added demand for more girls' schools. The number of girls, which is at present about one-third of the number of boys, is increasing more rapidly than the number of boys in school.

The actual number of girls entering school in 1932 was more than the number of boys entering. The enrolment of girls in primary education has increased 105 per cent. But even though the relative rate of increase of girls is greater than that of boys, there will be for a long time the disparity in the education of girls and boys that is characteristic of the East. The desire that eventually this should not be the case is evident from the new requests each year for more girls' schools.

This urge for girls' education is passing out of the few cities exposed to modern ideas into the smaller towns, where today a girls' school attracts an increasing number. Even from Najaf and Kerbela, the two shrine cities of Shi'ah Islam, requests for girls' schools were sent several years ago to Baghdad, but the reactionary forces in these Shi'ah strongholds stirred up such an opposition that the requests were withdrawn. More open to new ideas are the semi-nomadic tribes of the desert.

Growth in education may be measured not only in geographical extension and in the larger number of schools and of girls enrolled, but also in the ascending level of girls' education. It has moved steadily up from the little Quran school under the mollah to the primary school, then to intermediate and secondary schools.

The Central Girls' College in Baghdad has extended its course from eight to ten players, and-now gives the most complete education for girl's in Iraq. For the small town the new attitude toward girls' education is evident in the numbers in the primary school; in Baghdad the Central College is the index of the Muslim response to education for girls since over eighty per cent of the students are Muslim, and many do not live in Baghdad. The registration in this school each year exceeds the facilities so that a large number must be turned away. In Iraq conservatism has been disarmed by promoting the education for girls within the sanctions of Islamic tradition.

The Baghdad school is a good illustration of the general situation. Purdah conditions in this institution are carefully observed, the school following rather than directly promoting social change. But the atmosphere of the school is steadily becoming less purdah. At the beginning there was no man servant; now a young man janitor moves about the school freely. At first, no men visitors were allowed, not even the English Director of Education; now they are admitted but only with special permits from the Ministry of Education. When they were first admitted, all the girls veiled; now perhaps only one or two out of forty ever cover their faces before visitors.

Although none of the older girls take part in the school exercises, there is a tendency for parents, proud of their daughters, to waive their conservatism and let them appear in public even after they are really past the age of veiling. For example, a well-known family still allows a talented daughter of fourteen to perform in public. She is rather small for her age, and passes without criticism.

The consciousness of the veil is still very evident, however, outside the school. Visit the Baghdad School near closing time and you will find a group of old women, perhaps a few men, hovering about waiting to take the girls home. The older as well as the younger girls must have a special guardian, since according to Muslim custom, a veiled woman is helpless outside her own home. These caretakers are often disregarded by the girls; or perhaps "parked" somewhere while the girls manage to shop or go to the dressmaker on the way home.

An extra gift or *bakshish* smooths the way for this suspicious freedom and then the girl appears at home properly chaperoned. The elderly chaperone is required also to accompany the girls on 'We school excursion, a regular annual event for each class, and a great sign of advancing freedom. These excursions are an interesting illustration of the old and new. The girls go in motor cars, veiled, as far as the outskirts of the city, then up go the veils. Their regular attendants' a nurse or a chauffeur, or some old family retainer, enjoy watching the games and incidentally have a good exposure to modern ideas. "These caretakers," as the Principal of the school remarked, "are much more aware of the present-day schoolgirl's problems than are the girl's parents."

The slightest innovation in the Baghdad school, as in other schools in Iraq, must be carefully considered in reference to conservative opinion. The need for such care is illustrated by the protest which was made against having a lecture given at the Girls' College by a professor from the Men's Normal School.

One of the students commented on having heard a very interesting lecture. The father, a reactionary Muslim, reported it to the Parliament and the Minister of Education. Since then, the further use of men speakers has not been possible. Indicative of progress, however, is the occasional attendance of a group from the Girls' Normal School at lectures, cinemas or special national celebrations at the Men's Normal School. The girls are, it is true, carefully chaperoned, and sit as a group in the balcony without any individual contact.

The limited social *milieu* of girls' education in Baghdad is determined not only by public opinion, but also by the attitude of the authorities. King Feisal was very definitely interested in girls' education but believed that it should, be promoted within the social sanctions of Islam. King Ghazi has continued his father's policy. The advance of education, for girls, as for boys, will doubtless continue to receive the patronage of the Palace, but without any idea of changing social customs.

The change in the programme of girls' education along a number of lines indicates growth in effectiveness. Teachers are beginning to be aware that girls need other courses than the stereotyped programme required by an identical system for boys and girls. The difficulty of introducing new content in education becomes obvious from the fact that a girl in a civics class, working on a "Know your City" project, could not visit the post office, because girls are not supposed to go out and have no reason to see public buildings. In spite of difficulties new ideas are making headway. Physical education is progressing, even though slowly because of the veil.

Physical education is now interpreted in the larger meaning as an emphasis on normal recreation—clubs, school excursions, and general creative activities. This represents an entirely new idea in education as a whole, but especially in the education of girls. The use of the school as the centre for entertainments, recreation, cinema and radio performance is being promoted. The old Oriental idea of the crowds being entertained by the storyteller furnishes perhaps the germ for the new community usefulness of the school. Some teachers realize the need for vocational education for girls, but the time does not yet seem ripe for this emphasis.

Differentiation in girls' education, however, is emphasized through courses in home sciences, including homemaking, child care, sanitation and personal hygiene. With these new emphases the necessity for a closer relationship between the home and the school is obvious to thoughtful teachers, who realize that the real job of the modern school is social.

The Principal of the Baghdad Central College summed up the problem of the difference between the teaching of the school and the home thus: "Every Muslim girl who goes to the Baghdad School is exposed to two streams of influence which affect every act of her life-sleeping, dressing, and undressing at night, eating, walking, and thinking. The school teaches physical and mental activity; the home, passivity and fatalism. The school must seek to bridge the gap between its influence and that of the home."

This contrast between the ideals of home and school have led to a recognition of the need for adult education. There are some developments of adult education for the lower classes to raise the level of literacy, and also the higher level along the lines of social education. At the other extreme from adult education is the promotion of the modern kindergarten, an entirely new emphasis in Iraq. These kindergartens are in striking contrast to the mollah schools for little children, where they sat all huddled up together before an old sheikh or an uneducated elderly Muslim woman, chanting the Quran in high shrill voices, swaying back and forth in rhythmic accompaniment. The kindergarten in the Girls' School in Baghdad, which serves as a training centre for kindergarten teachers, would compare favourably in equipment with nine-tenths of modern American kindergartens. Another problem about which educators for girls in Iraq express concern is the question of social relationships. Under the regime of the veil the school does not encourage social contact, but the content of the teaching, as has been shown, lead toward the idea of unveiling.

Social change and education inevitably go together, since, as an Iraqi educator said, "You can't 'stagger' social advance" until the educational process is finished, and you cannot advance in education without some idea of social reform. The major difficulty in promoting a programme of modern education or even education along conventional lines in Iraq has been the securing of teachers. The steady development of a staff of trained women teachers in a decade has been accomplished to a large extent by the importation of Syrian teachers. The salaries paid by the Iraqi Government to these Syrian teachers have been very high, in comparison with salaries in Syria, but the need was urgent.

A real pioneering spirit and keenness for adventure together with their technical preparation for teaching, have been required of these Syrian teachers, who have been building a school programme for girls in a new country. This group of young Syrians has established the teaching profession in Iraq on a high educational level, has given prestige to teaching as a career and made it worthy of even the most conservative upper class. Their influence however has not been limited to the schools but has permeated the social environment.

Undoubtedly to the younger generation of Iraqi young men and women, the Syrian group of men and women teachers has presented, by their normal social relationships, a whole new way of life and inspired the desire in the younger generation of Iraq to be released from their traditional social restraints. The heyday of the Syrian teacher's opportunity, both for men and women-for there have been many of each has now passed.

The Syrian women teachers are now only in secondary and normal schools and there much less than before. Eventually, perhaps in four or five years, they will be entirely replaced, as it is considered desirable, both because of national economy and national amour-proper, for Iraq to have her own teachers. The preparation of Iraqi girls for secondary schools is being accomplished by sending them abroad to Syria or elsewhere on Government scholarships. The extension of Government subsidies to girls in itself signalizes progress in girls' education.

Until 1928 these foreign scholarships were limited to men. Since 1928, when the first group of eight girls went to Syria, their number each year has steadily grown. Now thirty or more girls are studying abroad, mostly in Beirut at the American School for Girls and the British Syrian Training College, also in the American junior College for Women and the American University of Beirut.

Naturally, the problem of sending girls is more difficult than boys because of social conditions. Furthermore there is less certainty of direct benefit to the Department of Education, since educating girls is something of a lottery because of the high probability of their marriage.

However, as an investment, not measured in direct returns to the schools, but to the community as a whole, this system of foreign scholarships has had great value. Especially worthy of note is the increase of Muslim girls on foreign scholarships. At first, only Christians were available, as Muslim parents could not think of sending their daughters abroad. The number of Muslim girls has increased; now about half the number or more are Muslims.

The attitude of Muslim parents has distinctly changed. Now training abroad is becoming every year a more natural thing, although it must still make quite a stir in a Muslim family to send a daughter forth across the desert five hundred miles, for ten months' study each year for several years, in a Christian Mission School, since these are for the most part the schools best fitted to serve the purpose. Muslim girls now go abroad for study not merely on Government scholarships, but also on private funds to gain a higher education, as a few Muslims as well as Christians have felt the urge for something beyond the Baghdad School. These Muslim girls from Iraq who are studying abroad are already exerting a social influence in their home environment. They come back from Beirut each spring with new ideas showing Anglo-Saxon influence in points of view and clothes of the French style. Often while abroad they have perhaps indulged in a vacation from the veil. All of these broader outside influences cannot fail to have their effects in Baghdad or in Mosul. Up to the present time the needs for higher education both for men and women in Iraq have been met by- study abroad, in very large measure in the American University of Beirut, which has become the university for the Arabic speaking world. There has been some agitation in Baghdad for the establishment of a university but this is not considered probable for some time, since this would involve an unwarranted expense for the small number of students who are as yet ready or desirous of higher education.

A medical college in Baghdad is, however, regarded as necessary to solve the most pressing national problem of health. The training of men and Women in medical-service is fundamental to the economic progress of Iraq and in the near future should be carried on in Iraq.

The admission of Muslim girls to the coeducational medical school in Baghdad would be an interesting parallel to the fact that the first university coeducation in Egypt was for women medical students. One of the special influences that has favoured the promotion of girls' education, especially in Baghdad, is the presence of a number of educated Turkish women, wives of prominent Iraqi officials. Their example has stimulated a spirit of competition in Baghdad mothers to have their daughters well educated and thus make a good marriage. The marriage motivation which is evident throughout the East in promoting girls' education, has thus an added force in Baghdad, because of the Turkish influence in the situation. The group of advanced Turkish women has created a desire among some of the Baghdad women for social progress. The contrast between the freedom of Turkey and the social conservatism of Iraq has made a special impression because the Turkish women are Muslims. The combined effect of the Turkish and Syrian groups has undoubtedly been influential in creating in Baghdad a certain dissatisfaction with existing social conditions and in stimulating the urge for change. In the development of modern education in Iraq, Anglo-Saxon-British and American-influence has played an important role. British ideas furnished the basis of the educational system which was organized during the first years of the mandate.

American educational influence has been evident in the later developments in Iraq, largely due to the fact that most of the Syrian teachers were graduates from the American institutions in Beirut and a number of them also had studied in America. Moreover the majority of the Iraqi students on foreign scholarships have also studied in Beirut in the American schools and hold key positions in the educational system of Iraq.

As a natural result of the predominance of Anglo-Saxon influence in Iraq, English is the second language. Compared with other countries of the Near East and Middle East, the work of foreign educational institutions in Iraq has been very limited. Girls' education, however, has been directly affected by the three American Mission Schools for girls in Baghdad, Mosul and Basra. These three institutions have contributed to a number of Muslim girls a sound educational preparation and have stimulated public appreciation of the value of girls' education. The primary impetus for general progress in Iraq and this, of course, affects the educational advance of women has come through the vigorous spirit of nationalism awakened since the World War. The example of Turkish nationalism, strong, aggressive, successful has been undoubtedly a stimulant for Iraq.

Leaders in Iraq repeatedly express the idea that the retarded development of women is a real handicap to the development of children and hence to the progress of the State. Iraq has adopted democratic institutions such as a constitution and Parliament, which are an anomaly in an illiterate country. Hence, the problem is to raise the whole educational level. The spirit of almost breathless nationalism of Iraq has stirred the public consciousness into a sense of need for education, and especially education for Muslim girls.

Girls' Education in Iran

Education in Iran has always in the past been identified with religion, largely connected with the mosques and maintained by the clergy, created an unfavourable atmosphere for promoting the education of girls. The general public has always considered it useless to educate girls.

The idea expressed in Iranian philosophy that education should be highly selective for those who can profit by it, has always been the current opinion and has debarred girls from educational privilege as expressed in the saying, "Where the innate capacity is good, education may make an impression, but no furbisher knows how to give a polish to bad iron." Although the new spirit is overcoming the old prejudicial attitude toward girls' education, such a handicap is not soon overcome.

The number of Government boys' schools, primary and secondary, is about four times the number of schools for girls, and the total enrolment of boys in all schools in Iran is slightly more than three times that of girls. More than half the education of girls in Iran is carried on by private schools, which have contributed also very greatly to boys' education.

Teheran of course represents the high-water mark of interest in both girls' and boys' education. Rural education receives little attention and girls' rural schools are practically nil. The opening of ten primary schools of three grades for boys and girls not only a numerical advance together represents also social progress in adopting in educational, facilities but coeducation. The teachers of these mixed primary schools are all women and over half the pupils are girls.

Education for the great majority of girls is limited to the elementary schools, which means a maximum of six years but often only a four-years' course. There are only a few middle schools and a normal school for girls, offering an eleven years' course and about thirty private middle schools, also of eleven years.

The American Mission institution for girls in Teheran, Nurbakush, with a course of twelve and sometimes thirteen years represents the top level of education for girls in Iran. Girls' education in Iran of any kind is the product of only about two decades and education on anything like a modern basis is the result of only about a decade. Viewed over a period of years there are distinct signs of advance. The fact that education for girls has begun is in itself the most hopeful evidence of progress. Aside from the growth in the extent of girls' education in Iran, it is worthy of notice also that education for girls has risen from the floor of the Quran school to the level of seats and desks of the modern primary school.

From the dull, damp room connected with some mosque with its crowd of little boys and girls huddled together on a mat in an atmosphere of disorder and all-talk-at-one-time casual heterogeneity under an old sheikh, whose method was to keep up an unbroken chanting of the Quran—from such a school it is a far cry to the present-day primary school with its well-ordered school room, its maps and blackboard, its orderly atmosphere, and young teachers, such as one finds in most of the schools in Teheran today. The fact, however, that some girls' schools are still held in private dwellings, ill-adapted for school use. And that many of the teachers are inexperienced, makes one realize that schools for girls, even in Teheran, are of recent origin.

The eagerness of girls for education and the inadequacy of their facilities are also evident when one visits a Teheran primary school, and found three girls wedged tightly in each seat in a room with fifty children, which could not comfortably hold more than thirty or thirty-five. With girls clamouring for places in school, it is easy to understand the statement that the Parliament does not disagree over the necessity to expand education for girls. It is safe also to affirm that there are no blast schoolgirls in Iran. For not only in Teheran, but also in a smaller city like Doulatabad, which is off the beaten travel route to Teheran, education is prized as a golden opportunity.

When the first girls' school was opened there, about ten years ago, a private venture of a wealthy Muslim woman, the key-bearded city fathers raised a strong opposition. "Why should there be a school for girls?" They said. Who believes that they can learn?" The answer to their protest was a model small town school, an attractive new building, very spacious playground and an alert young teacher from Teheran, well trained according to the present standards.

Any doubt as to whether girls can learn is dispelled by the bright-eyed little Iranian girls, one hundred or more, learning the elements of modern education, and also the useful vocation of carpet weaving, if they choose. The eager response of the girls must give deep satisfaction to the founder of the school, who herself is illiterate and therefore, perhaps, more keenly appreciates the value of education. She must feel that her annual expense for the school, the entire income from one of her villages, is a sound investment. But the city fathers doubtless still shake their heads at such rank and futile extravagance. In such a reactionary environment, modern education had been planted with great care.

The emphasis on religious teaching in the Government schools, however, has recently been greatly reduced. Iranian boys and girls in the public schools are no longer taught to intone the Quran and perform the prescribed Arabic prayers.

A book of quotations from the Quran has displaced the former meticulous religious teaching. This book plus a small book on the Sharia, the Muslim law, prepares them to meet the requirements on religion included in the Government examinations at the end of the sixth year. In the secondary schools no religious teaching is required, but in the normal school Muslim law is included. One questions, however, how long this may be a fixed requirement, as a modern spirit of inquiry is beginning to be evident.

The teachings of the Quran are no longer required: in the elementary schools the instruction is practically nil; in the secondary schools some attention is given to the Islamic law. Schools are given the choice between teaching religion and ethics. There seems to be a decided tendency to prefer the latter. There is a marked difference between the present attitude toward the teaching of Islam and the attitude of only a few years ago. The outward conventions requited by Islamic tradition—curtained inner and outer doorways and no men visitors or teachers—were always very carefully observed until the order from the Shah came in May 1935 suddenly abolishing the chaddur. Only girls who appeared unveiled could receive a diploma or school honours.

Most of the young girls discarded the chaddur, many for the first time, but a few paid the penalty of their parents' conservatism. In Tabriz the winners of the first and second honours at the Normal School Celebration had to relinquish their prizes because they could not receive these awards unveiled. These regulations against the veil both for students and teachers, have played a leading part in the emancipation movement which reached its dramatic climax in the official endorsement of the Shah at the Normal School Celebration, now an historic event. Perhaps more astonishing to the hundreds who have attended the graduation exercises of the Government schools in Teheran and Tabriz have been the gymnastic exhibitions, held within the last year, in which young Iranian girls in shorts engaged in active exercises and sports. The enforced freedom from the chaddur in girls' schools may mean a complete orientation in girls' education.

The physical schools has been developed along the more formal type of gymnastic exercise. The creative forms of recreation through various extracurricular activities are scarcely known. New emphases, however, are being introduced by an American adviser to the Ministry of Education. A class of thirty-two young women in 1935 finished a course of three months in scouting as a -preparation to develop this work in the girls' schools. Another group has been trained in sports to offset the programme of conventional calisthenics.

An effort is also being made to introduce more social plays, and games, and especially music, all of which are innovations. The programme of athletics in girls' schools has been given a great deal of newspaper publicity through frequent pictures of Girl Guide troops and girls in, active games and exercises. Thus the public is being effectively educated to this new idea of girlhood. School hygiene is also receiving attention.

A special medical officer visits the schools, inspects the sanitary conditions, examines the children and sends those needing special attention to the clinic or hospital where free treatment is given. But since these visits are not very frequent, perhaps only once a month, the regular teacher is expected to emphasize the fundamentals of health. A distinctive feature of the teaching profession in Iran has been the work of the women inspectors. The system of having women inspectors, which was established when the private schools were brought under Government supervision, was necessitated by the fact that it was impossible because of the veil for men to visit girls' schools. Thus a social handicap has led to a constructive educational benefit.

The women inspectors, many of whom are graduates of the American School for Girls in Teheran, represent a high type in the teaching profession. One of the best known of the women inspectors is Khanum Doulatabadee, the pioneer in girls' education already mentioned, who was one of the first women from Iran to study abroad.

As Iranian girls at that time did not leave their own country alone, the ever watchful police held up at the border this eager student on her way to Paris, until verification could be received from Teheran. Today Iranian women students as well as men pursue higher education abroad. But women students have not yet received Government scholarships for foreign study. For over eighty years Iranian boys have been sent abroad for foreign study. Practically all of the present leaders of Iran have studied in Europe, the large majority in France.

An increasing number have been sent from the different ministries—Education, Health, justice and others.

Although some of the other Ministries are still sending students abroad the Ministry of Education has now discontinued these foreign scholarships, at least temporarily, and is concentrating on the development of stronger institutions of higher learning in Iran. When a law was passed authorizing too foreign scholarships annually for five years for young men but making no provision for women students, the obvious inequality evoked a vigorous protest from some of the advocates of women's education. Ten to twenty scholarships for teacher training were urged for women. The question became the subject of heated discussion carried on in the Press. The opponents argued on the basis of unpreparedness of girls and the danger of Western contamination, contending furthermore that Iran offered adequate training for girls.

The advocates of foreign scholarships for girls, among whom were several women, cited as proof of the capacity of girls the number of successful candidates in Government examination, and maintained that women would be less contaminated morally than men have been by foreign contact. They emphasized the necessity of training in Europe because of the backward conditions in Iran, which make adequate training impossible.

The discussion brought into sharp relief the conflict in Iran today between conservatism and progress. In spite of a strong tide in favour of foreign scholarships for girls, the opposition prevailed. No girls have been officially included on the Government lists, but a few, six or eight, have been partially helped by Government funds. However, quite a number of Iranian girls, perhaps sixty or more, are now studying abroad, mostly in Europe on private funds.

Recently, higher education in Iran for girls has been the subject of much public discussion. The conservatives in Iran as elsewhere East or West have advanced the argument that girls not only do not need advanced education but should not have it, since it units them for home life. But quite aside from the opposition against higher education for women, there seems to be as yet on the whole very little demand for it in Iran. Nurbakush, Sage College, meets the needs as yet of the small minority who desire to go beyond the secondary school. The Government University will be eventually opened to women students in departments, beginning first with dentistry and pharmacy, for which courses several women students have already applied.

The prevailing lack of urge for higher education up to the present time is doubtless related to the fact that the interest in professional careers in Iran has not yet in any sense cut across the idea of marriage. Aside from teaching which, as has been said, is considered as an economic necessity rather than a career, there is practically no profession open to Muslim girls in Iran. Marriage is the main career. To ensure a good marriage, education up to a point is regarded as desirable. This explains in Iran as elsewhere the increasing number of girls in school beyond the primary and secondary stage. But higher education is not considered an additional marriage asset; perhaps this explains the lack of desire for it.

The fact that the education of girls is being extended, however, through the secondary stage is very important. The longer period of education and later marriage age point to the eventual solution of one of the major problems of Iran and of the East as a whole—the disparity between the literate husband and illiterate wife. Some few attempts are being made in private schools in Teheran to meet the problem of the present generation of illiterate wives, many of whom are pathetically eager to bridge the gap between themselves and their husbands.

Some of them are beyond the schoolgirl stage and can only laboriously overcome the handicap of illiteracy.

Many are still the age of schoolgirls and eager to attend the regular schools, which, however, are already overcrowded and cannot admit married women or girls. A few private schools for married women have been started such as, for example, the one carried on by a Women's Association in Iran. These schools are small but significant, showing what should be done on a much larger scale to meet this important social problem.

The growing consciousness of this problem—the disparity in education between men and women—is one of the main secrets of the present awakening of interest in education for girls and women in Iran, whether it finds expression in the primary or secondary schools or in meagre adult education efforts. A few years ago there was not as at present this poignant awareness of the fact that Iranian women without education are under a terrific handicap.

The social and intellectual cleavage between men and women in Iran was not questioned. But today there is a growing consciousness of a need for change. The younger generation of educated men want educated wives in Iran as elsewhere. The Iranian mother desires to see her daughter well married and enjoying an equality in marriage such as she, herself, has been denied. Perhaps just as in Baghdad the increase of foreign wives in the higher circles has made some Teheran mothers realize the desirability of educating their daughters.

Doubtless, Muslim women in Iran, especially in Teheran, have been affected also by a comparison of their social and educational position with that of women in other communities. The Armenians, in giving up the chaddur a number of years ago and availing themselves freely of educational opportunity have furnished a progressive example.

The Zoroastrian community with its freedom from social handicaps for women, and its active promotion of girls' schools may have also had an influence, although the forward movement of Zoroastrian women has produced no outstanding women leaders. More significant for Muslim women perhaps has been the example of the women of the Bahai community, who though still veiled, are quite free behind the veil, representing thus a halfway stage of progress.

The fact that in many communities the Bahai Girls' was the first and only school for a long time has undoubtedly stimulated Muslim educational effort, but the Bahaist influence is less important today than in the earlier period. The Muslim woman's desire for education and general advance has also been greatly affected by the social reforms in Turkey.

A direct influence on the educational progress of Muslim women has also come from the Anglo-Saxon schools, the British and American Mission girls' schools in different parts of Irani and especially Nurbakush in Teheran. These institutions have effectively presented to the community the highest value of education for girls. Without discussing freedom or apparently promoting freedom for women, they produce an atmosphere in which freedom is the natural result. At the commencement of Nurbakush in May 1929 for the first time the three Muslim graduates unveiled delivered their graduating addresses to an audience of eight hundred people, and were received with enthusiasm and applause.

The Mission Schools for Girls in Tabriz and Hamadan have deeply affected a whole area. The Shiraz Girls' School, formerly a Mission institution but now under private auspices has been a distinctive influence for education along modern English lines. It represents an adaptation of Anglo-Saxon ideals. Alborz College in Teheran, the American College for Men, has without question been a great force for the social and educational progress of women, in that it has given to its large student body of young men from all over Iran new social ideals.

The increasing penetration of Anglo-Saxon ideas, as represented in the British and American schools in Iran, is an interesting evidence of the new trend in Iran away from the European model of life and thought. For over eighty years French influence has been dominant. French is the second language; the educational system is modelled on French lines; Paris has always been the Mecca for Iranian students. But in the present period of awakening, a migration from French to Anglo-Saxon influence is evident, which is having a pervasive effect on the social and educational advance of women.

Although foreign influences, French and English, are exerting a subtle force toward change in various phases of Iranian life, the impelling motive of the present renaissance, of which the advance of women is a part, in Iran as in Iraq, is the newly aroused spirit of nationalism. This has for Iran the special meaning of a growth in the consciousness of national unity and a new appreciation of Iranian culture. The building of roads has facilitated travel and brought hitherto isolated cities into closer contact. The divided provincial loyalties of the past are being supplanted by a national loyalty and pride, which demands that Iran should not have an inferior position in the East. A few leaders in Iran recognize that the advance of women is a necessity for national progress and are therefore vigorously promoting girls' education. Even by the less thinking majority, education for girls is being accepted as a natural part of the new era.

Girls' Education in India

The obvious reason for the lack of education among Muslim women is purdah and general Muslim conservatism, an interrelated cause and effect. Purdah lays a detaining hand on the Muslim girl's education. It interferes not only after the veil is assumed, which is usually not until the age Eleven or twelve years, but also before that age; the prevailing purdah psychology often prevents even little girls, not yet veiled, from attending the primary school, which does not have a woman teacher. Because of the dearth of women teachers in the primary schools many Muslim girls never cross the threshold of a school.

The direct effect of purdah on the number of girls in school is shown by the fact that in purdah-bound provinces like the Punjab and the United Provinces, the attendance of girls in school is lower than in other provinces. Aside from the fact that purdah undoubtedly curtails the school privileges of Muslim girls, it presents very practical difficulties in education. At the opening or closing hour, or in a smaller town like Bhopal, the covered bullock-carts lined up at the school door, and have watched the shrouded figures scuttle from the entrance of the school compound into the curtained safety of the conveyance.

In addition to the purdah conveyance, the necessity for a female attendant to accompany the girl to see to it that purdah is not broken on the way to school, and the elaborate precautions necessary for preserving strict purdah in the school, for example requiring even the elimination of all male servants from girls' schools—these restrictions have vastly complicated school life for a Muslim girl in India.

Other social customs characteristic of India, but not peculiar to Muslims, have prevented Muslim girls, as well as Indian girls of other communities, from having full educational privileges. Although child marriage is especially associated with Hinduism, early marriage among the masses of Muslims is also quite common.

In 1921 out of eight and a half million brides under fifteen years of age one and a half million were Muslims. This means that number of girls were cut off from any education beyond the early primary grades. With attention concentrated on early marriage for their daughter, the Muslim parents' chief concern naturally is to find a suitable son-in-law. Hence, attendance of girls in the primary school seems unnecessary and in the middle school is obviously impossible. As girls are withdrawn from school just at the time when they begin to mature in mind as well as body, this not only cuts off the majority from ordinary education but reduces to a minimum the number of Muslim girls who might become teachers.

The education of Muslim girls has been impeded not only by the specific handicaps of purdah and early marriage, but frequently by the conservatism of the Indian Muslim community. This conservatism has been strengthened by the Nationalist Movement. Muslim India in its fear of absorption by the Hindus, has shown a reaction similar to the attitude the Muslim community in Palestine in reference to Zionism. Some Muslim leaders have always insisted on having special privileges in schools for Muslims, unwilling otherwise to avail themselves of the regular facilities of education in India.

The general situation, of education for Muslim girls shows a very slow but steady advance both in the number of schools for girls and of girls in schools. After 1920 the curve of elementary and secondary schools begins to ascend. This period marks also practically the beginning of higher education for Muslim girls, although the number of Muslim girls is still negligible. Isabella Thoburn College in Lucknow, and Kinnaird College for Women in Lahore, which may be taken as valid criteria, show a steady increase of Muslims as also of girls from other communities. The few Muslim women who are well educated often hold positions of unusual prominence.

A widely known Muslim woman in the Punjab, the first woman to take her doctorate, has an important post as an inspectress for girls' schools. She has maintained strict purdah and thus proved that in spite of the purdah, advance in education is possible. But it may also be questioned whether by such a policy she. Has not sacrificed an opportunity to exert greater influence for social advance, as the first highly educated Muslim woman in her part of India.

Of the widespread desire of Muslim parents for the education of their daughters there is no question today; even more evident is the eager response of Muslim girls themselves to these new opportunities.

The renaissance in education is affecting not only the extent but also the character of the Government programme for girls' schools. Under the old system the few girls who entered college found themselves well prepared for equal competition with men in professional careers; but preparation for marriage, the primary career for the great majority in India, as elsewhere in the East, has received little attention. The regular Government schools and the majority of private girls' schools have been bound by the straitjacket of the examination system.

Homemaking subjects, physical education, and hygiene have been only optional and difficult to promote, since the parents, as well as students, regard the school certificate based on the regular requirements as the final seal of education. There is, however, some loosening of the straitjacket bonds, through the beginning of vocational training and homemaking courses, and more physical education.

A certain amount of vocational education has been developed in connection with the regular schools. Some of the Mission schools' have pioneered in this field attempting to coordinate girls' education more closely with the needs of practical life.

The most distinctive development in the Government system is the Government Zenana Industrial Schools in Lahore of which there are now fifteen. In addition to regular elementary education these schools offer courses in home arts and crafts along very modem lines. Although these schools are open to girls and women of different religions, and social levels, and different ages they especially serve Muslims and offer particularly the uneducated *purdahnashin* a belated opportunity to overcome her lack of earlier educational development by the right type of useful vocational training. The response of Muslim schoolgirls to education, keen as it is, perhaps is not as eager as is the desire of some young Muslim women, who were married at an early age and thus deprived of education.

The growing demand for more educational facilities for Muslim girls today reflects in no small measure the effect of some of the non-Muslim communities The Parsees because of their social freedom of women, the Brahma Samaj community because of its aggressive social reforms, and the Christians because of their widespread facilities for education and the large number of Christian women pioneers in professional life have in different degrees helped to stimulate the social and educational advance of Muslim girls. A few outstanding Hindu reformers, men and women, have also undoubtedly exerted a strong influence in the advance of Indian women as a whole affecting Muslims as well as Hindus. Undoubtedly one of the main forces that has steadily promoted the educational and social development of Indian women of all communities, has been the Christian institutions for girls. These schools were very often the first school for girls in a community, and today they still constitute a large part of girls' education in India.

The study of progress in the education of girls and women in India, is virtually a study of the educational efforts of Missions. Certain institutions have had a special effect on the education of Muslim girls, notably the two Christian Colleges in North India already mentioned– Kinnaird College and Isabella Thoburn College, and the Women's Christian College in Madras. The increase in Muslim students in Kinnaird College is a special indication of a breaking down of conservatism since the Government College observes purdah strictly. A growing number of Muslim fathers desire the more liberal type of education.

In 1925 two Muslim girls, swathed in shroudlike -white burqas were awarded their diplomas from Isabella Thoburn College which issues its diplomas at the convocation of the University of Lucknow. In 1929 three Muslim girls on the same platform received their diplomas, unveiled with all the other men and women students. Their names were read off in the alphabetical list and no one in the audience paid any attention to whether they were Hindu, Muslim, or Christian.

Since that time all Muslim students have received their diplomas publicly in the Lucknow University. In the liberalizing atmosphere of these colleges for women, such an advance is regarded as merely the natural result of a modern education. Some of the men's colleges are also exerting a progressive influence on women's education.

The major factor in the promotion of educational and social progress today is the influence exerted by Indian women themselves, both individually and through collective effort. A decade ago, only a few Indian women were conscious of their responsibility as a force for advance. Today there is a growing number of educated leaders who are devoting themselves to the crusade of education for the hundreds of thousands of uneducated women who, still behind the purdah, arc voiceless to make known their needs.

In the small minority of highly cultivated leaders, who are advocates of education, one can single out from different parts of India the few outstanding Muslim leaders who are devoting themselves untiringly to the promotion of woman's education and social reform.

A number of women's organizations in India have as their primary objective education and social reform, and through collective effort are influencing public opinion and official policy. Viewed in the light of statistics, the appalling illiteracy of Indian women, the comparatively small number of girls in schools, the withdrawal from school of many girls after but one year, the growing disparity in education between men and women, the dearth of women teachers—and with all of these facts intensified in reference to Muslim women the situation does indeed seem depressing. But the upward curve in the education of girls, Muslims as well as others, has begun. Official and private agencies are increasing the educational facilities for girls. The general public, including even the conservatives, has awakened to the need to educate girls as well as boys. The eager response of girls to these new opportunities is everywhere evident. Progressive influences, foreign and Indian, are working unitedly on this common problem of education for girls.

Educational Ideals in Egypt

Due to the slow development of education, Egyptian women did not begin to emerge from illiteracy until after a spirit of nationalism asserted itself in 1919. Popular education, properly speaking, either for boys or girls, had its beginning in Egypt after that date. The previous unimportant position of education in Egyptian policy is shown by the fact that Lord Milliners's book *England in Egypt* devotes only a few pages to education and the *Encyclopaedia Britannia* gives it barely a page in small type. Up to this time popular education meant for the most part native schools, largely under untrained and even illiterate teachers, whose main qualification was their ability to chant the Quran. Under these conditions the figures for illiteracy and the disparity in education between girls and boys, are not surprising. Many of the women teachers could neither read nor write.

Anything above elementary schools for girls was obviously not considered. The Government in 1920 had only five primary girls' schools with 843 Pupils. Since that time there has been a definite forward movement in education. The new Constitution of Egypt, proclaimed in 1923, provided for free and compulsory primary education, with 1935 set as the objective date for realizing this educational aim. Obviously this achieve-ment has not been possible in such a limited period, but the country is moving toward that goal. There were in 1929 in contrast to 1919 almost twice as many elementary schools, and more than twice as many girls in elementary schools; almost three times as many higher elementary schools with almost three times as many higher elementary students; nine times as many schools for teachers' training for elementary schools with a little less than six times the increase in students; three times as many kindergarten schools and seven times the number of children; four times as many primary schools and four times the number of primary pupils.

This period marked also the beginning of secondary education for girls and the addition of a special college for girls; the transition from the old style makable school, often held in a mere hovel and taught by an illiterate teacher, to a well-organized modern school under a trained teacher; and the introduction of modern kindergartens on the Friable model. But the most significant progress of this first decade lies in the fact that it marks the beginning of modem education for girls and its advance from the elementary grade to the college and university level.

The real landmark as regards girls' education is the year 1925 when girls' secondary education was officially established. Before 1925 a great gulf divided the status of boys' and girls' education. The fact that lower standards were required for teaching in girls' primary schools than in boys' schools, illustrated the inferiority of girls' education. Teachers for the boys' schools had to complete their secondary education before being admitted for teachers' training; whereas women teachers for girls' schools obtained the primary certificate after only four years' study in primary schools, and in addition the four years' course of a training college. Graduates of unusual ability were sent to England, but few won this opportunity, because of their short period of training and limited scope of knowledge. Girls not desirous of teaching suffered from the lack of general cultural values in the course.

Egyptian leaders, however, have recognized the inadequacy of the preparation for teachers of girls' schools and the resultant inequality of the educational status of boys and girls, and have accordingly promoted the addition of secondary schools for girls. To serve the two types of girls—those of the leisure class, desiring general education, and those preparing to teach—secondary education was differentiated into two types of courses.

Some of the educators who are directing the policy of girls' education in Egypt, recognize the desirability of more differentiation in girls' education, especially in the secondary schools. The objectives of education for girls are not adequately met by the prescribed curriculum which was built to serve the needs of boys. Education of boys has been directed largely toward a Government Job and therefore based on the "white collar and clean hands" idea of education.

Such a system, which no longer fits the needs of boys, is obviously unsuited for girls. The difficulty of achieving differentiation in girls' education, however, is obvious because of the hidebound examination system. If equality in education for girls and boys means identical standards then differentiation in the girls' programme is impossible.

The important question is whether the special needs of girls can be met without sacrificing the principle of true equality. Opinion is divided on this subject. Some teachers advocate more attention to vocational education such as the industrial arts. An Industrial Arts Course is offered in the Elementary Teachers' Training Schools, but as a whole general vocational training is not yet considered necessary since the usual vocational lines, which constitute in the West the means of economic livelihood for the masses, do not exist for the Muslim girls. The girls' schools of Egypt are, of course, primarily geared to the needs of Muslims, because of the very large proportion of Muslims in the population.

Commenting on the question as to the need for vocational training for girls, the Director of Girls' Education some years ago said: "The public is not ready for economic liberty for women. It will be another twenty-five years before women will be in many professions in Egypt. We are pushing vocational training for boys, of course, as an economic necessity."

A gymnastics exhibition of two thousand primary

schoolgirls under the supervision of the Egyptian Directress of Physical Education, illustrated the development of physical education for girls in Egypt. The complete freedom of the Egyptian girls at that time seemed refreshing in contrast with the veil-restricted life of schoolgirls in most of the other Muslim countries. This exhibition, the Second Annual Exhibition of the Physical Education Department in Cairo was held in the Gezireh sports grounds before a very large and representative gathering.

The children, with complete abandon and schoolgirl enthusiasm, carried out the varied programme, which showed incidentally the influence of the Supervisor's training in England-relay races and games, English country dances, drills and marches. The Muslim Director was assisted by a group of teachers, all Muslims, a fact which one recognized by their neatly bound scarf headdress, which to the casual observer did not suggest a special Muslim style but gave only the impression of a distinctive fashion worn in preference to the hat. There was no suggestion of the veil or the psychology of the veil in their manner. And yet, one knew that it could not have happened a few years earlier in Cairo and at that time was possible in no other Muslim country except Turkey. Today Iran, as we have said, also endorses this full measure of freedom. Although the Islamic social customs have greatly changed, modernism in Egypt has not meant secularism in the schools. The teaching of Islam in the girls' schools is still being carried on but in a modern way by young teachers trained in the tenets of their religion.

The modern method of teaching religion in the Egyptian schools is appreciated in other countries. Palestine has occasionally turned to Egypt for a trained woman teacher of religion. The religious teaching in the training schools is given by sheikhs, not the elderly type as formerly, but often young sheikhs, some of whom have been trained in Europe. These younger sheikhs are the products of the new reforms of Al Azhar, the great intellectual centre of the Muslim world. The study of science and comparative religions in Europe can scarcely fail to have its effect.

Today the inclusion of the teaching of Islam in the school programme is a formal recognition of religion, one feels, rather than a vital endorsement of Islam, such as would characterize Muslim teaching in India. Girls in Normal School have always been supposed to keep their heads covered in classes taught by men, but this is no longer observed. Moreover, they do not now have the attitude of passive acquiescent deference before the sheikh as in the past. Sometimes the sheikhs have to call in a woman teacher to help in discipline. The freedom of the Muslim schools of Cairo today is in striking contrast to the general conditions fifteen or twenty years ago, as related by one of the English inspectresses, who had taught for a number of years in a private school in Lower Egypt. "Formerly the girls were always brought to school in covered conveyances; men clerks could not be employed. The girls were all closely veiled, visited very little even in the homes of girls with whom they had been special friends in school, and after their marriage rarely saw each other. There was no need for more than primary schools as early marriage was the rule. Contact with foreigners was very slight; in fact, the Egyptians were afraid of foreigners." This, she explained, was not true of Cairo, but of Zagazig, a typical large town in Lower Egypt. "When I opened the Girls' School in Zagazig twenty years ago," she continued, "the little girls were very much frightened. One little girl especially would not allow me to do anything for her for three days. Then when she finally allowed me to undo the little Quran amulet to wash her neck, I knew that her fear had been broken."

What a striking contrast to that day of seclusion and fear of contact one finds in modern Egypt today with its crowded primary and secondary schools and its public gymnastics exhibitions. The social conservatism of the authorities does not in any way seem to retard the educational development of girls. The schools remain technically in the frame of Islam, but each year the frame is widened. The modern spirit dominates in spite of the adherence to certain traditions. Undoubtedly, one of the greatest difficulties in promoting rural education in Egypt is the placement of teachers. As in India and elsewhere the difference in living standards and in social mores makes it practically impossible for young women teachers to live in backward village areas. Furthermore trained women teachers are reluctant to leave the interests and amusements of the large city. There are few special inducements offered for rural service; quite the contrary, in fact, as positions in Cairo are often given as the reward for merit and students of lower scholarship are sent to villages. This problem is a subject for serious consideration. The most noteworthy advance in girls' education in Egypt during the last decade and a half has been the successful establishment of a trained teaching staff. The growth from two training colleges for women elementary teachers in 1920 to fifteen in 1934 with an increase in students from 447 to 1,132 shows that women teachers have been poured out in increasing volume.

In spite of the rapidity of the process a high standard of training has been maintained by the English supervisors and English principals of the training colleges. The teaching profession has been made especially desirable. Egyptian women students in the training schools have received free board, and free tuition and sometimes even a stipend; whereas men in training have had only free tuition.

Women teachers have received better salaries in Egypt than teachers in any other part of the Near East, and often better than men in Government service. As a result, the supply has caught up with the demand, and in the elementary colleges even exceeded it. The definite Government endorsement of teaching has undoubtedly encouraged Muslim girls to enter the profession. Women have been given more official recognition in education than in any other field. A Muslim woman teacher some years ago was on the Government Education Board.

One of the inspectresses of women's education recently commented on the number of women teachers in evidence at the Ministry of Education and called attention especially to their complete freedom of expression. "There is no feeling of inhibition before the Director of Education; in fact, most of the women teachers would be quite free to express an opinion even to the Minister of Education."

The self-assurance and spirit of independence of Muslim women teachers in Egypt is especially worthy of comment because of the fact that Egyptian women have so recently entered professional life. Such an attitude is in sharp contrast to the hesitant attitude which is often characteristic of Muslim women of the old-fashioned type. The woman teacher typifies this new freedom of Egyptian women. In the establishment of the teaching profession for women, the system of foreign scholarships has been an important factor. From 1922 to 1930 the number of scholarships for women increased from ten to forty. The increase of applicants has made possible more careful selection, first from each school, then from the best from all the schools. Muslims, because of their larger number of applicants, have a practical though not theoretical preference.

Various lines of training are followed-Froebel

kindergarten courses, Domestic Science, Art, Physical Training, and regular courses for the B.A. degree. These students are naturally sent to England because of the language and the general English basis on which education in Egypt is being developed. English headmistresses are now being replaced by Egyptian headmistresses, of whom a number have been chosen since the appointment of the first Egyptian headmistress, Mine Mansour Fahmy, a widely known educator. One of the distinctive forces promoting educational advance for women in Egypt. Is the Feminist Union of Cairo which, from its inception, has promoted as one of its primary aims, equality of educational opportunity for girls, requesting first the opening of girls' secondary schools later the admission of women into the university, and the granting of foreign scholarships to girls. Through lectures, a woman's magazine, and in various other ways the Feminist Union has sought to promote the intellectual and moral advance of women as a necessary preparation for political and social equality.

The Feminist Union is also carrying on an interesting educational project-an industrial school where two hundred girls of the poorer class are given a general education, also domestic science, needlework and carpet making, as a means of earning a livelihood. There have been some interesting developments in adult education in Egypt. Several years ago a very ambitious programme of lectures for women was promoted by a movement called the Reconstruction Education Movement. We have already referred to the lecture on the advance of women given by Madame Hoda Sharawi Pasha at the American University of Cairo. Lectures of this type are a regular part of the programme of the University Extension Department, which has as its objective the education of the public along lines that are of national interest. There can be little question of the educational and social influence of having a Muslim woman deliver an address on the status of women before a mixed audience of perhaps a thousand people with two hundred women and a large number of white-turbaned sheikhs.

Foreign influence has had a more pervasive effect on educational and social advance in modern Egypt than in any other country of the Near East, exerting its influence with less shock. But French influence has been dominant ever since Mehmet Ali imported the body of French savants and Ismail followed a policy of conscious exposure of Egypt to French culture. The second language is French, the atmosphere and prevailing culture is French. As far as women are concerned, the upper class especially has been greatly influenced by French styles and French culture through private education, social contact and travel. It is interesting that British culture has not been the dominant influence in Egypt in view of the long period of occupation.

At the present time, however, there is a distinct increase in English influence, which is exerted primarily through the public school. English specialists in education, English methods of education. Egyptian students studying in England, the general use of English in the schools—all these are significant evidences and causes of the increase in English cultural influence. The Anglo-Saxon influence has been, in general, very favourable to a growth in social freedom and the educational advance of women.

Anglo-Saxon influence has affected Egypt not only through English, but also through American channels, especially through the American Mission schools. Many of these institutions antedate the Government schools and have been an outstanding educational force over a long period. The first girls' school in Egypt was opened by an American Mission seventeen years before the first Government school for girls was established by Ismail.

The Assiut Mission School through educating a large number of Coptic women as well as a smaller number of Muslims had Mach education for girls in Assiut recognized as a necessity.

The American College for Girls in Cairo, a junior college, the most advanced institution for girls in Egypt, has demonstrated the value of higher education and prepared leaders for various professional careers and for lives of general usefulness. The College has for a long period had a large proportion of Muslim students. The American institutions for men, Assiut College and the American University at Cairo, which admits women to its courses, have played an important part in promoting the advance of women by educating young Egyptian men to a proper understanding of the position of women in society. One can scarcely speak of Syrian influence as foreign in relation to Egypt because of the cultural unity between the two countries established through the language, but as an outside influence coming into Egypt, Syria has played an important part. A number of early Syrian leaders, who have contributed greatly to the thought life of Egypt, have now become entirely identified with Egypt. Syrian influence is recognized as a definite element of progress.

The effect of modern Turkey on progress in Egypt, especially on promoting the development of women, has been less direct and obvious than in Iraq or Persia. Although the Turkish reforms have not been taken as a goal in Egypt as in other countries, there is, however, little question of the indirect effect of Turkey, as an example of a progressive Muslim country. The day has passed in Egypt when foreign influence is needed to promote either directly, or by example, the appreciation of girls' education.

National pride actuates modernists and reactionaries alike to promote education for girls as well as for boys as part of the programme of progress. Nationalism in Egypt is not merely a political passion. It has had the deeper meaning of a birth of national consciousness. This new spirit has generated the dynamic power for national advance. But unlike Turkey, Egypt has not considered advancement of woman as a sine qua non of national progress.

Education in Palestine

Under the Turkish regime very little attention was given to the education of Muslim girls. Some improvement began after 1908 with the opening of a few girls' schools by the Government. But as the language of the schools was Turkish, they had a limited effect in an Arabic-speaking country.

For the great majority of Muslim girls education was confined as elsewhere to the very heterogeneous Quran schools. A few girls of the upper classes received from the convent schools a somewhat sketchy education, consisting of a smattering of French, and a bit of handwork and embroidery. A smaller number was given instruction of sorts at home, but the foreign governess did not play as important a role in Palestine, as in Egypt and Turkey, in bringing the education and culture of the West into the harem. Hence, comparatively few of the higher class Muslim girls in Palestine had any educational advantages. The situation for Christian girls was quite different because of the large number of Mission institutions in Palestine.

These Mission institutions practically left untouched the Muslim communities; hence, there was a great contrast in the educational advancement of Muslim and Christian women of the prewar generation. This explains the fact that the literacy of women of the Christian community is approximately eighty per cent in contrast to five per cent for Muslim women. There is a similar difference in the literacy of Christian and Muslim men, of ninety per cent for Christians and ten per cent for Muslims. The postwar period marks the beginning of the new regime in education for all, but especially for Muslim girls. Since that time a Government programme has been vigorously promoted and the Muslim community also has undertaken education for girls as well as for boys.

The growth through the Government programme is clearly shown by the steady increase in the number of girls in attendance in schools since 1919. More than twice as many girls were in the Arabic public schools, the Government system, in 1932-33 as in 1920. This increase in the girls in Government schools marks primarily an increase in Muslim girls who are being educated, since the great majority of Christians attend private institutions.

The lack of education for Muslim girls, however, is shown by the contrast between the number of Christian and Muslim girls in school. In 1932 a little less than half of the total number of girls in schools of Palestine, both public and private were Muslims, a fact which has special meaning since seventy per cent of the population of Palestine is Muslim.

A further evidence of the lack of education for Muslim girls is the difference in the number of schools for Muslim girls and boys, and also in the enrolment of each sex. In 1932-33 there were almost ten times as many schools for boys as for girls in the Arab public system, and in rural Palestine, one girls' school for thirty boys' schools.

As to the enrolment the total number of Muslim boys in school in both public and private institutions, was four times that of Muslim girls in schools of all kinds. The difference between the education of Muslim girls and of Muslim boys offers a significant contrast to the situation in the Christian community where there is practical equality in education for boys and girls.' Education for girls in Palestine is still in the primary stage.

The Government policy has been to promote primary schools throughout Palestine for the masses before raising the level of education for the few, who may be ready for the higher grades. In carrying out this policy of promoting primary education, the Government is developing village schools as rapidly as the villages will assume the cost of buildings.

The rural programme will benefit Muslims especially, as the rural population is very largely Arab. The great majority of rural schools, however, are as yet for boys. Muslim girls would receive more education if social conditions made possible coeducation.

The policy of developing education in harmony with general needs is shown by the emphasis on practical subjects. There is as yet no vocational training except courses in domestic arts and homemaking. In several places practical instruction in infant welfare is provided through visits of the students to the infant welfare clinic under the supervision of the doctor and trained nurse.

Emphasis in the Government schools is also given to physical education, singing and games, and drill. Interscholastic netball matches are held every year.

The Girl Guide Movement has been very popular in Palestine. There are over one thousand Guides-guiders, brownies and rangers. All of the companies except the Y.W.C.A. companies, are connected with schools. The Girl Guide displays and prize-giving programmes are limited to women and must be carried on under careful harem restrictions.

Training camps for leaders and small groups of girls which are held every year, make a marked appeal. A Western visitor to one of these camps finds it especially interesting to watch the arrival of Muslim Guides at camp; they arrive black-veiled and black-clothed and reappear from their tents completely different in their grey uniforms and picturesque white headdresses. This transformation is a symbol of the effect of the Girl Guide Movement, which unites girls of different religions and gives them all a wider, freer outlook.

In developing the general system of education for girls, Palestine faced the common problem of the East—the dearth of trained teachers. In 1932-33 there were only 172 women teachers in a total of 827 teachers in the Government schools.

The special importance of the Teachers' Training College is, therefore, obvious and the growth of this college is an index of the steadily ascending curve of girls' education. This institution, which has always had an English Principal, has shown a continuous increase in the number of students and especially in the proportion of Muslim girls. Some years ago it was necessary to take the Muslim girls free of charge. Only girls of the middle class, and those merely because of economic necessity, were willing to enter.

Today the inducement of free tuition is no longer necessary; the applicants for admission include daughters of some of the best families in Jerusalem. Hitherto teaching has been considered as a respectable profession, but in the general public mind no girl would enter teaching except as an economic necessity, and certainly no girl of social position would teach. The Training College is successfully changing this idea. In the beginning trained Egyptian and Syrian teachers were enlisted for service in Palestine. Now they are being replaced by graduates from the Training College.

The need for primary teachers was so urgent that the requirements at the beginning could not be too high nor the selection of candidates too rigid, but now higher standards for admission are required and greater care can be taken in selecting candidates for training. A more advanced course has also been developed, in addition to the regular teachers' training, in order to meet the need for a secondary school for paying pupils.

In promoting this programme of steady growth the Teachers' Training College has been very careful to stay within the conventions of the veil, which are still widely observed in Palestine. There are of course Christian students who do not observe Muslim customs but the general atmosphere of the school is in harmony with Muslim ideas. By its distinctly harem conditions the Training College has achieved its primary objective of winning the confidence of even conservative Muslim parents, and attracting Muslim girls for training.

Aside from the Director of Education, who visits the school freely, no men are allowed. But when the Director later visits the schools where the training students teach, often the teachers veil. This is an interesting contrast between Egypt and Palestine, as Egyptian teachers have never veiled before the Directors on their visits to the schools. When other men visitors come to the Training College, the girls are told in advance and given the opportunity of veiling. The girls are not allowed to receive any male visitors except the immediate family or relatives. The commencement exercises, sports, contests, and other school gatherings have only women audiences. For the classes in the Quran the girls all have their faces covered even though the sheikh is often an elderly man. In the Training College these elderly religious leaders have not been replaced by young sheikhs as in Cairo.

But some of the girls' schools now have women teachers. It is safe to surmise that no ethical teachings along modern lines are injected into these Muslim classes in religion.

Although the Training College carefully avoids promoting modern social or religious ideas, it is steadily laying the foundation for a future social freedom which seems inevitable. The impact of modern ideas is irresistible so that the individual girl is unconsciously being led toward social change. In order that the excellent training given at the College may not be lost, a careful plan of supervision during the first year of teaching is followed and the final certificate is withheld until after that apprenticeship is satisfactorily completed.

The allocation of graduates from the Training College to their teaching posts presents in Palestine as elsewhere a serious problem. Prevailing social attitudes make it difficult and often impossible for a girl to teach outside of her own village. Christian as well as Muslim teachers insist on teaching at home, or perhaps the parents insist. For example, the parents of a girl living in Safe were unwilling to have her teach in Tiberias, less than an hour's distance away.

Muslim communities that are especially reactionary such as Hebron and Nablus, demand a Muslim teacher but social conditions make it difficult for a Muslim woman from outside to live in these places. Christian teachers often find difficulties in teaching in an entirely Muslim town where social conventions make life very restricted. For what might pass as harmless in Jerusalem is often considered to be questionable morals in a centre of greater conservatism. To meet the need for teachers in the village schools, the Training College in Jerusalem has established a Rural Training Centre in Ramallah which is about twelve miles from Jerusalem. The curriculum includes mainly practical subjects—Domestic Science, Needlework, Gardening and Care of Poultry.

All of the students for the first year, thirteen in number, are Muslims. The standard of living in the school is that of a village, with the same type of convenience but with an emphasis on health and cleanliness. The Department of Education has established a small number of foreign scholarships for girls. Several have hid training in Egypt, in the American University of Beirut, and in England. Palestine has not, however, promoted the foreign scholarship plan as vigorously as have Iraq and Egypt.

The major task has been the training of women teachers for the primary schools, which is being achieved in the Training College in Jerusalem. Secondary education has not been undertaken and therefore the preparation of secondary teachers by training abroad has not yet been promoted.

In spite of evidences of conservatism, which one finds with interesting variation in different places, and in reference to different questions related to girls' education, there is today a general acceptance of the idea of education for girls as well as boys.

Even in reactionary centres like Hebron a distinct change is evident as the demand stage had already begun in 1930, when the pressure for a new school was being felt. The keen interest in girls' education in Jerusalem represents the other end of the scale from Hebron. The Directress of the Mamuniya School, a Syrian Christian, commented on the increase of Muslim girls in the upper grades, as shown in this leading Muslim girls' school in Jerusalem. Interest is also growing in education for girls beyond the elementary stage. As has been said the Government has not as yet provided secondary schools for girls. But the Teachers' Training College has a two years' course and the Jerusalem College for Girls and also the Friends' School at Ramallah offer secondary education. These two institutions represent Christian effort of a very high type; the Friends' School is a Mission institution, the Jerusalem College for Girls, a private Christian enterprise with missionary cooperation, and some Government support. The latter, founded in 1918, is the highest institution for girls in Palestine, offering a fourteen years' course, which extends from the kindergarten through the secondary grade to teachers' training and the first year of university. The American Friends' School for Girls in Ramallah, the first school for girls in Palestine, which was founded in 1869, has been a most convincing argument for girls' education.

As a boarding school with girls from all over Palestine, its influence has been widespread and very beneficial. Obviously these two private schools cannot long satisfy the demand for secondary education of girls in Palestine. In the last decade of Government primary schools the number of Christians who have attended Government primary schools has increased and therefore the demand for free secondary education has grown steadily.

Through the Government schools, moreover, an entirely new Muslim client We for girls' primary and therefore also for secondary schools has been created. Today Palestine has passed beyond the period in which private schools can adequately meet the needs for girls' education. The growing demand for both primary and secondary schools is the real criterion of progress in girls' education in Palestine.

Aside from the educational facilities for girls, provided by Government schools and private Christian agencies, girls' education in the elementary stage is also being advanced by the Supreme Muslim Council, through funds from the mosque endowments. More money is expended for boys' schools, but the necessity for girls' education is recognized, and also the need for education on modern lines, which is shown by the effort to secure well-trained Muslim and Christian teachers from Syria.

In addition to the regular Government programme these schools of the Supreme Muslim Council stress especially Arabic and Islamic teaching. The objective in these schools, both for boys and girls, is to strengthen the Muslim influence and safeguard Islamic culture, which Muslim leaders have felt to be endangered by the, Zionist influx since the Mandate. "Strictly Muslim education is necessary," as the secretary of the Supreme Muslim Council explained, "because the Government cannot give the Arabic language adequate emphasis; nor Muslim tradition its full value."Although the veil is carefully maintained in these Muslim schools under the Supreme Council, the need for a modern programme and for modern methods of education is fully realized.

Whatever may be the reason, well-trained teachers are employed in these Muslim schools; games, Guide activities, dramatics are all encouraged as a part of the programme. The Supreme Muslim Council has also taken a very advanced step in establishing a number of foreign scholarships for Muslim girls; four in Helouan Training College in Cairo, and one in the Sidon Mission School for Household Economics in Syria, the only school of its kind in the Near East.

In addition to these foreign scholarships, a scholarship has been granted for nurses' training in the Jerusalem hospital. The influences which are producing an active interest in girls' education on the part of Muslim leaders are an interesting complex of conflicting tendencies.

Undoubtedly the presence of an aggressive Zionist minority, which is increasing in numbers and power, has affected the Muslim attitude and strangely enough along two opposing lines. The necessity for competition on an equal basis and consciousness of a lack of education and general Muslim lag, have spurred the Muslim community to progress.

The contrast between the educational development of Muslim women with that of the women from other communities, also furnishes the urge to promote education for Muslim girls as a necessary part of their general advance. On the other hand, the presence of an entirely different civilization nothing—could be more different than the conservative Muslim and the modern Zionist—has aroused a fear of absorption, and has therefore produced a defence psychology that tenaciously protects Arab and Islamic culture; hence the extreme social conservatism of the Arab community in Palestine, which adversely affects the position of women.

A leading citizen of Jerusalem who voices the policy of the Supreme Muslim Council expressed very clearly this double motivation of progress and conservatism: "Zionism brought an awakening of national consciousness and a sense of necessity for social uplift which must affect women. To oppose Zionism we have realized the necessity for the same weapons that the Zionists have. The Jews maintain a high educational level both for men and women. Hence, to bring up the Arab level we must educate Muslim women.

The inner life of Palestine, until after the World War, was singularly unaffected by foreign influence. The Christian groups from abroad which were concentrated in Jerusalem did not fuse into the life of the country as a whole. The very fact that Jerusalem is the sacred city of three great faiths has always divided the community into compartments.

The adherents of each religion leading segregated lives, Muslims and naturally most of all Muslim women, were quite isolated from the other currents of life, practically cut off from contact with the outside world. But the postwar period has brought Palestine as a whole, and especially Arab life, sharply into contact with modern forces.

The impact of foreign influence has not aroused as keen a desire for change as in Iraq. But the insistent exposure to modem life is undoubtedly having its effect. The promotion of school's for girls as for boys by the Government has presented the opportunity and thus stimulated the desire of the Muslim community to advance. Education for girls will doubtless develop more slowly than boys' education, but the forward movement seems assured.

In Trans-jordan education is the third item in the Government expenditure is an evidence that it is of primary interest in this newly formed political entity but very old country. Schools in Trans-Jordan under the Turkish regime were few and far between—seventeen schools for boys, four for girls, the traditional Quran schools. Practically all that remains of the Turkish school system now is the war-wreck of a rather good school building in Kerak, the former Turkish seat of government. The rest of the country seems to have been untouched by education save for a few Mission schools, which were and are very meagre in comparison with Mission schools elsewhere. But the postwar period has brought to Trans-Jordan, along with cinemas and automobiles, the development of education both for boys and girls.

For girls especially, the present period represents a clear gain over the prewar period, and steady progress in overcoming the disparity between girls' and boys' education. Fortunately Adib Wahby has remained Director of Education for a number of years and has been able to witness the results of his efforts. In 1930 there were eight times as many boys' primary schools as primary schools for girls; today the proportion is three to one. There is as yet, however, no girls' secondary school but four for boys.

In the beginning it was necessary to import women teachers from Syria and Palestine and pay them higher salaries than were paid to men teachers. The lure of the desert—Amman is just on the edge of the desert—did not appeal to the girl from Beirut or Jerusalem, accustomed to more "civilization." Today over half the women teachers are from Trans-Jordan, and their salaries arc no longer higher than those of men. Progress in education has equalized the salary standards so that the women teachers have lost their advantage. To attract Trans-Jordan girls of the better class into teaching has apparently not been very difficult, as there is less prejudice to break down in this breezy town of Amman on the desert's edge than in many more sophisticated cities. Moreover the well-paid young teachers from outside, representing the latest styles of Beirut or Jerusalem, doubtless have made the teaching profession singularly attractive and *comme il faut* for girls of the first families. The difficulty in training Trans-Jordan girls has been, until the present time, solved by scholarships in Jerusalem or Syria. Six girls are now studying in Jerusalem. But eventually there will doubtless be a training school for women teachers in Trans-Jordan. The danger of a purely academic education, unrelated to the simple environment of Trans-Jordan girls, is recognized. But a special Arts and Crafts school for girls, corresponding to the very modern Trade School for Boys, although frequently discussed, has not yet been achieved.

In the promotion of the new educational programme Trans-Jordan presents an interesting contrast to Palestine. In Trans-Jordan the programme depends entirely on local initiative. The English Adviser for Trans-Jordan has no direct relationship to internal affairs; such as, health and education. The primary interest of the Mandate in Trans-Jordan is in the problem of security, without which, of course, there could be no constructive development along any line.

The attention of the Mandate is centred in the air over Trans-Jordan, rather than on the land itself, as the maintenance of the air route across the desert through Trans-Jordan and Iraq is vital to the route to India. The English Adviser, although personally interested, assumes no direct responsibility for social or educational developments.

In Palestine, education is directly promoted and administered by the Mandate under a more direct foreign administration than in any other country of the Near East. Efficiency of method and speed in promotion are the result. The desire of the people, however, under the direct foreign promotion in Palestine is no keener than in Trans-Jordan.

Education in Syria

In Syria there is a lack of any united system of education and therefore a divergence of cultures and educational trends. This means that there is not merely a difference between the backward and progressive sections as in other countries, but also a distinct variation in the type of education and culture in different parts of the country and even in the different communities in the same section. The lack of a single educational system has retarded the education of Muslim women much more than the Christian, especially in the Lebanon, since Muslim girls for the most part have not taken advantage of the many Christian schools. Before the war, a few Muslim girls of the upper class in the Catholic convent schools and the Protestant schools, were the great exception.

Since the war the number of Muslim girls in foreign schools and in Muslim schools has increased but they represent a selected class, which are less conservative and not averse to foreign influence. The great middle class of Christians as well as Muslims has felt a lack of free public education, since the middle class in any country is cut off from educational advantages as long as there is no public system. During the war, an interesting attempt was made to lay the foundation for a school system on definite national lines. The leading educator from Istanbul, Halide Edib, was sent to Syria with a staff of fifty or more teachers to establish primary, secondary and normal education for girls. Schools were opened in Beirut and Damascus on very modern lines, with Arabic as the basis for instruction and French and Turkish as additional languages. This excellent effort, however, was brought to an abrupt close by the fortunes of war, but has left permanent results, as the present Government system is based on these schools.

Under the French Mandate, schools have been promoted through the local governments, on French and Arabic lines. An attempt is being made to standardize courses and certificates according to the French system. There has been no interference with the programme of foreign schools, although it is to the advantage of their students that the foreign schools meet the requirements of the French school certificates for different grades.

The foreign schools have remained practically autonomous and constitute as a whole the major educational influence in Syria. The Government schools do not compete with the foreign schools; the main value of the Government system consists in its extension of education to the masses.

The Muslim Philanthropic Educational Society has been recently developing facilities for secondary education of girls. Thus education on modern lines is reaching down further into Syrian life. Muslim girls especially are profiting from the development of Government schools. It is estimated that at least ninety-five per cent of the girls in Government schools are Muslims; since the girls and also boys of the Christian population, especially in the Lebanon, are educated in the various Christian schools, local and foreign. Hence the Government schools have had their primary benefit in reaching the Muslim community.

That this extension of education for Muslim girls is greatly needed, is obvious. Although the Muslim population of Syria is over one-half the total, the proportion of Muslim girls in schools was only a little more than one-fourth of the total enrolment in 1928. The hopeful feature in the situation, however, is the trend of increase. The number of Muslim girls in both the Government and private schools is practically a clear gain in view of the meagre prewar Government facilities and small prewar attendance of girls in private or public schools. A distinctly constructive new factor in the situation is the active promotion of girls' education, both primary and secondary by the Muslim Philanthropic Education Society.

In addition to promoting primary education for girls, the Government has provided a certain amount of secondary and higher education for girls; in the Lebanon the New School with secondary grades and two years of normal training; in Damascus, a normal school and the Syrian University open to women; in Aleppo, a secondary school and normal school. Secondary education for girls in Syria is largely provided by foreign institutions, the majority of which are in Beirut. The beginning of secondary education in the Government school in Beirut is a hopeful trend, as it is primarily intended to provide secondary education for girls of the middle or poorer class, who cannot afford the private school.

The Government schools for girls in Syria give the impression of a decided mixture of French and Arabic. The atmosphere is distinctly French with Arabic as a second language and culture. In the kindergarten the picture of a French kitchen, a French home, a French barnyard, build up the child's vocabulary in a French atmosphere. The group of little five-year-olds sing with great enthusiasm *C'est la musique du Moulin.* But they also sing with equal fervour the anthem of the Lebanese Republic, a good example of Syrian adaptability.

Muslim girls after leaving school, which is usually not later than the fifth grade, are cut off from any educational influences. The eager and grateful appreciation of some of these ex-primary schoolgirls throws light on the empty veiled leisure of the average Muslim girl's life. Those who are in touch with the problem of girls' education in various, parts of Syria, it is interesting to note, find certain similar signs of progress, however different the actual situation may be. There is little question that the best educational facilities for girls in all stages—primary, secondary and college—are afforded by foreign institutions.

Before the war these schools were largely attended by girls of the Christian community; since the war there has been a marked increase in the attendance of Muslims. Schools such as these offer an interesting index of the present attitude toward secondary education for girls. The need for higher education for girls, Christian and Muslim, is being met by the American junior College for Girls, and by coeducation in the American University of Beirut. Originally apart of the American Girls' School, the junior College is now an independent institution, preparing girls to enter the junior Year of the University of Beirut. Its influence is steadily increasing.

As the highest institution for girls in the Arabic-speaking countries, exclusive of Egypt, the junior College attracts students from Iraq and Palestine on Government scholarship and also on private support. Of the twenty-five Muslim graduates from the junior College, a number are holding important teaching positions. Aside from the regular academic college course, the junior College stresses homemaking, health, recreation and community service, such as a special club project for a group of forty to fifty homeless Muslim boys. Summer programmes of village welfare carried on in the Lebanon villages, by groups of Muslim and Christian students under faculty supervision, illustrate a creative approach to major problems of rural education. Such attempts to bring students in direct contact with backward village life, may have a helpful bearing on the problem which is caused by the growing cleavage between the educated urban minority and the underprivileged rural population, one of the critical problems of the East as a whole.

Coeducation at the American University of Beirut has met with a favourable response as is shown by the increase in numbers each year, although the demand for higher education for women is still very limited. Of the twenty eight women students in 1934, two were Muslims. The first Muslim woman graduated in 1929, Madame Ihsan Shakir el Kousy, an Egyptian, whose example doubtless encouraged other Muslim women students to enter a coeducational university. The fact that she was studying with her husband, prevented any adverse reaction to the idea of an unveiled Muslim woman attending classes with men.

Coeducation for Muslim girls is still distinctly in the pioneering stage in Syria. There is perhaps little awareness of its significance; in some quarters there may be active opposition. But the student body has accepted coeducation as an established fact, recognizing women students on an equal basis, as members of the same classes with men, and in the normal relationships of study and discussion group contacts. Women share also in student activities and also hold student offices; for example, a woman student, the only one in a class of fifty, recently was elected class president. Viewing the present situation of education in Syria with special reference to Muslim girls, one is conscious of a general awakening of interest, not only in advanced but in backward areas, and a slow but sure advance from the primary school to the university. Foreign influences have played a larger part in this advance in certain areas of Syria than in any other Eastern country. The absence of foreign contact in some parts explains perhaps in large measure the greater divergence in Syria in the development of different sections than is characteristic of other countries of the East.

The growing awareness of the disparity in education between men and women; the marriage motif, which causes parents to realize the impossibility of their daughters' making a good marriage unless educated; the presence of the more advanced educated Christian community, especially in the Lebanon, which stimulates in Muslim girls and women the desire for progress; the urge to adopt modern ideas, due to the irresistible pressure of Western life; and finally the spirit of keen nationalistic self-determination and aroused self-respect—these are the conscious and unconscious motivation, for progress in Syria

A composite of progressive influences and personal desires is thus actively operating in favour of the educational advance of Muslim women of Syria. The forces for education are not, however, Pari passu leading to an immediate social transition as symbolized by unveiling. Nationalism under a Mandate Power is driven back into itself and seeks defence for its own traditions. The assertion of self-determination which is politically discouraged finds its outlet in the insistence on its own social conventions. The Muslim community in Syria and Palestine, in the presence of foreign influences, tends to become socially conservative; and social conservatism in Islam is not conducive to a change in the social status of Muslim women.

Education in Turkey

Education for girls in Turkey was the sudden product of the new regime. The almost passionate drive to educate the masses is the distinct result of the new republic, but a period of preparation came before. A few Turkish women of the upper class began to receive the, private cultural education. Of the home soon after Turkish men came under the influence of French ideas, even as far back as Mahmud the Great (1809-39). Later, during the period of the Tanzimat reforms (1839-79) foreign governesses were introduced into the harem for the privileged few. Even the severity of Abdul Hamid could not stop the flow of Western influence, although it dammed up the outlet and made the open acceptance of Western ideas and attendance at Western schools difficult, especially for girls.

For the great majority of Turkish women, however, aside from the Quran schools and a girls' normal school for training elementary teachers, attended primarily by orphans and poorer girls, there was no real educational provision for girls, until after, the Constitution in 1909.

The first serious efforts at more than mere elementary education for girls came in 1913 with the establishment of a coeducational or secondary school for girls by Bayan Nakiye Elgun, for over thirty years the outstanding educational leader of Turkey, now a Deputy in the Grand National Assembly. The extension of primary education followed, and also the reorganization of the Evkaff (Mosque Foundation) schools was undertaken and effectively carried out by Halide Edib and Bayan Nakiye. These schools were consolidated in 1916 under the Ministry of Public Instruction. The adverse fortunes of the World War, the period of despair and defeat that followed, the Allied Occupation, the Turkish struggle and triumph in the Greek War constitute the all-absorbing, later sequence of events, in which the interest in education was lost in major issues. Then came the birth of the New Nation, and the realization of the necessity for strengthening its foundations.

Under the new regime, education has been assumed as a vital national responsibility and, as a consistent part of the promotion of general education, girls' education has moved steadily forward. The decade between 1913 and 1923 shows a gradual development and improvement of girls' education but with no distinctive change in direction. The next decade between 1923 and 1933 reflects not only the strenuous drive for increasing girls' education, but also the introduction of coeducation.

Most of the elementary education for Turkish girls is now provided through mixed schools. As a primary mean of solving the tremendous problem of the disparity in education of girls and boys, Turkey adopted coeducation in 1925, beginning with the elemntary schools, later introducing it to a certain extent in other stages. The success of coeducation, as a national programme is shown by the rapid increase of girls in primary schools, an achievement which would have been obviously impossible under the system of separate schools because of the double expense as well as the lack of teachers.

In the adoption of coeducation Turkey differs from all oilier Eastern countries, which have not yet cut the Gordian knot of their difficulty in promoting general education and especially education of girls. A trip through Asia Minor from Marash to Marsovan several years ago revealed how widely coeducation is being extended. Strangely enough or perhaps naturally enough, coeducation has been introduced especially in the Interior rather than in Istanbul. The primary reason is doubtless economic. The only possibility of extending education has been through the economy of mixed schools. Hence, not only primary but also some middle schools and *lycees* in the Interior are coeducational; whereas in Istanbul there are separate girls' middle schools and lycees, and coeducation has not replaced the already well-established system. But if new schools are built in Istanbul as elsewhere they will doubtless be coeducational.

In addition to its economic value, coeducation is serving a definite purpose as a leverage in lifting social conditions, especially in the Interior. Since one still sees veiled women in Asia Minor, the idea of coeducation may seem strangely incongruous, but the very fact that the veil has not entirely disappeared in the Interior is a logical social reason for coeducation. The present generation of women in Asia Minor may not all discard the veil, although there are indications that unveiling may be more aggressively promoted.

In order, however, that the best social as well as educational values may be safeguarded in the coeducation system, certain wise precautions are being taken. Only mixed activities that belong properly to the school programme are encouraged. Mixed dramatics and mixed recreation are under careful guidance and subject to certain restrictions; for example, in school plays no girls can take boys' parts, or vice versa. Moreover, care is taken that teachers shall not present extremes in modern social customs. Rouge and lipstick and lurid fingernails are frowned upon, and a frown often equals an order. Teachers, moreover, are not allowed to enter the Turkish beauty contest. The need for careful social guidance of coeducation in order to meet its inherent difficulties and avoid possible social dangers, is fully recognized by thoughtful Turkish teachers in mixed schools.

One of the major problems in Turkey, in the extension of schools in rural areas, is the provision of trained teachers. To allocate an individual teacher to rural schools is always difficult, because of the social adjustment to an isolated village life. This problem is being met in some places in Turkey by the appointment of a married couple to a village. The married couple conducts the school on modern lines, creates a modern home, which invites imitation, and adds greatly to the general community life.

As a further effective use of teachers in rural areas, to facilitate the spread of rural education, the idea is being developed of establishing a school with a number of teachers and a boarding home for students in a central village, perhaps also a clinic and small hospital, the whole unit thus serving the needs of the surrounding area.

The boarding school is required as a modification of the usual consolidated school because of the lack of bus lines and the great distances between the villages. A very interesting demonstration of this concentrated plan of rural reconstruction in education and health has already been achieved in Etemetsu, a model village half an hour's distance from Ankara. To see the very up-to-date, small, but adequately equipped hospital with a keen young doctor in charge, and an attractive midwife, and to visit the modern school and boarding home near by, staffed by several young married couples, was like catching a glimpse into the future of rural Turkey, if such a plan could be carried out more widely. The alternation of the regular school programme with practical work for boys, several hours each day in the garden and fields, and for the girls, the same amount of time spent in weaving and sewing, showed that this modern school was avoiding the danger of educating village children away from village life.

The boarding home for more than a hundred children, some of them under the special support of the Child Welfare Society, showed that the influence of the school was extended into villages beyond walking distance. Adjoining the school, but with a separate entrance and a small garden, was an attractive building for the teachers, in which each married couple had a little private apartment. Such a plan undoubtedly ensured the continuity of the teaching staff and their full contribution to the community life. Between this small group of teachers and the people of the village evidently there is an intimate contact, as a visit to several homes clearly showed. The way one of the young mothers proudly displayed her baby to the midwife for her approval was an evidence that the home and hospital are closely related. The promotion of education in the new Turkey has meant the modernization of the whole educational programme.

Of central importance in this process of building Turkish education on a modern basis is the policy of secularization of schools. The starting-point for all of the reforms in education was the elimination of the power of the ecclesiastic authorities. For example, coeducation, which has increased especially the education of girls, could scarcely have been accomplished under the old regime, when schools were dominated by religion. Following out this policy, the schools have been completely secularized.

The Turkish girls of today, therefore, have no formal religious instruction in the school. The chanting of the Quran, the teaching of the Islamic formula, the proper ritual and prayers, as far as the schools are concerned, are all things of the past, since definite religious instruction is regarded as the function of the home, not the school. Religion as such is not repudiated, but is regarded as an entirely individual matter. Not only in reference to religious teaching but in general because they did not assert complete inde-pendence, there is a distinct trend in education away from the old traditional ideas.

One of the most important developments is the introduction of physical education on modern lines, given by well-trained teachers. Mild calisthenics directed by the regular class teacher in high-heeled shoes, giving her commands passively in a colourless voice, constituted the physical education of the earlier period.

Today one finds a vigorous young Turkish Physical Director, well trained, conducting her class in a regular uniform and flat-heeled shows, issuing commands in vibrant tones and actively leading the gymnastic exercises. The present teachers of Physical Education are graduates of the course given in Ankara at the Men's Normal School, or at the Istanbul Normal School.

The course in Ankara is one of the most recent developments in coeducation. The lectures in theory for men and women students are held together; the courses in practical gymnastics are separate. The men and women students use the same gymnasium, but at different times. At one end are the dressing-rooms and showers for men; at the other, those for the women. The freedom of this joint physical education training course for men and women is the natural result of the new social attitude in Turkey.

Another significant emphasis in the education of Turkish girls is the promotion of vocational education. A number of excellent vocational schools have been established to teach practical arts, as their name Sanat schools signifies.

The Ismet Pasa Institute in Ankara serves as a model for the rest of Turkey for schools of this type, with its fine modernistic building, its excellent classrooms and laboratories, its splendid equipment, adequate dormitory facilities, and well-trained staff. In addition to regular middle school subjects—a primary certificate is required for entrance—two main courses are offered, household economics and a clerical course.

The Household Economics Course is very complete, including home arts sewing, tailoring, embroidery, cooking, laundry and millinery, which has a rather special interest in Turkey, because of the discarding of the veil. As the veil was less expensive than the hat, there is a distinct economic value in having Turkish girls learn millinery. Two enterprising graduates of the school have set up hat shops in Ankara and are doing a flourishing business. The Clerical Course also meets a timely need in view of the recent entrance of Turkish girls into business life. In addition to one of these two special courses, Home Economics or Clerical Training, all of the students have a simple course in Homemaking and Child Care, taught by a well-known young Turkish woman doctor, a specialist in child welfare. This Institute offers an interesting illustration of the consistent year-by-year growth of education in Turkey. In a five-year period it has become established in its very spacious new building. The French Directress has been replaced by a Turkish Director, with a Turkish woman assistant, both of whom have studied in Europe. Turkish teachers, several trained abroad, have replaced all of the foreign teachers except one, the French specialist in millinery. In addition to the clerical course at the Ismet Pasa Institute, training along commercial lines is offered for girls in the very up-to-date Ankara Commercial School, a coeducational institution under a Russian Principal. This school has a number of modern emphases in education; such as student cooperatives, student savings department, a student shop and the student management of the library.

In the development of Turkish education along modem lines, the problem of the training of women teachers is receiving serious consideration. Training for primary teachers is provided in a number of normal schools throughout Turkey; training for secondary teachers is given in the Higher Normal School in Istanbul, connected with Istanbul University. The requirements for teaching have been advanced: to teach in a lycee, a diploma from the university is necessary; for the primary or secondary grade, a normal school certificate. The relationship of the teacher to the community is for Turkey today a vital question.

The young normal-school graduates from Istanbul, fully emancipated young Turkish women wearing hats, fond of dancing and a normal social life, face a difficult problem of social adjustment when they find themselves planted in backward communities, where perhaps some of the women are still veiled and old social customs are still observed. Moreover these young teachers in the Interior have the responsibility of interpreting by their own example the meaning of social freedom. For all this they must be adequately prepared. Hence, the task of the normal schools is not merely to give academic training in methods of teaching, but to socialize education and interpret the career of teaching on a very high moral level. Some of the directors of the normal schools and teachers have grasped the significance of the problem, and are working creatively to develop in every way possible the social values in education.

The young graduates on their part, eagerly take advantage of all opportunities, especially extra-curriculum activities, such as folk-dances and games for recreation, in order to prepare themselves for the varied demands of teaching service in the Interior. In addition to the regular training courses in normal schools, which are given on a Government scholarship for a contract of five years' obligatory service in the interior, the plan of short-term summer training courses, especially designed for the untrained village teachers, of whom there are still many, has been developed within the last few years.

For foreign scholarships to prepare for teaching along special lines, women students compete on equal terms with men. The competition for foreign scholarships is open primarily to lycee students both boys and girls, but in some special cases, students in the *orta mektep*, junior high school, also compete. The principle of equality of boys and girls for foreign scholarships does not necessarily mean that the same number of Turkish men and women students receive foreign scholarships. The needs of Turkey for special types of service naturally have a direct bearing on the situation.

Higher education in Turkey is open to women on a basis of full equality with men. Women were admitted to the university in 1915 during the World War, but attended at first as quite a separate section; the men's classes were held in the morning, the women's classes in the afternoon. This involved a duplication of time and effort on the part of the faculty, and hence a double expense.

In the summer season of 1921 accordingly mixed classes were begun, with men and women students on different sides of the room and with no contact outside of classes. The women students entered the classes veiled, raised their veils during the class, and lowered them when leaving.

The fact that this first group of pioneer women students was in a conspicuous and difficult position, was shown by their extreme care in the details of veiling. These early days of coeducation in Turkey are typical of the present situation in some countries in the Muslim East, where coeducation is regarded as a doubtful social experiment.

Since 1922, when the Medical Faculty was opened for women, there has been a continuous increase in the number of Turkish women in the University of Istanbul, studying law, science, letters, medicine, dentistry, pharmacy, and even engineering. In 1934 the total number of women students was over one-fourth the number of men students.

An interesting evidence of the increasing response of Turkish girls to the opportunity of a higher education is the number of out-of-town students now attending Istanbul University. It is a distinctly new development for a hundred or more Turkish women students to come from the Interior to Istanbul for higher education. Many of these nonresident women students live with relatives or friends, but soon a regular dormitory provision for them will doubtless be needed.

Aside from the opportunities for higher education offered at the university, facilities for cultural studies are provided in special schools in which women students are registered together with men. A Government school for the training of teachers of music in Ankara usually has an equal number of men and women. This School of

Music is of interest because it shows the present effort being made to Westernize the music of Turkey. The students from this school will fill positions in teaching music all over Turkey.

The study of art, also on Western models, is offered in the Beaux-Arts School in Istanbul, situated in one of the palaces on the Bosphorus, which shows the way the old regime serves the new. There is a fair proportion of women students in the various departments. Girls from the *lycees* compete for entrance. Commercial art, poster making, interior design are all given special attention. In addition to promoting regular education in all its phases, Turkey has vigorously attacked the problem of general adult education.

The illiteracy of Turkey some years ago was estimated at eighty-five per cent; the general illiteracy of women was higher than men, as is usually the case. The adoption of the new Turkish script in 1928 presented the opportunity and drastic necessity for a nationwide drive for literacy. The change from the old to the new letters meant for the time being that the whole nation was reduced to the level of illiteracy. It was immediately necessary for all—the learned and the unlearned—to go to school.

Consequently, a campaign for literacy, unparalleled perhaps in world history, wag launched. In October 1928 the nation's schooling began, including Kamal Ataturk, Cabinet ministers, officials, teachers, peasants, men, women, and children of all classes. Attendance at these National Schools the first year was compulsory for everyone between the ages of sixteen and forty. As soon as the student learned to read and write and could pass an examination, a certificate was issued which served as exemption from further study.

Enforcement of the law was vigorously prosecuted by the Turkish police. The course was taught by regular teachers, who received a small supplementary salary for this extra teaching. School buildings and other public buildings were utilized. The courses were held outside of regular school hours, classes for women for the most part in the daytime; for men, at night.

The courses during the second year were of two types: the simple course for literacy, and a more advanced course including geography, higher arithmetic, additional reading, letter writing and civics. Women constituted over half of the million students in the National Adult Schools, which were established in September 1928, when the new language was officially adopted, and continued during two years.

According to reports, women made equal progress with men. Women of all classes took advantage of the opportunity to learn to read, even mothers attending classes with babies in their arms. The upper class of women, highly educated in the old Turkish language, entered into this pursuit of literacy in new Turkish with best as in a game, studied at home or in one of the national schools, passed their public examinations along with the masses, and proudly received their diplomas with their pictures attached as on a passport.

The women of the people especially have profited by this drive for learning the new letters. Illiterate before, with little thought of ever learning to read and write, they have suddenly, through the national schools, been awakened to an idea of their ability, hitherto unknown. The number of women reading newspapers on the trams and boats is a visible proof of their new literacy.

Foreign influence has permeated the life and thought of the country. It is difficult to estimate what was the full measure of this foreign influence silently pervading the Turkish harem, and bringing glimpses of a different world, for such subtle influences are not summed up in statistics. In the later period foreign schools began to play their part in the education of Turkish women.

Throughout the Interior of Turkey the American Mission Board has had a chain of girls' schools for a considerable time, until recently when their number has been reduced and their influence concentrated in a few selected centres. Although these schools have been attended primarily by girls of the non-Muslim population, they have undoubtedly benefited the cause of education in Turkey as a whole, giving a successful demonstration of modern girls' schools at a time when the need for education for girls was not generally recognized.

The French and Italian convents have contributed primarily to the education of girls of their religious community with also a limited contact with the Turkish population. The influence of the convent schools has been directly mainly along the lines of home-training and culture. None of the foreign institutions perhaps has exerted a greater influence on the education of girls over a longer period than Istanbul Women's College, which was founded as a high school in 1875 and became a college in 1910.

Through its general influence and through the individual example of some of its distinguished graduates, this college represents one of the major educational forces which has prepared for the forward movement of the Turkish women. The last decade shows an increased number of Turkish women students in the College, a fact which indicates the growing interest in higher education for Turkish women. The Turkish graduates and former students at the College are contributing in many ways to the life of Turkey; as homemakers, women in business and professional life, in public affairs, and more recently in the Councils of the State, as the recently elected group of Turkey women deputies includes several graduates of the College.

In the promotion of higher education for women, Istanbul Women's College has exerted an influence not only in Turkey but widely throughout the East. In relationship to the work of Istanbul Women's College, Robert College for men has had a direct effect on the education of women in Turkey, through creating an understanding of modern social values and an appreciation for the necessity of a higher educational and social status of women.

Foreign educational influence in Turkey are working in close relationship with the Turkish Ministry of Public Instruction, seeking to make their distinctive contribution in accordance with the educational policy and ideals of Modern Turkey.

The national system of Turkish education, highly centralized and closely integrated in all of its branches, determines the general trends as well as specific emphases of the present programme. In its general attitude toward foreign influences, Turkey differs from other countries in the East.

In contrast to the laisser-faire attitude in Syria, or the unconscious absorption and assimilation of foreign influence in Egypt, or the acquiescent acceptance of foreign educational benefits in-Palestine, the New Republic follows a policy of careful selectivity and appraisal of foreign influences. There is little question that Turkey recognizes certain values in the educational systems in Europe and America.

The presence of foreign educators in the Turkish school system is ample proof of this fact; for example, an American woman specialist in primary education, made a practical demonstration of modern methods in a Turkish primary school; an American specialist in teaching English to foreigners gave a series of courses to Turkish teachers of English; several American teachers of English are at present in Ankara schools, and a few in Istanbul.

A large group of noted German professors are aiding in the re-establishment of the University of Istanbul on advanced modern lines. French and Russian specialists are contributing in their special technical and cultural fields to the educational development of Turkey on modern Western lines.

But modern Turkey today does her own shopping for education and culture and for scientific progress—it may be in Berlin, or Paris, Moscow, London, or New York. It has been of special significance to the education of girls that this process of selecting foreign values has indicated a definite interest in Anglo-Saxon and perhaps especially in American methods.

In speaking of European culture and education, a former Minister of Public Instruction said in a personal conversation that the culture of Europe was more suited to the old regime than the new. Turkish girls have come out, of the harem and need now an education of practical emphasis and social value, so that they may be better fitted for civic and national responsibility.

It is important, however, that one should remember that the choice of foreign values is only a means to an end. The primary basis of Turkish education and culture is not foreign but Turkish. The sense of direction in Turkish education as in Turkish life is singularly clear.

4
Leisure and Recreation

Women's Clubs

In ancient society the frame of a Muslim women's life was her home. But within last decades the radii of her interests have been lengthening from the frame of her family and its ramnofications, so that today the periphery of her life has been extended beyond the quiet protected environment of the past into the rush and confusion of the modern world.

Today almost every town and city has its club or gathering-place for women. These clubs for women developing in the East are not unlike the clubs in the small towns of America a generation ago, in their enrichment of life through wider interests and contacts. But the women's clubs in the East have a greater significance than a club in America, even in that early day, could possibly have had, as life for the Muslim woman hitherto has had no outside relationships. Through these new club groups women are beginning now to think of themselves not merely as member of a family, but as units in society.

Moreover, the feeling of mutuality of interest with other women is quite a new experience, which has come to many Eastern women within the last decade. It is also an entirely new. Idea for the East that women through their collective effort can make a distinctive contribution to society. The devélopment of women's societies in different places has followed similar lines.

In many cases child welfare has given the initial urge which has brought the Muslim woman out of her home: for example, activity along these lines often has grown out of the purdah clubs in India. Sometimes other lines of welfare and philanthropy, care of orphans and charity relief, or perhaps some simple embroidery workshop employment scheme furnishes the objective for a club. Some of the organizations along welfare lines are very well developed.

Often a mixed club of foreign and local leadership furnishes the beginning and centralizes the social effort of Eastern women. This has been especially true in the purdah clubs in India, many of which owe their inception to foreign leadership. The Palestine Women's Council is also a significant organization of this type which for a number of years has been a force for the general social welfare of the women of Palestine--Muslims, Christians, and Jews. The Cairo Women's Club in another interesting association of Egyptian and foreign leaders.

Education of women furnishes the *motif* in many places for group action among women; for example, the Awakening of Women Society in Damascus, which for a time had a girls' as its major project. The educational purpose of the women's clubs in the East is basic to their central objective, which is the promotion of the general advance of women.

A typical illustration is the first women's club in Teheran, the Vatan Khahan, Well-Wishers of the Fatherland, which for a number of years has had a small school for adult women, and promoted the extension of girls' education and legislative social reform. The club has had a large number of nominal members but only a small nucleus have worked steadily under the leadership of Mastureh Khanum Afshar on an ambitious programme for the general advance of women. The Women's Section of the Red Lion and the Sun (the Persian Red Cross) under the patronage of the Palace—the fifteen-year-old daughter of the Shah, Princess Shahdokht Pahlavi, is the honorary president—has enlisted a large number of members. Over five hundred women attended one of the annual meetings held in the Ivory Hall of the Palace, a most unusual evidence of the new day, as hitherto Muslim women practically never entered the Palace, save in the harem.

Recently a new Women's Club, Kanun-i-Banuan, has been started in Teheran also under the official patronage of the Crown Princess Shahdokht Pahlavi. Sufficient funds have made possible a club centre on a prominent street, in a large building which has offices, a lecture hall with a stage for dramatics, and outdoor recreation space for tennis, basketball and other sports. Under the direction of the president and committee of twenty-five prominent women of Teheran a varied programme is carried on along intellectual and cultural lines with ample recreational privileges.

A large number of the members are teachers. No woman with a chaddur is admitted. This new club has been made the centre of the emancipation movement, where a number of noteworthy gatherings for the promotion of the advance of women have been held, attended by the Prime Minister and other notables. This Women's Club in Teheran is regarded as the symbol of the new social status of women.

In contrast to Iran, the idea of a woman's club in Iraq for the advancement of women has not been cordially received. In Baghdad a few years ago a very simple venture with a harmless and constructive programme of education for orphan girls in a small rented house aroused the fears of the conservatives by the high-sounding sign over the door: "The Elevation of Women." As a result of the opposition in the Press and a protest sent to King Feisal, the club was closed. Perhaps it may be reopened at some later date when Baghdad is ready for a woman's club.

In some cities important groups for the future promotion of collective effort of women are the Alumnae Club of Girls' Schools and Colleges, which may develop into organizations devoted to women's interests and activities. These young women's organizations in the East which are directed toward the general advance in the status of women are an interesting evidence of the growing similarity of Eastern women's interests whether in Cairo or Teheran.

The stages of development of these different associations, their type of leadership, the social and political background which determines their progress show great variety but all have the common goal of women's welfare and social advance. Some of these organizations have reached a position of national importance. The Federation of Women's Clubs in Syria, which unites clubs from Beirut, Tripoli and Damascus, has special significance in that it represents the cooperation of foreign and Syrian, Muslim and Christian leadership.

In the Federation are several Muslim societies, the Awakening of the Feminine Youth and the Society of Philanthropic Deeds in Beirut and the Awakening of Women in Damascus already mentioned, and a club from Tripoli. The Federation holds a biennial conference and carries on general social welfare. The Feminist Union in Egypt represents a much more conscious women's movement in the usual meaning of the term, than the Syrian Federation. Although not widely representative of Egyptian women, the majority of the members being wealthy women of leisure, the Feminist Union is significant as the spearhead of a forward movement for women, under the influential leadership of Madame Sharawi Pasha.

Since its inception this society has advocated political equality, suffrage and women's representation in parliament, privileges not yet granted. At the present time the Feminist Union is not aggressively advocating suffrage but awaiting a timely opportunity for further effort along this line, meanwhile promoting general social reform.

Turkish Women's Organizations

A programme of social welfare and education is carried on in connection with an Industrial School project. An effective propaganda for the advance of Egyptian women is promoted through *L' Egyptienne*, the magazine of the Feminist Union which is published in French and thus effectively interprets Egyptian women to the outside world. This society, through Madame Sharawi Pasha especially, has had for a number of years a close connection with international women's movements. The *Turk Kadin Birligi*, the Turkish Women's society, has been quite a different type of organization from the Egyptian Feminist Union.

Organized shortly after the beginning of the New Republic, and discontinued in April 1935 after the International Suffrage Alliance Congress in Istanbul, this society of Turkish women has been in a sense the symbol of the social transition through which Turkish women have passed in the last decade. This society has not initiated advance but by its existence has registered progress.

In its study of various social questions of importance to women, the Kadin Birligi received the endorsement of the Government and in various ways was recognized by the Government, as the collective representative of Turkish women's interests. In organizing and successfully carrying through the International Suffrage Alliance Congress in Istanbul, the Kadin Birligi received a remarkable degree of Government support.

The use of Yildiz Palace with its excellent facilities for an international gathering, the series of entertainments in other palaces, the special railway and customs facilities for all delegates, the front page publicity in the Turkish Press throughout the Congress, and as the final climax of official endorsement of the Congress, a day's excursion to Ankara for a selected number of delegates with a reception by Kamal Ataturk at his residence near Ankara—these were all unquestioned evidences of official interest in helping the Kadin Birligi make the Congress an undoubted success.

In the light of all this, it is not strange that the dissolution of the Kadin Birligi immediately after the Congress should have called forth expressions of surprise and regret from the leaders of the Woman's Movement outside of Turkey, as this seemed a strangely paradoxical situation, in fact, almost a refutation of the advanced position of Turkish women. Perhaps the closing of the Kadin Birligi may be explained as a logical result of the prevailing interpretation of the primary objective of a Woman's Movement—namely to secure equal rights.

If this is the main objective and justification of a Woman's Movement, then the Kadin Birligi may have been considered no longer necessary since these rights are now so fully secured in Turkey. Or perhaps the closing of the Kadin Birligi may have been the natural result of the general concept of the new State which has as its ideal the unity of efforts of men and women in the service of the State. Whatever may be the correct interpretation as to the reason for the dissolution of the society, it has evidently been considered that the Turkish Union has served its primary purpose and the members have disbanded. The Kadin Birligi has now merged its efforts and finances into the Himayei Etval, the Child Welfare Society of Turkey, a mixed organization of men and women.

The closing of the Turkish Union has not in any sense raised a question in Turkey as to the equality of women and full recognition of their importance in the State. This event called forth very little comment of any kind. It was merely accepted as an indication that women's efforts are to be redirected along other channels.

For the Western observer, however, this interesting development raises the fundamental question, as to whether the collective efforts of women's organizations do not have a contribution to render the State and Society, which is quite distinctive from their efforts with men in mixed organizations.

Indian Women Organizations

Women's organizations in India are more widely representative and national in scope than those of any other country of the East. The All-Indian Muslim Women's Association represents the united efforts of Muslim women to promote the educational and social interests of the women of that community.

The Women's Indian Association has been the primary champion of the suffrage cause, has promoted also a general education programme through its centre in Madras and exerted a wide sphere of influence which reaches all communities, through publishing Stri Dharma, the leading women's magazine in India.

The National Council of Women in its constituent councils all over India carries on an active programme of educational and social reform. Its membership and leadership are widely representative of different racial and religious communities of India. The National Y.W.C.A., one of the oldest women's organizations in India, which antedates the present forward movement of women, has promoted a national programme of a varied character with a strong emphasis on the preparation of Christian leadership and on the well-rounded development of women and girls. It brings into close relationship women of the foreign, Indian and Anglo-Indian communities, and works- in close cooperation with all of the other women's organizations.

From the point of view of a woman's movement in the usual sense of the term, the most powerful force of collective women's effort in India is the All-India Women's Conference. Uniting as it does on a common platform of progress women from all over India, of different races and religions, conservatives and progressives, the All-India Women's Conference, since its inception in 1926, has become recognized as the most effective instrument of propaganda in India in educating public opinion for the social and educational advance of women.

The resolutions passed at each Annual Conference cover a wide range of reforms needed; such as, increased facilities for girls' education, better health standards, improvement of rural life, moral training based on spiritual ideals, abolition of purdah and polygamy, enforcement of the child marriage law, equality of opportunity in public service, and equality of legal rights.

The Home Science College, established at Delhi by the All-India Women's Education Fund, is a demonstration of the practical service rendered by this movement in the promotion of educational advance. This movement actively participates in the promotion of legislative measures for the improvement of the status of women. The demands- made by the All-India Women's Conference to the Provincial Governments and to the Government of India carry great weight, of the Kadin Birligi may have been the natural result of the general concept of the new State which has as its ideal the unity of efforts of men and women in the service of the State. Whatever may be the correct interpretation as to the reason for the dissolution of the society, it has evidently been considered that the Turkish Union has served its primary purpose and the members have disbanded. The Kadin Birligi has now merged its efforts and finances into the Himayei Etval, the Child Welfare Society of Turkey, a mixed organization of men and women.

The closing of the Turkish Union has not in any sense raised a question in Turkey as to the equality of women and full recognition of their importance in the State. This event called forth very little comment of any kind. It was merely accepted as an indication that women's efforts are to be redirected along other channels.

For the Western observer, however, this interesting development raises the fundamental question, as to whether the collective efforts of women's organizations do not have a contribution to render the State and Society, which is quite distinctive from their efforts with men in mixed organizations.

Women's organizations in India are more widely representative and national in scope than those of any other country of the East. The All-Indian Muslim Women's Association represents the united efforts of Muslim women to promote the educational and social interests of the women of that community

The Women's Indian Association has been the primary champion of the suffrage cause, has promoted also a general education programme through its centre in Madras and exerted a wide sphere of influence which reaches all communities, through publishing Stri Dharma, the leading women's magazine in India. The National Council of Women in its constituent councils all over India carries on an active programme of educational and social reform. Its membership and leadership arc widely representative of different racial and religious communities of India.

The National Y.W.C.A., one of the oldest women's organizations in India, which antedates the present forward movement of women, has promoted a national programme of a varied character with a strong emphasis on the preparation of Christian leadership and on the well-rounded development of women and girls. It brings into close relationship women of the foreign, Indian and Anglo-Indian communities, and works in close cooperation with all of the other women's organizations.

From the point of view of a woman's movement in the usual sense of the term, the most powerful force of collective women's effort in India is the All-India Women's Conference. Uniting as it does on a common platform of progress women from all over India, of different races and religions, conservatives and progressives, the All-India Women's Conference, since its inception in 1926, has become recognized as the most effective instrument of propaganda in India in educating public opinion for the social and educational advance of women.

The resolutions passed at each Annual Conference cover a wide range of reforms needed; such as, increased facilities for girls' education, better health standards, improvement of rural life, moral training based on spiritual ideals, abolition of purdah and polygamy, enforcement of the child marriage law, equality of opportunity in public service, and equality of legal rights.

The Home Science College, established at Delhi by the All-India Women's Education Fund, is a demonstration of the practical service rendered by this movement in the promotion of educational advance. This movement actively participates in the promotion of legislative measures for the improvement of the status of women.

The demands made by the All-India Women's Conference to the Provincial Governments and to the Government of India carry great weight, since these enlightened Indian women leaders represent a powerful influence, a small minority speaking for the great silent masses. As Lady Irwin said, "Through the All-India Women's Conference the voice of Indian women is being heard."

The women's organizations in India and perhaps in much less degree the Feminist Union in Cairo, differ from similar bodies in other countries in the East, in that they are more definitely the cause for the advance of women, whereas women's societies elsewhere are not the cause but the result of advance.

The very existence of women's organizations in the East is a striking indication of change. The Turkish Society, the Kadin Birligi, is a good illustration of this fact, as it registered the progress of Turkish women but cannot be interpreted as having produced it. Even though as we have already seen, the Indian women's organizations are definitely a conscious instrument for effecting reform, still the general liberating movement affecting the status of women in India as elsewhere has antedated most of these organizations, and is scarcely the result of any of these special efforts to promote progress.

These Women's Movements in India, therefore, as in other countries of the East, may be interpreted not merely as Women's Movement with capital letters, working for a

Cause as for example the Suffrage Movement in England or America, but also as the evidence of a deep inward movement, stirring in the life of Eastern women. They represent something more fundamental than a single Cause such as Suffrage. These movements of women throughout the East are allied with powerful forces working toward general social and educational advance, which will mean a higher status women. Undoubtedly an impelling motive of this steady outward movement of women in the East is the spirit of nationalism which since the World War has surged through the Eastern world. In this awakening of national consciousness women have become deeply imbued with the sense of their relationship to national life. The sudden appeal of patriotism has swept away, at least temporarily, all hampering social and religious inhibitions, and given Muslim women, with other Eastern women, a sudden realization of their power and responsibility for service to the nation.

The Nationalist revolution in 1919 in Egypt offers a dramatic illustration of the awakening of women to national consciousness. Large crowds of women, Muslims and non-Muslims, thronged the streets, the upper classes and lower classes alike, veiled and unveiled, all demanding independence, shouting "Down with the English," waving banners and exulting in a frenzy of patriotism. Even the usually inarticulate fellaheen women joined in the general national outburst. This participation of Egyptian women in an uncontrolled turbulent demonstration of nationalism had doubtless certain temporary bad effects.

It is, however, of permanent significance in that it marks the first awakening of national consciousness in. Egyptian women, and has perhaps been the germ from which has developed a sane and constructive interest in national life among a number of thoughtful Egyptian women. Two incidents in Palestine that show the releasing effect of the spirit of nationalism have already been mentioned the protest against Zionism at the I-High Commissioner's residence by a group of unveiled women, and a later protest also against Zionism that occurred at the Holy Sepulchre at Easter 1934. Similarly women in Syria have been vocal in their demands for the national cause.

When the French and Syrian Treaty was being presented in Parliament in November 1934, a crowd of veiled Muslim women met in the Salahiyah suburb, one of the best residence sections, and marched to the National Parliament to protest against the Treaty since they felt that it meant a long period of national dependence. An accident in the crowd near the Parliament, which led to the death of one of the women, created a grave situation which was associated with the demonstration.

The long sustained part played by Turkish women in the National Struggle during the Allied Occupation and Greek-Turkish War is well known. In 1921 a mass meeting of Turkish women was held at Sultan Ahmed to protest against the occupation of Smyrna by the Greeks. Accusing the Turkish men of inaction, the Turkish women threatened to take up arms themselves in national defence.

In the forefront of the Turkish patriots of that period Halide Edib (Madame Adnan Bey) will always be especially remembered. As a powerful speaker inspiring the masses to action before the War of Independence; as a refugee in Anatolia with a price on her head; as an active participant in the Councils of War in Ankara; as a nurse in military hospitals and a member of the Intelligence Service at the front in all these ways actively identified with the Turkish life-and-death struggle, she demonstrated the educated Turkish woman's capacity for sacrifice in national life. Perhaps an even more stirring evidence of the Turkish woman's patriotism is symbolized in the monument on the public square in Ankara. One of the statues shows a Turkish peasant woman in the native costume of full trousers and with unveiled face, struggling forward, bent under the burden of a great bomb carried on her shoulder. This simple figure presents the grim reality of the sacrifice of hundreds of Turkish peasant women, who literally won the war, as Refet Pasha on the General Staff of the victorious Turkish army said: "We owe the greatest part of our success to the Anatolian peasant women. For hundreds and hundreds of miles they transported the ammunition on carts or on their backs along roadless wastes, protecting the ammunition with the scanty covers with which they covered their babies, who accompanied them strapped on their backs."

A more recent expression of the patriotic urge in Turkey was the request, in 1933, that came from some Istanbul high school girls that they should be liable for compulsory military service. This called forth much comment. There is little probability of such a regulation, but the request offers an interesting illustration of the eager spirit of nationalism in the younger generation. Iranian women even before the World War gave an interesting demonstration of their patriotism.

During the revolution of 1910-11 three hundred women came to the Majlis (Parliament) and, throwing off their veils ' exhorted the men to uphold the liberty and dignity of Iran. Behind the mosque curtains mass meetings of women were held, where fiery speeches were delivered on Iranian independence. The men read these documents later in the Majlis and said: "The women teach us how to love our country." The women not only held meetings but gave their jewels saying: "We are women and cannot fight but we can give to our country."

Another outburst of national feeling came at the time of the Treaty of Great Britain with Iran in 1919. The Tongue of Woman, an Iranian Woman's magazine, made such a violent protest against the treaty and stirred up such strong opposition that the magazine was finally closed. But the nationalist movement in India has offered the most striking evidence of the active response of women to the urge of nationalism, suddenly calling them forth from sheltered seclusion into the limelight of world publicity. Inspired by Gandhi, Indian women eagerly pressed into the national struggle, participating fearlessly in the Civil Disobedience Movement.

Processions long and wearisome in crowded city streets, picketing of wine shops and cloth shops in the heat and dust of the Indian bazaar, exposure to lathi charges from the police, and imprisonment for months in ordinary gaols-all these results of civil disobedience were not only accepted willingly by Indian women, but courted as a personal privilege to sacrifice themselves in the national cause. It is estimated that at least three thousand women were imprisoned during the Civil Disobedience Movement.

Indian women have participated not only in the Civil Disobedience Movement and in national political congresses, but also in less public though no less patriotic service; for example, in the promotion of Indian home industry, swadeshi.

Many Indian women have preferred this less spectacular expression of nationalism, and showed remarkable initiative and ability in the organization of individual and collective efforts to increase the use of Indian goods. In the nationalist movement Muslim women in India as a whole, because of the purdah, have played a less important role than the women of other communities, especially Hindus. A number of individual Muslim women, however have taken a prominent part in the national cause, for example Amman Bibi, the mother of the famous Muslim political leaders, Mohammed and Shaukat Ali, appeared veiled on the platform Of the Calcutta Congress of 19, as a protest against the imprisonment of her sons. More significant than the role of individuals has been the mass demonstration of Muslim women in the nationalist cause such as one in North India in which hundreds of veiled women took part.

The growth in national consciousness among women has led in some countries to their active participation in political life. Interest in public affairs is obviously limited to the enlightened few, since the masses are politically unawakened.

In Egypt a small minority of women, both Muslims and Copts, has been actively identified in politics. Madame Zaghloul Pasha, since the death of her husband, has been the head of the Wafd party, often in personal danger because of her political activity. The interests of Madame Zaghloul Pasha and her group are focussed entirely on party politics.

The Feminist Union under Madame Sharawi Pasha's leadership, has a more general interest 'in public affairs and advance in the status of women. This group is politically conscious but does not direct its activities along partisan lines. In contrast to the political awakening of women's groups in Egypt the women of the Middle East, Iran and Iraq have not yet been stirred to interest in political affairs.

There are, however, interesting exceptions, as for example the wife of a religious leader in Baghdad, a Member of the Parliament, who shows an avid interest in politics. Although still behind the veil, she telephones freely to different Members of the Parliament to get the political news. In Palestine and Syria there is little or no expressed desire for woman's suffrage. But political issues, as identified with nationalism in Syria and with the reaction against Zionism in Palestine, are a subject of deep concern to the women of these countries, even though they may not take an active part in public life. The era of nationalism in Turkey, in addition to its social and economic benefits for women, has brought them full political equality. First municipal suffrage and the eligibility of women for election to city councils was granted in 1930; four years later, December 1934, national suffrage was accorded to women, and seventeen Turkish women Deputies were elected to the Grand National Assembly in Ankara out of a total of three hundred and ninety.

Equality of political status for women has been considered by the leaders of the Turkish Republic as a logical part of national development, and the natural climax of the reforms in the status of women which began in 1923. When the municipal suffrage was granted, it was tacitly understood that the full vote would come in due time. Because of the lack of struggle for suffrage, doubtless, many women in Turkey have little appreciation of its meaning. But at least a small number, the thinking minority, realize the value of their newly acquired political opportunity. Fourteen of the seventeen women Deputies who were elected as the first women representatives in the Grand National Assembly are teachers, and several are from small towns and rural areas.

In India political privileges for women have come during the ascendency of the national movement. In the postwar period the major Indian States and all the provinces of British India granted women's suffrage and equal rights of election to municipal councils and legislatures. Since gaining political rights, Indian women have participated in public life as magistrates and members of legislative assemblies in steadily increasing numbers.

The new Constitution of India, adopted August 1935 has now extended the opportunities for women in political life by granting national suffrage on a preferential basis, which increases the ratio of women voters, and allots to women a definite number of seats in the Federal legislative chambers. Provision is also made for a fixed representation of the religious communities. This preferential basis of women's suffrage has met with a sustained opposition from the leading women's organizations in India, since the beginning of the discussion of the new constitution in 1931.

The collective opinion of Indian women has registered itself strongly in favour of equal adult suffrage and against the principle of preferential suffrage. This view was strongly expressed by a woman's committee of three outstanding women leaders—Muslim, Christian and Hindu—before the Joint Select Committee appointed by the British Parliament to consider the Indian Constitutional Reform.

This delegation of women, representing three. Great religious faiths, expressed a united opinion against suffrage based on communal divisions, which was in striking contrast to the proverbial spirit of communal discord, that has always been considered the main barrier against national unity in India. As their view was not incorporated in the final Parliamentary Report, a memorandum of protest was sent jointly from the All-India Women's Conference, the Women's Indian Association and the National Council of Women. After expressing appreciation for the recognition that Indian women in public life have received, and for the genuine desire of the joint Parliamentary Committee to extend suffrage to women in larger numbers and include them in legislative offices, the memorandum strongly opposed the suffrage provisions in the new Constitution.

The substance of the protest is that the preferential suffrage basis for women favours certain classes and vested interests, and that sex equality has not been observed. The sentence "With Lord Lothian, we are unrepentant believers in a system of direct election," succinctly summarizes this clear and fearless expression of a number of Indian women leaders in regard to political rights. The memorandum closes with the statement: "We wish to make it quite clear that even if we had secured or secure for ourselves all that we have wished or wish to secure and if, at the same time, we felt that the recommendations as a whole, were not in the true interest of India, we would, as women, the natural guardians of future generations, feel it our bounden duty to deny all privileges for ourselves for the sake of the common good."

The 1936 All-India Conference at Trivandrum reiterated its disapproval of the franchise qualifications for women but urged that women should avail themselves of the full privileges granted. It especially called upon "all educated women to see that all women qualified for the vote should apply for registration of their names on the electoral roll and use their votes to the best advantage. In reading such a vigorous statement one must of course bear in mind that it reflects the political consciousness of a very small minority of Indian women, among whom there are comparatively few Muslim women. But this small minority of women leaders in India is more articulate in political affairs than the women of any other country in the East.

A few Indian women have played an active part in securing political rights but not in conflict with Indian men as the leading Indian nationalists have favoured political rights for Indian women. The special efforts for women's suffrage have been merely a part of the general nationalist effort, the divergence of opinion concerning woman's suffrage, as granted in the new Constitution, has a deeper meaning than merely the idea of rights for women. A spirit of genuine concern for national welfare rather than the desire to promote merely women's interests is the keynote of the political activity of Indian women leaders. Their primary motivation is social and educational reform, but since such reforms cannot be divorced from political issues, the All-India Women's Conference, although definitely non-political in its origin and objective, has found it impossible to remain outside of the political field.

Hence the growth in political activity of Indian women has come as the inevitable result of their awakened social consciousness and passion for national progress. Women elsewhere in the East are not yet as keenly aware of the intimate relationship between social and political issues. But feminism in the East as a whole is characterized by the same growing desire, so evident in India, for women to play their part effectively in the common good. During the postwar period the horizon of Eastern women has been steadily widening, not merely beyond the home into civic and national life but also into a growing range of international relationships. This new contact of the women of the East with the world beyond their own national boundaries has come through many channels, but especially through the women's international organizations with which the Eastern societies are affiliated.

Formerly in the conferences of these world movements, Western women, who had knowledge of the

Orient, often represented the East, interpreting problems and point of view of the East. But today Western women would not have the temerity to try to interpret the changing East, since Eastern women themselves now represent the East.

A world conference of women today is not complete without its Eastern delegates. During the last decade the attendance of women delegates from the Near East and India in international conferences has steadily increased. Madame Huda Sharawi Pasha for a number of years has represented Egypt in international gatherings. Members of the Kadin Birligi in Turkey have for the past six years attended world meetings and the conferences of the Balkan area; Indian women for a longer period than women in the Near East have been in contact with the major international organizations for women. No one who attended the International Suffrage Alliance Congress in Istanbul (April 1935) could fail to realize the important role of the women of the East today in their international relationships.

Three women from India (as it happened all three were Muslims), a young woman from Teheran, a number from Egypt, both Muslims and Copts, a large delegation of Syrian women, representing Christians and Muslims, and also a group of students from the American junior College in Beirut-all these Eastern delegates, together with a group of very active Turkish delegates, the total number of Eastern women constituting perhaps half of the Congress, gave one the very definite impression of the active participation of women of the East in international life. Not only in women's conferences but in mixed gatherings on specific international problems, Eastern women have begun to play an effective role.

Women leaders from India especially have quickly found a place in international conferences of a political nature, receiving recognition more quickly in fact than have the women of the West, when one considers how recently Eastern women entered public life. After a little less than a decade of political rights two Indian women—one a Hindu, the other a Muslim—were appointed delegates to the Round Table Conference of India with England. These women delegates were regarded, not as charming feminine additions only, but as active members of the Conference, capable of intelligent deliberation on the future relationship of these two countries. Their presence at the Conference table on an equal basis with Indian men was an irrefutable evidence of the new day in India.

5
A Legitimate Community

In December 1947, very soon after the partition of India and in view of the large-scale abduction of women in both countries, the governments of India and Pakistan entered into an interdominion agreement to recover and restore all such women to their respective countries and original homes. Albeit humanitarian in intent, the Recovery Programme, through its covert and overt rhetoric and operations, was as much an index of how India and Pakistan constituted themselves vis-a-vis each other as it was a contest of competing claims by Hindus, Muslims, and Sikhs over one another's women and children.

To this extent, both countries were engaged in a redefinition of each other's national character as demonstrated by a commitment to upholding honour and restoring moral order. The proper regulation of women's sexuality was essential not only in itself but because the moral depravity and sexual chaos that mass abduction represented had to be reversed. Thus, the individual and collective sins of men who behaved without restraint or responsibility in a surge of communal "madness" had to be redeemed by nations who understood their duty in, once again, bringing about sexual discipline and, through it, the desired reinforcement of community and national identity.

In India, the concern of the Social Reform movement with widow remarriage, *sati* (widow immolation), and the age of consent was, in fact, a concern with women's sexuality. The movement's intention was to lift it out of the domain of the traditional and insert it into the political and social agenda of modern nationhood. But as various analyses have shown, the enterprise was confounded at the outset by the clear demarcation of public from private, and by the need to emphasize the purity and cultural superiority of Indian womanhood.

The rhetoric of modernity, however, could hardly be abandoned by a modernizing state: it was constrained to undertake the kind of transformation that would enable it to weld a nation, build a citizenry that would recognize its fellow members as part of the same nation, sharing nationality. It would have to grant rights, assign responsibility, and guarantee equality in an undifferentiated manner to all its citizens.

Definitions of "modern" take place in a political field where certain identities are privileged—even while equality is promised—and others subordinated. Wherever women serve as boundary markers between different national, ethnic, and religious collectivities, she says, "their emergence as full-fledged citizens" with concomitant rights will be jeopardized. Women have been subsumed only symbolically into the national body politic because no nationalism in the world has ever granted women and men the same privileged access to the resources of the nation-state. Moreover, as Mosse points out, "nationalism had a special affinity for male society and together with the concept of respectability legitimized the dominance of men over women".

The passionate brotherhood of "deep comradeship" that Benedict Anderson talks about is an essentially male fraternity, in which women are enshrined as Mother, and the trope of nation-as-woman "further secures male-male arrangements and an all-male history".

Floya Anthias and Nira Yuval-Davis have pointed out how central dimensions of the roles of women are constituted around the relationships of collectivities to the state, and that equally central dimensions of the relationships between collectivities and the state are constituted around the roles of women. This particular nexus has lately come in for sustained scrutiny by researchers and activists in South Asia amid escalating ethnic tension and regional chauvinisms that have resulted in fundamentalism and communitarian violence, the crystallization of regressive cultural practice, and selective reinterpretations of tradition, especially with regard to women's "proper" role in society. Bitter and violent conflict amongst Hindus, Muslims and Sikhs led to the division of India along communal lines.

In the wake of this the reconfiguration of relationships between communities, the state, and gender in postpartition India took place around the body and being of the abducted women of all three communities. By extension, she also delineated the relationship between India and Pakistan as they typified the two principal "communities," Hindu and Muslim, eternally and irrevocably locked in battle with each other. Each was projected as an essentialised collectivity: Hindustan, land of the Hindus, and Pakistan, Muslim homeland, closed to non-Muslims.

Most theorists of nationalism have posited that nations are haunted by their definitional Others. Implying "some element of alterity for its definition," a nation, according to Perry Anderson, is ineluctably "shaped by what it opposes." Benedict Anderson further suggests that nationalism should best be conceived "not as an ideology" but "as if it belonged with kinship or religion rather than with liberalism or fascism".

Three significant factors in the constitution of the Indian state set it apart from—and in its perception, above—Pakistan: it was statedly secular, democratic, and socialist. Pakistan was avowedly Islamic, basically feudal, suspiciously "un-modern." This was at the level of ideology. At the "imagined" level, however, other factors informed the self-perception of the Indian state and its male subjects. Both are important for an under standing of the uncommon zeal and commitment with which the Indian government set out to recover women.

The idea of Pakistan as embodying/representing the larger collectivity of Muslims, by definition inimical to Indian national interest; the sexuality of women as transgressed by abduction and forcible conversion and cohabitation; and the question of the "legitimacy" of children born of such "wrong" unions as future members of a community are the three elements, as forging the link between secularity, sexuality, and the state.

Muslim Women Abducted

In December 1949 the Legislative Assembly in India debated a bill—when subsequently passed, the Abducted Persons (Recovery and Restoration) Act of 1949 to facilitate the return of all Muslim women abducted during the partition disturbances to Pakistan. It was an extension of a reciprocal agreement with Pakistan, whereby both dominions pledged to locate and recover all such women with the greatest possible speed. The bill under discussion set out the terms of reference for such recovery in India. Its provisions were explicit and wide ranging in the powers given to the police for what we would today call to search and seizure"; exemption from any civil or criminal action against any officer or constable for excesses committed in the course of recovery; and virtual suspension of all democratic and fundamental rights of the women and children—"abducted persons"—in question. There was considerable disquiet expressed by members regarding all of these, but there seemed to be a general agreement on Pakistan's duplicity in the matter of recovering non-Muslim women from its territories.

For the Indian government, as for many leaders, Pakistan's intentions as far as the restoration of women was concerned never quite squared with its performance. Pakistan disallowed the MEO (Military Evacuation Organisation) from conducting recoveries after July 1948; was tardy in promulgating an ordinance based upon the November 1948 agreement; appeared not to be cooperating on the speedy recovery of those whose details had been furnished by the Indian government; desisted from taking action against the government servants who were believed to have possession of two thousand women; and failed to ensure that its police and social workers honoured the spirit and letter of the agreement.

Members of the Assembly continually urged Minister Gopalaswami Ayyangar to impress upon the government the need to put greater pressure on Pakistan for this purpose. One, Smt. Durgabai from Madras, even went so far as to say, "Thanks to the leadership in our country, we have been able to get social workers who are not only public-spirited but non-communal in their outlook, and therefore, they are inspired by the noble example set up by the Father of the Nation, Mahatma Gandhi, and also other leaders whose support and help are available in plenty for recovery activity." Another member, Pandit Thakur Das Bhargava, declared, "So far as we are concerned, we know how to honour our moral obligations, implying that the Pakistanis did not. As the discussions in the Assembly continued, it became clear that in most members' view, Pakistan itself had become the abductor country, mimicking at a national level the behaviour of its subjects and guilty of the same moral turpitude.

By contrast, India behaved like a responsible parent-protector, in turn reflecting what was generally the responsible behaviour of its people. There were aberrations, of course–"Some of our misguided brothers also share the responsibility to a certain extent"–but in the words of one member, "Greater fault lies with the people and even with the government of Pakistan."

Pakistan's duplicity regarding the return of women was consistent with its duplicity in all other matters under dispute–Kashmir, canal waters, and evacuee property–and provided proof enough of its indifference to honouring agreements in general. By proceeding as if Pakistan would indeed keep to its side of the bargain, India was guilty of weakness and irresolution. In the face of such provocation, it had no choice but to depart from its moderate and "civilized" course and speak Pakistan's language. Pandit Thakur Das Bhargava stated:

> The Pakistan government does not understand the language of morality, it only understands the language of force and retaliation.... If this were a matter of mere international morality, I am at one with the Honourable Minister. But all the same when we have entered into a bilateral agreement-and with all solemnity they entered into the Agreement-let us see how it has been honoured in letter and in spirit by Pakistan.

In at least two very significant instances, Pakistan had betrayed its intentions:

> We knew on the 3rd of September 1947 an

> agreement was signed between the two governments and the ink was not dry when the Pakistan government, along with the Azad Kashmir government, raided parts of Kashmir and took away our women.... For a government to be party to this loot, to this raid upon women and property and then to say that they were not... and ultimately to accept that they were... nobody on earth can justify the Pakistan government.

Two thousand Hindu women were in the custody of Pakistani government officials and not being returned. That India should have signed a cease-fire agreement before the captured women had been returned indicated that it was neither "bold enough, good enough, sagacious enough nor honest enough."

Women had been spirited away to the closed districts of Jhelum, Gujarat, Campbellpur, the Northwest Frontier, and Rawalpindi, where no Indian recovery official was allowed to enter; they were stripped and paraded in Kabul; they were passed from hand to hand and sold in *bazars*—still India stood silently by. If retaliation was the only language Pakistan could understand, then that was what India should speak, and speak it through those same sisters whom "our country has a tradition of protecting." They would be the hostages.

If the state had cast itself in the role of father to the women, then its male citizens would safeguard them like their "brothers" Sir," said Pandit Thakur Das Bhargava, "there is no reason why... a country is not justified in keeping these [Muslim] girls as hostages for some time.... I don't see any harm in employing this tactic in getting our girls. As a matter of policy, of strategy, it should have been done."If India could think of cutting off relations with Pakistan on economic matters, why could it not do so to "get our sisters back?"

It could not, because then India would be no different from Pakistan. "Now I wish this to go on record," said Minister Gopalaswami Ayyangar, "that [making recoveries] is a thing which, as a civilized government we ought to continue to do. Our own policy is that whatever may be done in the other Dominion, whether recoveries... are adequate or not, we owe a duty to the large number of Muslim women who are abducted within our own territory'.

After March 1947, communal tension and the ensuing violence escalated at such a rapid pace, that leaders and representatives of the Indian and Pakistani governments met in Lahore in September 1947 and resolved that steps be taken to "recover and restore abducted persons."

On 17 November 1947 the All India Congress Committee passed a resolution:

> During these disorders large numbers of women have been abducted on either side and there have been forcible conversions on a large scale. No civilized people can recognize such conversions and there is nothing more heinous than the abduction of women.

Forcible Conversions

From the very beginning the concern with abducted women or persons went hand in hand with alarm at "forcible conversions." This preoccupation continued throughout the debates and, in fact, underlined another important factor in India's relationship with Pakistan: the loss of Hindus to Islam through such conversions, in addition to the loss of territory.

Abduction and conversion were the double blow dealt to the Hindu "community," so that the recovery of "their" women, if not of land, became a powerful assertion of Hindu manhood, at the same time that it demonstrated the moral high ground occupied by the Indian state. Nothing like this concern was evident with regard to the abduction of Hindu women by Hindu men, or Muslim women by Muslim men, presumably because here no offence against community or religion had been committed, nor anyone's "honour" compromised. Although there seemed to be general consensus on both sides that large numbers of women had indeed been "abducted", a working definition of an "abducted" person was attempted by the Indian government only in 1949 in the bill under discussion:

> In this Act, unless there is anything repugnant in the subject or context, 11 abducted person" means... a male child under the age of 16 years or a female of whatever age who is, or immediately before the 1st day of March 1947, was a Muslim and who, on or after that day and before the 1st day of January 1949, has become separated from his or her family and is found to be living with or under the control of any other individual or family, and in the latter case includes a child born to any such female after the said date... If any police officer, not below the rank of an Assistant Sub-Inspector or any other police officer specially authorized... has reason to believe that an abducted person resides or is to be found in any place he may, after recording the reasons for his belief, without warrant, enter and search the place and take into custody any person found therein, who in his opinion is an abducted person, and deliver or cause such person to be delivered to the custody of the officer in charge of the nearest camp with the least possible delay...
>
> [6] Determination of question whether any person detained is an abducted person:
>
> (1) If any question arises whether a person detained in a camp is or is not an abducted person, or whether such person should be

> restored to his or her relatives, or handed over to any other person, or conveyed out of India, or allowed to leave the camp, it shall be referred to, and decided by, a tribunal constituted for the purpose by the Central Government.
>
> (2) The decision of the tribunal shall be final; provided that the Central Government may, either of its own motion or on the application of any party interested in the matter, review or revise any such decision.

Looseness and arbitrariness of these definitions provoked intense debate in the Assembly. Many members were justifiably disturbed by the bill's implications and by the extremely wide powers given the police to determine exactly who would fall into this category. Some demurred at the absence of judicial recourse available to either abducted persons or their families. Others drew attention to the significant departures made in this definition from the legal definition of "abduction" and the consequent culpability of the government in a court of law. Their misgivings were often fully borne out, not only by the actual process of recovery but also by the very impossibility of establishing, beyond reasonable doubt, that the person/woman "recovered" had in fact been "abducted." Search officers and social workers told us that they used all kinds of tactics in order to locate and "rescue" the women. They would go disguised as bangle sellers or in *burqa* (veil), and cajole, threaten, and even physically intimidate families.

The circumstances of the "abductions" varied widely. Some women were left behind as hostages for the safe passage of their families; others were separated from their group or family while escaping, or strayed and were picked up; still others were initially given protection and then incorporated into the host family; yet again, as in the case of Bhawalpur State, all the women of a single block were kept back. Some changed hands several times or were sold to the highest or lowest bidder, as the case might be; some became second or third wives; and very many were converted and married, and lived with considerable dignity and respect.

As defined by the act of 1949 any and every woman located in the home or under the control of a family or individual of the other community, was eligible for recovery, regardless of any indications to the contrary. Resistance to being "recovered" came not only from their "abductors" but also from the women themselves. Many escaped from the centers to which they had been brought and returned to their "captors," sometimes by the most extraordinary means. The women often protested that their liaisons had been made freely and under no compulsion; indeed, we learned that many had taken advantage of the social turmoil to marry men of their choice from outside their community, something that would have been almost certainly disallowed in more normal times. Very many such disputed cases came up for arbitration at the special tribunal set up by India and Pakistan, as recounted by Kamlabehn Patel and the police officers in charge, and they readily admit that the resolution of these cases was beset with difficulties.

Of the women who were forcibly repatriated, an appreciable number simply refused to return to their natal families or husbands; some, in protest, refused to change out of the clothes they had been wearing when they were picked up by the social workers; and at least two search officers told us that, as far as they knew, not a single woman had come to a recovery center of her own volition. "Who are you to meddle in our lives?" they shouted at the social workers when they were forced to go back. "What business is it of yours?" "If you were unable to save us then, what right have you to compel us now?

Exactly how widespread this resistance was is difficult to ascertain, especially given the coercive powers of the police. But every social worker or police officer we spoke to referred specifically to it; in fact, the act was allowed to lapse in 1956 when social workers and the police said they could no longer continue with Operation Recovery.

As early as 1949, Rameshwari Nehru, Honorary Advisor to the government in the Ministry of Relief and Rehabilitation, resigned in protest against a policy that she believed worked against women. She recommended that recoveries be discontinued altogether because she was "convinced that we have not achieved our purpose.... By sending women away, we have brought about grief and dislocation of their accepted family life without in the least promoting human happiness.

Both the governments had agreed that neither forced conversions no forced marriages would be recognized by either country. It followed that all children born of such unions would then be illegitimate, and for the purpose of the act were defined as "abducted persons" if they happened to be born to any able woman within the time frame set out in it. Now, those very members who had protested that no forcible recovery or return could be countenanced, and those who believed that every abductor had been guilty of a "shameful crime", was a murderer, and could not be relied upon to provide either security or dignity to the woman he had forcibly converted and married, found that there were no grounds for their children to be treated as abducted persons.

An important point about the abducted persons Act was that it needed to be legislated at all, because the maximum number of recoveries had been made between 1947 and 1949, before the bill was introduced in Parliament. Why then, was the Indian government so anxious to reclaim women, sometimes several years after their abduction? Why should the matter of national honour have been so closely bound up with the bodies of women, and with children born of 'wrong' unions? The experience of Pakistan suggest that recovery programme was neither so charged with significance nor as zealous in its effort to restore moral order. Indeed, informal discussions with persons involved in the work there indicate that pressure from India, rather than their own social or political compulsions, were responsible for the majority of recoveries made. There is also the responsibility that the community stepped in and took over much of the daily work of rehabilitation, evidenced by findings that the level of destitution of women was appreciably lower in Pakistan.

For India, a country that was still reeling from partition and painfully reconciling itself to its altered status, reclaiming what was by right its "own" became imperative in order to establish itself as a responsible and civilized state, one that fulfilled its duties toward its citizens, both in the matter of securing what was their due and in confirming itself as their protector. To some extent, this was mirrored in the refugees' own dependency in turning to the sarkar (government) as its ma-bap (mother and father) at this time of acute crisis. But the notion of recovery itself as it came to be articulated cannot really be seen as having sprung full-blown in the postpartition period as a consequence of events that had taken place during and after the violence that accompanied the exchange of populations.

If we pause to look at what had been happening in the Punjab from the mid-nineteenth century onward with the inception and consolidation of the Arya Samaj and the formation of a Punjabi Hindu consciousness, we might begin to discover some elements of its anxiety regarding Muslim and Christian inroads into Hinduness and the erosion of Hindu *dharma* (religion), values, and lifestyles through steady conversions to these two faiths by Hindus (Sarkar, this volume). With the creation of Pakistan, this anxiety found a new focus, for not only had it been unable to stem conversions to Islam but it had also actually lost one part of itself to the creation of a Muslim homeland. Recovery then became a symbolically significant activity (its eerie resonance in the current frenzy to recover sacred Hindu sites from the "usurping" Muslims is chilling), just as earlier the shuddhi (purification) program of the Arya Samaj, even if it resulted in bringing only one convert back into the Hindu fold, served to remind the Hindu community that losing its members to Islam or Christianity was not irreversible.

Recovering women who had been abducted and, moreover, forcibly converted, restoring them to both their own and the larger Hindu family, and ensuring that a generation of newly born Hindu children was not lost to Islam through their repatriation to Pakistan with their mothers can be seen as part of this concern. Because, in fact, such a recovery or return might not be voluntary, necessary legal measures had to be taken to accomplish the mission. In one sense, it seems that the only answer to forcible conversion was forcible recovery. The key to understanding the anxiety surrounding the matter of the children of abducted women lies in the importance attributed to legitimate membership of a family, a community, and ultimately, a nation.

The sanctity of all three lay in keeping the boundaries intact, in maintaining difference, and in refusing to allow sexuality to be contaminated by secularity. This was why the forced alliances resulting from abduction could be neither socially acknowledged nor legally sanctioned, and why the children born of them would forever be "illegitimate". This was also why the fake "family" had to be dismembered by physically removing the woman/ wife/ mother from its offending embrace and relocating her in the "real" family, where her sexuality could be suitably supervised.

The Abducted Persons Act was remarkable for the impunity with which it violated every principle of citizenship—fundamental rights and access to justice—and for contravening all earlier legislation with regard to marriage, divorce, custody and guardianship, and eventually, inheritance—not so much in regard to property but, more critically, in regard to membership of a community.

The freezing of boundaries, communal and national, calls for what Kristeva terms "sexual, nationalist, and religious protectionism' reducing men and women, but especially women, to "the identification needs of their originary groups", imprisoning them in the "impregnable aloofness of a weird primal paradise: family, ethnicity, nation, race."

6
Institution of Marriage

Marriage in Islam is regarded as a strong bond and a total commitment to life, to society and to being a respectable human. It is a promise that the married couple make to one another and to God. This undertaking on the part of the married partners would allow them to find mutual fulfilment and self-realisation, love and peace, comfort and hope. This is because marriage in Islam is essentially a righteous act and an act of complete devotion. As such, celibacy is discouraged not only for men, but for women as well. This is in consideration of the fact that their needs are equally legitimate and valid.

Islam views marriage as a natural course for women in the same way as it is for men, and probably even more so in view of the fact that marriage guarantees women some form of economic security. It must be stressed here that this benefit for women is in no way an indication that marriage in Islam is sheer economic transaction. Indeed, the economic factor is the least aspect of the whole enterprise; the emphasis has been always on the religious qualities of the spouses.

From the collective point of view the most significant benefit is of course procreation, but not just the physical perpetuation of the human race; rather, the institution of marriage ensures that this procreative function will be both sanctified and orderly, not vulgar and chaotic. From the specifically religious point of view, having children entails the following: the realisation of God's desire;' the fulfilment of the Prophet's call to marry and increase his followers' number; gaining the fruit of a child's prayer.

Muslims believe that when parents die and leave a child, his prayer would benefit the dead parents. However, if the child dies before his parents, he would make intercession on his parents' behalf. Fulfilling one's sexual desire is another important aspect of marriage. Marriage, from the Islamic viewpoint, helps control sexual passion and channel it in the right direction. Also, it functions as a shield against committing adultery and fornication, both of which are forbidden in Islam. Marriage, moreover, brings peace and tranquillity of spirit and implants love and compassion between the married partners. These are great supports for one's worship of God. Intimacy between spouses is viewed as catalyst for the development of their souls.

In other words, the intimate relationship that develops between a husband and wife is crucial for relieving the heart from its burdens and thus enables the mind to better focus on accomplishing the Divine requirements. Al-Ghazali beautifully explains this point in the following account: 'The third benefit of marriage is that the heart finds ease through intimacy with women, because of sitting and joking with them. This ease then becomes the cause of an increase in desire for worship. For diligence in worship brings weariness, and the heart contracts. But ease acquired in this way brings back the heart's strength. Ali said, 'Do not remove rest and ease completely from the hearts, lest they become blind'. It sometimes happened that the Prophet was overcome by such tremendous unveilings that his bodily frame was not able to tolerate it.

The marital link helps the partners to work together and co-operate amicably in the management of the domestic affairs of their house; hence sufficient time could be spared to meet the Divine commandments. Therefore, the Prophet is reported to have advised his followers to choose the right spouses who would help them attain Divine blessings.

Marriage, in addition, is seen as an opportunity to develop for oneself a good and sound character as a result of the added family responsibility which both spouses have to endure during their married life. Hence, success in carrying out family commitments (which are equally regarded as divine duties) would ensure Divine reward. The Prophet said 'A man will be rewarded for what he spends on his wife, even for putting a morsel of food into her mouth'.

Also, 'Whoever performs his prayers correctly, and spends on his children in spite of his modest means, and does not speak ill against others, will be in paradise as close to me as these [two fingers of mine]'. Finally, marriage ensures social stability and a dignified form of living for both partners (the husband and the wife), probably even more for women since it guarantees their rights both as wives as well as mothers (of course alongside their fights as individuals).

Since Islam takes marriage seriously, its concern has been always to ensure that the marriage bond stays relatively stable and durable. To achieve these goals, it has laid down certain rules and regulations to meet these objectives. First, the couple have to be of proper marriageable age; also, there should be no discrepancy between their ages. It must be stressed that the claim by some scholars that the groom has to be always senior in age so as to ensure a healthy marriage relationship has no religious grounds and in practical terms does not make any sense. In fact, it contradicts the practice of the Prophet, two of whose wives (Khadija and Sauda) happened to be older than him; despite this, the record shows that they lived in peace and harmony.

Second, there should be a degree of compatibility between the two partners in terms of social status, educational standards and physical attraction (again the claim by some scholars that the bride has to be more beautiful and more attractive than her groom is a fallacy). Third, the dowry of the bride should be of a reasonable level: neither too high, which could cause hardship for both of them, nor too low which might give the impression that the bride is of no worth. The dowry—which is in its essence a gift from the groom to the bride—should be affordable and manageable so as to ensure satisfaction and happiness on both sides. Fourth, the consent of the couple is crucial for the stability and durability of the marriage. Both have to enter into the wedlock with free will and without coercion.

Compelling the couple (or even just one of them) to contract an unsatisfactory union would be detrimental to the interest of both sides and could lead to a disastrous end. Fifth, the prospective partners have to be pious and of good moral conduct. Both have to be kind, sympathetic, considerate, patient and loving, caring to one another; this encourages peace and harmony in domestic life. Sixth, the two parties have to declare, from the beginning, their intentions to keep the marital bond as permanent as humanly possible. This commitment requires that the marriage contract should be free of any hidden agenda such as casual or temporary unions.

Islam is against all marriages that have been described as experimental, casual and temporary. In a clear statement, the Prophet outrightly denounced those men and women who enjoy the frequent change of marital partners and warned against their unacceptable behaviour. Having stated the importance Islam lays on the permanency of marriage, it is essential to stress that in Islam there is no concept of 'indissoluble' marriage.

Although Islam endeavours to keep the marital link stable and intact, this does not mean that the wedlock cannot be brought to an end if there are compelling circumstances. Indeed, Islam recognises that if the marriage is not working, it is in the interest of both sides to terminate it on good terms. Hence, divorce in Islam is a legitimate act, although it is discouraged by the Prophet. Islam, as we know, encourages both men and women to marry. Just like a man, a Muslim woman (virgin or non-virgin) has the freedom to propose to a man of her liking, either orally or in writing (I wonder how many Muslim women these days would dare to initiate an oral proposal, let alone put it in writing!).

The Muslim woman has the freedom of marital choice: she is at liberty to choose her prospective husband, look at him and get to know him" without coercion on the part of the father or other relatives. If force or pressure takes place, she has the right to appeal to the court to redress the wrong. Her consent is essential for the validity of the marriage contract.

The Prophet is reported to have made the following statements: 'A previously married woman shall not be married till she gives her consent, nor should a virgin be married till her consent is sought'. 'A previously married woman is more a guardian for herself than her guardian, and a virgin should be asked permission about herself, and her permission is her silence'. 'A grown-up girl shall be asked permission about herself. If she is silent, it is her permission; and if she declines, there shall be no compulsion on her'.

According to Islam, a divorced or widowed woman has the right to remarry without any shame or denunciation. In fact, the Quran allows the betrothal of a divorced or widowed woman even during her period of transition (idda). 'It shall be no offence for you openly to propose marriage indirectly to such women or to cherish them in your hearts. Allah knows that you will remember them. Do not arrange to meet them in secret and, if you do, speak to them honourably. But you shall not consummate the marriage before the end of their waiting period. Know that Allah has knowledge of all your thoughts. Therefore take heed and bear in mind that Allah is forgiving and merciful'.

Neither age nor previous marriage would impede a woman from contracting perfect matches. Many are the examples which can be cited from the early Muslim community during which women were, very often, re-married after they were divorced or widowed, and this was done without stigma or discredit. Take, for instance, Umm-Kulthum bint Aqba, an early convert from Mecca. She emigrated to Medina in defiance of her family, who tried to force her to return to Mecca, but to no avail. She stayed in Medina and married her first husband, Zaid bin Harith. When Zaid was killed in one of the battles she contracted a second marriage with Zubayr bin al-Awwam. Zubayr was rough with her, so she decided to part with him. After the separation, she married Abdel Rahman bin Awf, her third husband, and bore him two sons.

Upon Abdel Rahman's death, Umm Kulthum once more contracted herself into marriage, to her fourth and final husband, this time with the conqueror of Egypt, Amr ibn al-As. She stayed with him until she passed away. Atika bint Zaid is another good example. She was a woman of exceptional abilities who had managed to contract four marriages during her lifetime. Her first husband was Abdullah ibn Abu Bakr, son of the first Caliph Abu Bakr. He died, leaving her a fortune on condition that she would not re-marry.

For a while she was content with the idea of living a celibate life, but later she decided to go against his wish and not to spend the rest of her life alone; hence her decision to accept Umar ibn al-Khattab, the second Caliph, as her second husband. When Umar was assassinated in 642 she married her third husband, Zubayr ibn al-Awwam. After his death in 656, she took her fourth husband, Hussein ibn Ali, son of the fourth Caliph Ali; by this time she was around forty-five years old.'"

Marriage in Islam requires a contract between two equal partners. Hence, in Islamic terms, the woman is to be a subject rather than an object in the marriage contract. The contract, in sum, is a legal written document between two adults, which entails an offer by one partner and an acceptance by the other in the presence of two witnesses. The Qadi, or official, usually solemnises the marriage in a mosque or court or any other location.

The consent of the prospective wife is crucial for the effectiveness of the marriage contract. Any force or blackmail on the part of the relatives would automatically render the contract invalid. The bride, moreover, has the exclusive right to stipulate her own conditions in the contract. These conditions include mainly (though not exclusively) such issues as marriage terms (the right, for example, to have a monogamous relationship whilst she is still living with her husband) and divorce terms (the right, for instance, to dissolve the marital bond at her own initiative if she deems it necessary). In addition, dowries—one initial and another deferred in case of divorce—must be specified and written down and they should be of substance. The dowry (or *Mahr,* in Islamic terms) belongs to the wife; it is her exclusive right and it should not be given away, neither to her family nor to her relatives. The Quran says 'Give women their dowry as a free gift; but if they choose to make over to you a part of it, you may regard it as lawfully yours'."

When the marriage is consummated, the couple assume a new relationship: that is, a husband-wife relationship. It is a kind of reciprocal and interdependent relationship. The Quran says 'And of His signs is that He gave you wives from among yourselves, that you might live in tranquillity with them, and put love and kindness in your hearts. Surely there are signs in this for thinking people'. The verse implies that in a marriage bond the two partners are a comfort to each other. They should find and enjoy peace and tranquillity in each other's company and be bound together not only by a sexual relationship but also by love, compassion and mercy. As such, both have to demonstrate mutual care, affection, respect and be prepared to make sacrifices.

There should be no servility on the part of either side, for they are two equal partners in a healthy, loving and caring relationship. The Quran eloquently illustrates this equal partnership in the following statement: 'They are an apparel to you, as you are an apparel to them'. The verse explains that just as a garment covers a person completely and provides him/her with warmth, protection and decency, in the same way a husband and wife provide each other with the necessary warmth, comfort, intimacy and protection. The realisation of these principles in actual life depends, mainly, on the way both partners react to each other. In this context, the Quran expects them to behave in the best manner toward each other. The husband, on the one hand, is commanded to treat his wife gently and with kindness, affection and consideration. The Prophet said 'The best of you is the best of you to his wife, and I am better than any of you toward my wife'. He is to deal with her with dignity and in an equitable manner, not to hurt or injure her feelings. He is to show her that he loves her, appreciates her good qualities and he is to give her the impression that he needs her and depends on her to attain happiness in life. Also, he is asked to ensure that his tasks as husband and father are fulfilled to the utmost. Besides, the husband has to meet his legal responsibility to provide full maintenance of the wife: a task which he has to accomplish with good cheer and gladness.

The wife, on the other hand, is similarly required to reciprocate in kindness towards her husband, treat him with respect, admire his good qualities and express her love and affection to him. Also, she is called upon to ensure that her duties as wife and mother are performed to the best of her abilities. To maintain a happy conjugal relationship, both partners must be loyal, honest, direct, and trustworthy. They should be thoughtful, sympathetic and sensitive towards each other's feelings; in particular, they must avoid raising each other's suspicions and jealousy and try to maintain their integrity as husband and wife, united together in a matrimonial link. Concerning their sexual intimacy, both must be pleasing' and receptive. They should endeavour to attain and give maximum gratification.

Moreover, in order to keep the marital link intact, stable and healthy, both partners have to demonstrate their willingness to share the burden of looking after the welfare of the family. They must share the ups and downs of married life, be prepared to make sacrifices, pay attention to each other's point of view, consult each other and adopt joint decisions on important matters that affect the entire family. These joint decisions have to be delivered or enforced by the husband since, in

Islam, he is the head of the family. This is based on the following Quranic verses which give the husband the right to be in charge of the family: 'Women shall with justice have rights similar to those exercised against them, although men have a degree above women. Allah is Mighty and Wise'. 'Men have authority over women because Allah has made the one superior to the other, and because they spend their wealth to maintain them'. These verses were and still are a source of much discussion and debate throughout the Muslim world, generating a host of different interpretations. These interpretations range from liberal to moderate to conservative.

Our view in this context is that the headship of the husband should on no account be a license for dictatorship; it should entail no absolute freedom on the part of the person in charge; if the husband misuses or abuses his status, the wife has the right to interfere to rectify the situation. After all, the whole issue of being a chairperson is to ensure the smooth running of the family. Any neglect on the part of the husband to fulfil the task which is designated to him justifies his replacement by the more able person (the wife).

However, God-conscious pairs would always act responsibly because they are aware of their commitments to God as well as to each other. Also, because they are conscious of the fact that if they live up to their promises and act rationally in their married life they would invoke God's pleasure, hence making their lives a perpetual joy and paradise. But, sadly, this kind of paradise, envisaged by the Quran and practised briefly during the Prophet's time, has hardly ever been realised.

The Plights of the Muslim Women in Society

In fact, the case has nearly always been the reverse. Slowly but surely, attitudes towards women and marriage changed. The Quranic principles which bestowed honour, dignity, kindness and respect on women were gradually eroded and went into limbo. Customs, rather than Divine laws, shaped and continue to shape the social fabric of society and govern people's attitudes towards women and marriage. The outcome has been a steady deterioration in the status of women as far as their marital rights are concerned. Take, for example, the right to initiate a marriage proposal. This has been completely abandoned: not even in her wildest dreams would a woman dare to propose orally or in writing. The disappearance of this early practice has been so total that most women, even educated ones, are not aware of its existence, let alone practise it. The right to exercise her choice in selecting a marriage partner has, in most cases, been forgotten.

Most marriages that currently take place in Muslim societies are arranged unions, during which force and intimidation are quite often employed to obtain the girl's consent. Moreover, her freedom to sign the marriage contract has been considerably curtailed. The majority of Muslim marriages nowadays are contracted through agents (guardians, especially on the part of the woman), very often a male member of the family (father, brother, or uncle), who formalises and signs the contract on her behalf. In doing so, her opportunity and right to negotiate marriage and divorce terms are deliberately denied.

In most cases, a woman is subjected to considerable pressure to avoid stipulating in her marriage contract a divorce right or any other rights which might be viewed as a constraint on the freedom of the husband. If she did so, the social pressure on her would be so tremendous that in the end she would be obliged to give up, otherwise she would be accused of endangering the whole enterprise. Divorce has become a stigma and women are always regarded as being culpable.

The prospects for a non-virgin (divorcee or widow) getting remarried is dim. Indeed, in many cases they are forced to spend the rest of their lives cherishing the memories of their dead husbands and serving the male members of their own families. Within the context of a husband-wife relationship, authoritarianism and dictatorship have replaced the ideal and equal partnership advocated by the Quran.

The husband assumes the role of ruler, superior, controller, oppressor and master, while the wife, on the other hand, is reduced to a slave, a captive, a low, inferior and submissive creature. Listen to what the so-called Council of Ulama (that is, people with knowledge about Islam) of South Africa has to say about the relationship between the two spouses: 'She (the wife) should mould herself to wholeheartedly submit to his whims and fancies. His likes must become her likes and his dislikes, her dislikes. She should step out of her way to comfort him and to console him in his worries and distress. Her wishes and desires are subservient to his wishes and orders.... After all (God) has created her for her husband's comfort and peace'. The Council goes on to say 'The Shariah has accorded the husband the highest degree of authority over his wife. Likewise it will transpire that the wife has to offer the higher degree of submission to her husband... with humility and patience she should tolerate his shortcomings and even his injustice... men are the rulers of women and they have a superior rank... (as such) it is the husband's right and role to dominate and dictate (and) it is the duty of the wife to submit and serve. The wife should understand that she can never conquer her husband by confrontation and seeking to set herself up as his equal or superior'.

Concerning the financial arrangements between them, the Council stresses:. 'It is significant that in spite of the wife remaining the sole owner of her wealth... (she is encouraged) to put her wealth at his disposal and pleasure'. What about his money? 'She should not attempt to appoint herself as the controller of his finances. It is none of her business on whom her husband spends his wealth'. What if the husband fails to perform his duties properly?

The Council emphasises: 'She must not adopt a legal stand and a technical attitude, demanding from her husband perfect and total fulfilment of her legal rights.... The wife has to remember that despite her husband's failure to fulfil his duties to her, she is under... obligation to obey her husband..., obedience to the husband will ensure the everlasting happiness... for her'

The mutual responsibilities on both sides to demonstrate to each other their loyalty, honesty and respect have become exclusively the wife's domain and obligations. The husband has been deliberately left out of the equation. So whether he is honest and loyal or a cheat it does not matter. What matters most (and this is important to him and to the male-dominated society) is the faithfulness and loyalty of the wife. There is no question of reciprocity between them in this matter. The emphasis has always been on the wife, as if she is a creature with no control over her sexuality.

Dissolution of Marriage in Islam

The word 'divorce' 'traces its origin back to the Latin derivative and conjures up the splitting of a unit, the permanent physical separation of the spouses', while the Arabic word '*talaq*' is derived from the verb *itlaq* which means to set loose, set free or to leave. *Talaq*, therefore, within the context of the marital link means to terminate the bond created by a marriage contract.

In every society there are ways and means which allow the marital link to be dissolved if it fails to fulfil its objective. The reasons for the dissolution of marriage are, generally speaking, common and almost universal. They apply to human society irrespective of time, place or level of civilisation from the unavoidable death of a spouse or involuntary barrenness to the trivial cooking mistake of burning the husband's food or putting too much salt in it, not to mention the man's arbitrary dislike of his spouse or capricious preference for another woman who seems more pleasing to him. So the termination of marriage is sometimes inevitable and no system can afford to ignore this reality, otherwise it is doomed to failure.

Any system which insists on the indissolubility of marriage and overlooks the fact that under exceptional circumstances the dissolution of the family becomes a necessity is static, impractical and does not respond adequately to human needs. A system under which marriage is indissoluble would inevitably lead to the abuse of marriage, because people will always find ways around it, hence defeating the whole purpose which the system stands for in the first place.

In principle, Islam regards marriage as a lifelong commitment. However, sometimes there do arise situations wherein marriage ceases to fulfil its purpose. Hence, divorce can be invoked by either side or both of them in order to accommodate the realities of an unsuccessful marriage. It must be stressed that divorce can only be exercised as the last resort after all efforts for reconciliation between the spouses are exhausted. Therefore, in Islam divorce is considered a necessity if the married partners are not happy. However, divorce is heavily disapproved of and discouraged.

The Qur'an discourages divorce in the following verses: 'And (remember) when you (Muhammed) said to the man (Zayd, Muhammed's adopted son) whom Allah and yourself have favoured: keep your wife and have fear of Allah'.In this verse there is an implicit disapproval of divorce.

In other verses the Qur'an clearly discourages Muslims from having recourse to a hasty divorce, even though they might be dissatisfied with their marriage partners. 'Treat them with kindness; for even if you do dislike them, it may well be that you may dislike a thing which Allah has meant for your own good'.

The Qur'an not only discourages divorce, but it prohibits the slandering of one's wife in order to take back her dowry 'If you wish to have a wife in the place of a (divorced) one, do not take from her the dowry you have given her even it if be a talent of gold. That would be improper and grossly unjust; for how can you take it back when you have lain with each other and entered into a firm contract?

Divorce was also discouraged by the Prophet, who is reported to have said: 'Of all things licit, the most hateful to God is divorce,' Also: 'Let not the faithful man hate the faithful woman; if he dislikes some of her habits, he may like others." Ali, the son-in-law of the Prophet, said, 'Marry and do not divorce your wives, for divorce causes God's throne to tremble.' These disapprovals notwithstanding, Islam concedes the possibility of divorce as the lesser of two evils when the alternative is a disastrously unhappy marriage and it devotes much attention to dealing with it both in the Qur'an as well as in the Sunnah.

There are many causes for divorce. If the spouses discover that they are incompatible because of their ideas and opinions, their modes of behaviour and their temperaments, then they should resort to divorce. The conflict and tension that would inevitably arise as a result of their incompatibility would certainly give rise to ill-feeling and contempt between the spouses. This would adversely affect not only the couple but their children as well as their relatives and closest friends. As a way out of this difficult situation, Islam therefore prescribes divorce.

Furthermore, spouses locked forcibly in an unhappy union would surely be forced themselves—in an attempt to satisfy their sexual urge—to seek sexual intimacy outside the marriage tie, hence falling into the trap of committing adultery, which is forbidden in Islam. To prevent partners from indulging in such indecency, Islam allows the couple to be divorced so that they can go their own separate ways.

Divorce is also granted if the husband is impotent. Divorce, moreover, can take place if both spouses or one of them suffers a serious disease that renders the continuation of the marital relation either impossible or unsafe, or if the husband is put in prison for a long time or fails to support his wife.

In order for the divorce to be effective and valid, the person who is performing it has to be adult (*baligh*), sane (*aqil*), free from any confusion or coercion and full of clear and good intentions (*qasid*). In addition, the witnesses have to be reliable, trustworthy and of good conduct.

Divorce in Islam is one of those issues which has generated considerable controversy and debate among Muslims and non-Muslims alike; this is probably because it has been grossly abused by Muslims and certainly misunderstood by both Muslims and non-Muslims.

Islam is against divorce and is strongly in support of the family unit: hence, both spouses have to do their utmost to build up a strong and harmonious marital relationship. If, however, tension arises between them, they should not rush into a hasty divorce. First, they should try and make some serious efforts to save their marriage. For example, they should attempt to stand the causes of their differences and try to solve them in a private and amicable way. If this proves to be unsuccessful, then they are advised to ask representatives, one from each side, to mediate and try to restore peace between them.

The Quran says, 'If you fear a breach between a man and his wife, appoint an arbiter from his people and another from hers. If they wish to be reconciled, Allah will bring them together again–Allah is Knowing, Wise'. The arbiters have to be close to the parties involved and command their trust and respect. They should conduct their task impartially and discreetly. Also, they should try and settle the differences between the spouses without publicity; they should especially attempt to avoid the embarrassment of revealing such issues that might be regarded (by the married partners) as very private and intimate. The decisions reached by the arbiters are binding on both spouses. However, if one or both of them refuse to abide by them, then the rulings have to be enforced by the court.

The Quran clearly protects the right of the woman in this matter. By insisting here that two arbiters one from the side of each party (the husband as well as the wife) have to be called to investigate the matter between them peacefully and objectively, it has in fact put the interests of the wife on an equal footing with those of her husband, by giving her the opportunity to present her case and viewpoint before the arbiters. This is surely a fair and just way to deal with divorce matters because it takes into consideration the interests of both sides. More importantly, it protects the weak (the wife) from being abused by the strong (the husband) an outcome which all too frequently occurs in our society these days. For example, it prevents the husband from arbitrarily divorcing his wife without any due consideration for her mental or physical wellbeing, a practice very often used by the husband to punish his wife in contemporary Muslim societies.

In light of the above it would seem sensible to favour and recommend the adoption of this orderly divorce process by the judicial systems of all Muslim countries for it is simple, civilised and, most importantly, authentically Islamic: it has been described and recommended by the Quran. So, it is not something foreign or alien to Islam; on the contrary, it is an integral part of the Islamic tradition. Indeed there are many examples in which divorce cases were judged according to this procedure in early Islamic history.

For instance, it has been reported that during the reign of the fourth Caliph Ali (son-in-law of the Prophet), a man and his wife approached him complaining about each other's behaviour and stating that there were gross differences between them that had made their lives miserable. Ali immediately acted as Judge and asked for representatives from both sides to be despatched to him. Upon their arrival, he commissioned them to look into the matter carefully and decide whether there would be any possibility of making peace between them.

Also, he reminded them of their responsibility and sacred duty to handle the case with tact, due consideration and impartiality. He told them that if they sensed that there was a chance that they could be reconciled then they should spare no effort in doing so, otherwise they had to be separated with honour and in dignity. When the arbiters reached a decision, Ali made it legally effective by forcing the spouses to abide by it.

If the arbiters realise that there is a good chance for patching up things between the spouses, they are encouraged to do so, but if they think otherwise, the partners have to be allowed to go their own separate ways. It is most unfortunate that such a humane understanding of the verse and such a civilised practice of it failed to materialise throughout most of our Islamic history. For one reason or another, both the jurists as well as the rulers decided to ignore and shelve it.

Nevertheless, there were a few scholars who continued to stress the importance of utilising the directions contained in this verse and use them as guidance to promote legal or judicial divorce systems in the Muslim world. One of the most respected Egyptian scholars, Muhammed Abduh, advocated such reform.

In his book *Women and Islam*, Abduh explains as follows:

> The call in this verse if you fear a breach between a man and his wife, appoint an arbiter from his people and another from hers] is a general, not specific, one. It cannot be the responsibility of every person or every group of people in society. Therefore, there are two opinions among the interpreters: one says that the call is directed to the people who are concealed with the general affairs of the Muslim people, namely the rulers or representatives who are responsible for their overall well being.

Abduh continues:

> both opinions are right, for the first one allocates the responsibility of looking after the interest of the people in the hands of the representatives who have

> to endeavour to do their jobs properly, while the second one assigns the duty to the general public who have to team up and be cooperative with one another.

As far as the representatives are concerned, Abduh explains that there are two different views: one sees that the arbiters as mere mediators with no legal authority, while the other insists on regarding them as judges with legal power to enforce their decisions. Concerning the part which states, 'If they wish to be reconciled, Allah will bring them together again. Allah is, Knowing, Wise', Abduh interprets it thus: this part means that, God favours peace and harmony between spouses and wishes that they would be reconciled, because of the emphasis Islam lays on the family unit in society. As such the arbiters are exhorted to ensure that peace can prevail between them. However, if the arbiters fail to bridge the gap between the couple, they are not to blame.

Abduh then introduces his own version. He says: when conflict erupts between husband and wife and proves difficult to solve amicably, the spouses are advised to take the matter to the judge of the county. The judge here has to appoint two mediators—one represents the wife while the other acts for the husband. Both representatives have to be of good character and highly respected people. The judge, after briefing them, has to send them to the spouses in an attempt to solve the dispute. If the arbiters' efforts culminate in success, then it is good news. But if they fail to bring the two spouses together again, then they have the legal power to divorce them. The representatives, after completing their mission, have to report to the judge and the judge has to enforce their decision. It must be stressed here that the mediators—when they decide on separation have to give only one revocable divorce, so that time may be given to the spouses to reflect on their situation before final separation can take place. Abduh's view on the judicial process of divorce found acceptance among the reformers in some Muslim countries who thought that improvement in this area was badly needed because the unlimited power of the husband to repudiate his wife was grossly abused, hence making the lives of many Muslim women unbearable. His view was, therefore, incorporated into their legal systems and helped them to introduce such reform. Tunisia, for example, was one of a few Muslim countries which decided to introduce legal, reform based on Abduh's view on judicial divorce.

The Tunisian reformers argued that; 'In the case of discord between spouses, the Quran orders the appointment of arbitrators—yet what more obvious case of discord between spouses is there than a pronouncement of repudiation by the husband? And who is then better qualified to undertake the necessary function of arbitration than the official tribunals? On this ground,therefore, the right of a husband to repuditate his wife extra judiciously, was abolished.'

Thus, all divorce actions were prohibited, henceforth taking place outside, the domain of the court. The introduction of such reform has heralded two things. Firstly, it has empowered the court with an unrestricted power to compensate the wife for any injury endured as a result of the divorce; secondly, it ensures that both spouses am heated on an equal basis in this regard.

The Quran deals with divorce issues in another verse which states:

> Divorce may be pronounced twice, and then a woman must be retained in honour or allowed to go with kindness. It is unlawful for husbands to take from them anything they have given them, unless both fear that they may not be able to keep within

> the bounds set by Allah; in which case it shall be no offence for either of them if the wife ransoms herself.

In this verse, God explains that divorce may be pronounced twice, during which period reconciliation can take place; hence it is a revocable type of divorce, since the couple can still resume their marital life if they wish to do so.

However, a third pronouncement would lead to irrevocable divorce, after which the spouses cannot remarry, unless the woman marries another person first and that person also divorces her. In this case, she is allowed to remarry her former husband if she desires to do so: 'If a man divorces his wife, he cannot remarry her until she has wedded another man and been divorced by him; in which case it shall be no offence for either of them to return to the other, if they think that they can keep within the limits set by Allah. Such are the bounds of Allah. He makes them plain to men of understanding.'

Divorce must be pronounced when the wife is in a state of purity (*tuhr*), otherwise it is regarded as invalid. The reason for not allowing the husband to divorce his wife during the state of impurity is that the husband is physically separated from her and this might induce him to press ahead with the separation. While if she is in a state of purity, he is physically close to her and in this case he might be persuaded to reconsider his decision.

Anyway, if divorce takes place, the wife has to observe *idda* or the waiting period. This lasts for three months, during which time sexual intercourse is not allowed between the spouses. By the end of this waiting period, the separation becomes final and legally effective. The reason for making the waiting period obligatory is to ensure the achievement of the following: first, to give the spouses more time to reconsider their attitudes and resolve their differences; second, to determine whether or not the wife is pregnant, for if she is expecting a child there is always a good chance that the spouses might be willing to effect a reconciliation.

Both spouses are encouraged to recognise and respect each other's rights, after the separation. In particular, the Quran exhorts the man to be considerate and kind to his former wife. Also, he is enjoined to act with due care and not allow her to be thrown out of her house. He must ensure that she may stay, if she wishes, with respect and dignity. Moreover, he should properly maintain her and give her sufficient support. Here, it must be noted that there are differences of opinion among scholars regarding the maintenance of divorced women. Some recommend that a divorcee is entitled to sustenance, which includes both the dowry as well as a financial allowance, whilst others insist that the payment of her maintenance should only continue for the period of *idda*, which is not more than three menstrual cycles.

Under Islamic Law, the marriage contract may be dissolved in three ways: first, the death of one of the spouses; second, by act of the husband or the wife or both of them; third, through Judicial process or a decree of court. The dissolution of the marriage contract by the husband is called *Talaq* (divorce), which is usually translated as repudiation. It can be done unilaterally by the husband without his having to produce any reason. This form of divorce or *talaq* has been classified (by the jurists) into three main types:

1) *Talaq al-Ahsan*: This is the most approved form of repudiation. In this kind of Talaq the husband has to pronounce one single divorce during tuhr or the period of purity of the wife. Then he must abstain

from having physical contact with her during the waiting period. This form of repudiation is revocable. For the husband can, before the end of the idda, revoke the divorce and resume the conjugal relationship. It must be noted here that the approval of the wife is essential in this context. The husband cannot force her back, even if he regrets divorcing her. She must first give her consent before the couple can resume their matrimonial relations. In order for him to signal his intention to retain her, he may express this desire either explicitly or implicitly. The former is the preferred one, and is usually done by pronouncing the revocation of the repudiation. If, during the waiting period, one of the spouses dies, the other can still inherit the estate. If the husband allows the waiting period to elapse without reclaiming his wife, the repudiation becomes irrevocable or absolute (*bayan*).

2) *Talaq al-Hasan*: This is a less approved form of divorce. Here the husband repudiates his wife three successive times over a period of three months, once each month during the period of tuhr. As with Ahsan talaq, the husband can revoke his divorce after the first or second repudiation, but after the third repudiation the divorce becomes absolute (*bayan*). The only difference is that the wife cannot remarry her former husband until she has first married someone else and then dissolved that marriage. The reason for adding this condition is to prevent a hasty repudiation on the part of the husband.

3) *Talaq al-Bid'ah*:. This is the least approved method of divorce in the Muslim world but, unfortunately, it is the most widely used. It is highly condemned by women and civilised men and regarded as sinful. Nonetheless, it is considered legally effective once it

is pronounced. This form of divorce is effected by three repudiations, which may be pronounced at any time (not merely in clean periods) and without definite intervals'. It is an irrevocable form of talaq and the husband can only remarry his ex-wife after she has contracted a new marriage with a second man and dissolved that marriage (after proper consummation). *Bid'ah* divorce lacks any Quranic support. Also, it was strongly denounced by the Prophet, who is reported to have reacted angrily when he heard that somebody had divorced his wife by the triple pronouncement of talaq in a single sitting and said 'How would you play with the book of Allah while I am alive and amidst you? He then ordered the man to take back his wife. Nonetheless, this innovative divorce acquired legitimacy under the reign of the second Caliph Umar, who decided to make it legal in an attempt to prevent any careless use of the formula. However, his efforts in this context proved to no avail as his decree eventually produced counterproductive results. Since then it has remained lawful and legally effective among Sunnis (the Shia do not recognise this type of divorce), and men have continued to make use of it to their own advantage. We are therefore strongly in favour of banning it outright. It is a bizarre and odd practice; most importantly, it is very degrading to the dignity of Muslim women.

The great jurist, Ibn Taymiyyah, was against it. He stated that the erratic use of such a practice (triple pronouncement on a single occasion) was invalid and had no impact on the statutory position of a marriage. His aim was to protect women, as he thought that they were victimised by such a ruling (Umar's validation of *Bid'ah* divorce). It is a shame that his position has been forgotten and disregarded in contemporary Muslim societies.

The dissolution of marriage by the wife takes two forms:

1) *Talaq al-Tawfid*, or delegated divorce. In this form of divorce the husband, at the time of marriage, agrees to delegate to his wife the power of pronouncing the talaq, thus allowing her to dissolve the marriage contract. It must be stressed here that once the husband consents to give his wife the right to divorce him, he is no longer in a position to reclaim it. Tawfid divorce is indeed a powerful weapon in the hands of the wife, since she can easily use it if the conditions in the marriage contract are violated by the husband.

2) *Khula,* also called ransom by some jurists Here, the wife initiates the divorce, but the husband has to agree 31 to free her in return for repayment of part or all of the dowry or *mahr.* A woman seeking khula, however, may lose her right to maintenance during the waiting period. Women's right to khula was acknowledged and respected during the early Islamic era; they were very often allowed to exercise it without fear or intimidation. For a woman to request khula she does not have to quote any specific reason; the fact that she is unhappy with her husband would be enough to grant her separation under khula.

Divorce through mutual consent is usually called Mubara'ah. This form of divorce centres around an agreement between spouses to release each other from the marital link" with no exchange or payment on either side.

The final method of dissolving the marriage contract is through a judicial process, at the instigation of either the wife or husband.

This can be obtained in the case of (a) Lian and (b) annulment.

- *Lian*: It is the divorce by oath and it occurs when the husband accuses his wife of committing adultery without evidence. The court, after studying the case and hearing particular oaths from both spouses, would issue a decree allowing the marriage to be dissolved. This form of separation is irrevocable and the partners cannot remarry each other again.
- *Annulment*: The annulment of the marriage takes place when the wife lodges a complaint against her husband on the basis of the following: impotence, failure to fulfil the marital obligations, maltreatment, insanity and any other causes which might justify the annulment of the marriage.

7
Legal Status

In the Arabian peninsula (the birthplace of Islam), the situation of women prior to Islam was markedly worse. Women in this time of ignorance before Islam (*Jahiliyya*) were in subjugation either to their kinsmen or their husbands. They were considered a chattel to be possessed, to be bought, to be sold or to be inherited. Men had absolute domination over them. They were not individuals themselves, they either belonged to their father or to their husband. The widows of a man were very often inherited by his sons just like any other property.

After inheriting them from their father the sons could then easily marry them. Women had no independence or power over issues relating to their well-being and they were excluded from any active role in the social and political affairs of their society. It has been stated that at annual gatherings and fairs women were made to dance naked and poets sat around composing poems on various parts of their body and movements. In other words, they were treated as sex objects with no respect at all for their dignity. Women in pre-Islamic Arab times were also considered to be a heavy burden on the family. The birth of the daughter was embarrassing for the father, who considered it a disgrace and a matter of shame. Therefore, the Arabs of that time practised widely 'female infanticide': burying their female child alive. This custom was common among the Arabs and it was even viewed as a generous act.

One of the social reasons for such a,) attitude was that, in pre-Islamic times, there were often inter-tribal blood feuds, which demanded male members to defend their tribes. Hence men were in much greater demand than women. In addition, in the tribal conflict, the enemy always aimed at capturing women and taking them as prisoners so that they could collect heavy ransoms. Failing to do so, they would keep them as slaves. In both cases women were considered a liability to their own tribes. For if they paid ransom, they would lose money, if not, then the chastity of their women as well as their honour were at stake.

The Arabs did not welcome the birth of a baby girl, and this was so because of the nature of their society. Wars and invasions never ceased and taking revenge never stopped. All these things depended on the male, but a woman was unable to do any of these tasks, in addition to it, she was the desired loot for the service (of the enemy) in the eyes of the enemy, or she was for his entertainment. For these reasons, the Arabs believed that their own daughters constituted a heavy burden on them and the easiest way to get rid of them was to kill them immediately after they were born.

Men in the *Jahiliyya* society enjoyed an absolute right over women in matters related to marriage and divorce. He, the man, had unlimited rights of marriage and divorce. He could take as many wives as he wished and could discard a wife at will. The idea of a fixed institution of marriage was absent from the pre-Islamic era. There were only different kinds of sexual union which were characterised by the looseness of marriage bonds and the lack of any defined legal system: 'If one takes into consideration the preceding facts in conjunction with other factors such as the absence of any contract or legal guardian, the exclusion of the wife from her husband's inheritance, the easy methods of divorce, the lack of a period of seclusion after divorce and widowhood—the *idda* (waiting time)—the conclusion must be reached that there was no fixed institution of marriage and that marriage ties were in no sense regarded as binding'.

The result was that a man was at liberty to contract as many marriages as he wished; al-Tabari mentions that men in Arabia before Islam used to marry four, five, six, or even ten women simultaneously and nobody could ever stop them from marrying more than that 'Before Muhammad, the capacity of the Arab's purse would appear to have provided the only limitation to the number of his wives, and though there were established conventions about the status of the women he married, there were neither conventions nor laws to dictate to him how many they should be'.

When Islam emerged, the issue of marriage was regulated. It encouraged men to have one wife, but reluctantly allowed them to have up to four wives under special circumstances. Men before Islam also used to force their women, especially their slave girls, into prostitution (*Zina*). With regard to divorce, there was no formula for severing the marriage relationship. The husband, in general, enjoyed absolute power over the divorce issue and this led to constant abuses. As there was no check on the powers of the husband to dissolve the marriage tie, Arab men used to divorce their women very often and for any reason, even if it was a trivial one such as, for example, speaking highly of their family or tribes. However, the most obvious ones mentioned by the historians of the *Jahiliyya* were: the man could not find the love he was expecting in his wife; the couple were unable to establish friendship and intimacy or a man thought that he was marrying a young and beautiful woman who turned out to be otherwise.

The pagan Arabs also used to revoke the divorce and resume the marital relationship. A man, for example, would pronounce the formula 'I divorce you"' many times and then take his wife back; he could then divorce her again and yet could still take her back. When women were divorced or widowed there was no fixed period" for *idda.* Some women had to wait for a year before they would be able to re-marry, others contracted marriages immediately after the separation.

Divorced women had no right to claim for maintenance, men were exempted from any financial responsibility and endured no legal punishment for their actions. This inhuman treatment had contributed to the degradation of womanhood insofar as the woman herself believed that she should not be more than a servile and submissive creature, and had no fight to expect any respect and honour in the world. Such a deplorable situation illustrated that the fights and the liberties of women in those ancient societies were not only trampled upon, but were entirely denied them. It must be stressed that some scholars have argued that women in pre-Islamic Arabia had some rights, citing the case of Khadija, the Prophet's first wife, who was a highly successful business-woman.

Our response is that Khadija was an exception, one among a small elite of that society, and we believe that her case does not genuinely reflect the general condition of women in that society, which was one of subjugation. This view is shared by B. Stowasser 30 who writes 'we hear of publicly visible, independently wealthy women who are active in their own right. The best-known example here is, of course, Khadija, Muhammad's first wife... (but) aside from such rare figures of public visibility, involvement and independence as Khadija, the majority of pre-Islamic urban women appear to have lived in a male-dominated society in which their status was low and their rights were negligible.

Most women were subjugated to male domination, either that of a male relative, or that of the husband. The men's rights over their women were as their rights over any property. This seems to have been so not only in marriages by capture, where the captured woman was completely under the authority of her captor, but also in marriages by purchase or contract. Here, the suitor paid a sum of money (the *mahr)* to the guardian of the bride-to-be (and possibly another sum, the *sadaq,* to the woman herself), thereby purchasing her and making her his exclusive property. The marriage contract, in other words, was a contract between husband and guardian, with the bride the sales object.

Furthermore, neither conventions nor laws seem to have existed to put a limit to the number of wives that a man could have simultaneously, so that the only restrictive considerations were economic ones. As to divorce in the *Jahiliyya,* it was a matter entirely up to the will of the husband who, having purchased his wife, could discharge his total obligation to her by payment of any portion of the *mahr* that might remain due to her father or guardian, and be rid of her by pronouncement of the formula of dismissal. This formula, pronounced three times, was effective instantly. Finally, there is some indication that women in pre-Islamic Arabia were not allowed the holding, or in any case the uncontrolled disposal, of their possessions'.

Position of Women in Islam

In relation to the absolute, woman is equal to man in all essential fights and duties; God makes no distinction between man and woman. They are to be equally rewarded or punished for their deeds. The Quran says: "Their Lord answers them, saying: I will deny no man or woman among you the reward of their labours. You are the offspring of one another'. 'For Muslim men and women, for believing men and women; for devout men and women; for men and women who are patient; for men and women who humble themselves; for men and women who give charity; for men and women who fast; for men and women who guard their chastity; for men and women who remember Allah much—for them all has God prepared forgiveness and a great reward'.

'We shall reward the steadfast according to their noblest deeds. Be they men or women, those that embrace the faith and do what is fight We will surely grant a happy life; We shall reward them according to their noblest actions'. And again 'The true believers, both men and women, are friends to each other. They enjoin what is just and forbid what is evil; they attend to their prayers and pay the alms-tax and obey Allah and His Apostle. On these Allah will have mercy. He is Mighty, Wise. Allah has promised the men and women who believe in Him gardens watered by running streams, in which they shall abide forever. He has promised them goodly mansions in the gardens of Eden. And what is more, they shall have greater favour from Allah. That is the supreme triumph'.

In terms of moral responsibility, both men and women are equally accountable for their actions. For example, the Quran decrees that the same punishment has to be applied on the thieving men as well as the thieving women. Also, both the adulterer and the adulteress have to suffer the same punishment. In fact, in a situation where the husband accuses his wife of committing adultery, her oath weighs more heavily than his accusation and hence Islamic law would work in her favour. To rehabilitate the status of women in society, Islam denounced the old myth of Eve as temptress and source of evil, as the cause of original sin and the fall of humankind. According to the Quran the woman is not responsible for Adam's first mistake: both were equally wrong in disobeying God. Both asked for forgiveness and both were forgiven.

Quranic Guidelines of Equal Rights Women

Islam also changed the mentality of both men and women and created a new relationship between them based on respect and mutual understanding; taking care of the woman and respecting her were also emphasised. The status of women was also raised in Islam by granting her the legal right to enter into contracts, to run a business, and to possess property independently from her husband or any kinsmen. From the beginning, Islam stressed that women, as half of the society, should be offered all opportunities which could enable them to develop their natural abilities, so that they might participate effectively in the development of society. It also emphasised that women should be allowed to attain to the highest ranks of progress materially, intellectually and spiritually. It is within this context that Islam has granted women broad social, political and economic rights, education and training rights and work opportunity rights. To protect these rights from being abused by men, Islam provided firm legal safeguards.

The right of independent ownership involves the right to manage her own money and property independently. She is at liberty to buy, sell, mortgage, lease, borrow or lend, and sign contracts and legal documents. Also, she can donate her money, act as a trustee and set up a business or company. 'For men is a portion of what, they earn, and for women is a portion of what they earn. Ask Allah for His grace. Allah has knowledge of all things'. This right cannot be altered whether she is single or married. When she is married, she enjoys a free hand over the dower while she is married and after divorce. This independent economic position is based on Quranic principles, especially the teaching of *Zakat,* which encourages women to own, invest, save and distribute their earnings and savings according to their discretion. It also acknowledges and enforces the right of women to participate in various economic activities.

Islamic Cencept on Marriage

Islam regards marriage as a meritorious institution and attaches great importance to its well-being. Marriage in Islam is a union between two consenting adults. Its aims are to perpetuate human life and achieve spiritual and emotional harmony. The Quran says 'And of His signs is that He created you from dust and behold: you became men and multiplied throughout the earth. And of His signs is that He gave you wives from among yourselves, that you might live in tranquillity with them, and put love and kindness in your hearts. Surely there are signs in this for thinking people'. Also, the Prophet is reported to have said 'women are the twin halves of men'. Therefore, the consent of the two partners is essential to start a happy and stable family. Hence Islam is against the idea of forcing women to marry against their wishes. On the contrary, it encourages women to choose their spouses.

According to the Prophet, 'A widow (or divorcee) is not to be married before her consent is sought' and 'No virgin girl is to marry without first consulting her, and her approval is her keeping silent'. This freedom to choose her partner is guaranteed by the law which insists that the dowry has to be paid to the bride and not to the parents. The Prophet emphasised that although parents were to be consulted and obeyed, the fact remained that the woman's individuality and independence had to be recognised and respected. Hence the marriage contract has to reflect the interests of the woman in the first instance and be designed to meet her specific needs. The woman has to express her desire and impose conditions if necessary to secure her position. A Muslim woman, therefore, cannot be forced to enter into marriage without her agreement; indeed she has the right to revoke a marriage to which she did not agree in the first place.

The Prophet set a precedent for Muslim women when he invalidated marriages which were imposed on daughters by their parents. Let us see the Prophet's response when he heard that a girl was forced by her father to marry against her will: Ibn Abbas reported that a girl came to the Prophet complaining that her father had forced her to marry against her wishes. Upon hearing the story the Prophet granted her the choice between accepting the marriage or invalidating it.

As a woman has the right to have a say on issues concerning her own marriage, equally she has the right to initiate divorce if the partnership proves to be unsuccessful. If the marriage contract states that she has the right to divorce her husband, she could divorce him instantly; otherwise, she would have to resort to the court to dissolve the marital relationship.

Overall, the Quranic legislation concerning divorce allows time for reflection and insists on kind treatment of the woman. For example, whilst in pre-Islamic times a woman could easily be repudiated and thrown out by her husband, under the Quranic legislation he is no longer allowed to do so. If divorce takes place, the husband has to pay her back the deferred dowry and a reasonable sum of money as maintenance. He has to support her throughout the idda period (three months and ten days) to determine whether she is pregnant. If so he is legally obliged to support her until she delivers and nurses the baby to a certain age.

Education for Women—an Islamic Point of View

Both the Quran and the Sunnah advocate the rights of women and men equally to seek knowledge. The Quran commands all Muslims to exert effort in the pursuit of knowledge irrespective of their sex. It constantly encourages Muslims to read, think, contemplate and learn from the signs of Allah in nature: 'Are the wise and the ignorant equal? Truly, none will take heed but men of understanding'. 'Allah will raise to high ranks those that have faith and knowledge among you. He is cognizant of all your actions'. 'Say: Lord, increase me in knowledge'.

The Prophet moreover encouraged education for both males and females and even ordered that slave girls should be educated. He made it clear that seeking knowledge was a matter of religious duty binding upon every Muslim man and woman. His teachings were widely sought by both sexes and at the time of his death it was reported that there were many women scholars. So in Islam there can be no restriction of knowledge to one sex at the expense of the other. Today, however, family circumstances, together with the traditions and customs of specific Muslim countries, may work to the detriment of the girl, in terms of depriving her of education, for reasons which have nothing to do with Islam.

A woman in Islam has always been entitled, by law, to keep her family name and not take her husband's name. Therefore, she is always known by her family's name as an indication of her individuality and her own identity. So, in Islam, there is no process of changing the names of women be they married, divorced or widowed.

In Islam lawful sex has always been held in high esteem and regarded as an act of religious devotion for which rewards in the hereafter are acknowledged. It is meant to lead to a healthy way of human reproduction, release tensions, meet natural and psychological needs and strengthen the marriage ties between spouses.

Contrary to the present situation in which talk about legitimate sex has disappeared from religious thinking and writing and has become a matter of shame and stigma which ought to be suppressed, early Muslim scholars were fascinated by the idea and were quite open about it. They wrote chapters on the subject in which they elaborated on issues such as the anatomy of sex, the religious merits of lawful sexual activities, the intimate theme of coitus, its initial foreplay and its proper conclusion. They cautioned against an abrupt coitus and crude departure at the end of the act. Instead they advised an initial gentle approach and a slow courteous departure.

Moreover, they emphasised the fact that the husband should be considerate and gentle, never too rough and that he should prolong sufficiently for his wife to attain climax. A wife is encouraged to take the initiative and not be content with the role of being submissive. In their writings those early Muslim scholars were guided by the following traditions which have been attributed to the Prophet: 'It is a rude manner of a man to proceed to have intercourse with his wife without first playing with her'. 'Let not any of you fall upon his wife in the manner a male animal suddenly jumps upon his female partner. Let there be a messenger (to go) between them' (said the prophet). He was then asked: What is the Messenger, 'O you Messenger of God?' He said: 'kissing and endearing speech'. When one of you copulates with his wife, let him not rush away from her, having attained his own climax, until she is satisfied'. 'Wash your clothes, brush your teeth. Trim your hair. Keep always clean and tidy. A nation before you neglected themselves, thereby driving their women into adultery'. It is a vice in a man 'to assault his unprepared wife, seeking to satisfy his own lust and leaving her before she could achieve her own fulfilment'." Accordingly, if a woman feels that she is not sexually satisfied or her husband is impotent she has the right to seek divorce.

The Quran has allotted a share for the woman in the inheritance of her parents and kinsmen. Her share is guaranteed by law and it is completely hers. No one can have any claim on it. The Quran says 'Men shall have a share in what their parents and kinsmen leave; and women shall have a share in what their parents and kinsmen leave; whether it be little or much, it is legally theirs'. However, very often in reality the culture of specific Muslim countries subject women to social pressure to renounce their shares to the immediate male members of the family. This constitutes a gross violation of the Quranic verses concerning inheritance.

Islam encourages women to be active politically and to be involved in decision-making. In fact Islam is the only religion which acknowledges a political role for women.' In early Islam women were given every opportunity to express themselves, to argue," and to speak their mind in public. They led delegations," mediated and granted refuge and protection.

Political Rights of Women in Islam

Their judgements on political matters were highly valued and respected and they exercised great influence in shaping their own societies. Aisha and Umm Salama (the wives of the prophet) are clear cases in point. Umm Salama was a shrewd political adviser to the Prophet and very often acted as *imam* for women. Aisha, on the other hand, played a dominant part in the political arena she lived in. She lodged complaints, criticised the policies of the rulers and led opposition groups. Together with Umm Salama she played a crucial role in compiling the traditions of the Prophet, which are considered one of the main sources of Islamic Jurisprudence. For a considerable time she acted as a judge correcting and guiding the leaders of her time.

Islam regards women to be equal to men as human beings; hence it emphasises mutual understanding and respect between the two sexes. From the Islamic viewpoint, women as human beings and as half of the society should be treated with care, tenderness and affection. Indeed, the Prophet insisted on kind and gentle treatment of women and demonstrated this not only through his attitude towards his wives but also in his teachings to his followers. He constantly encouraged them to be kind, civil and considerate when dealing with women: 'The more civil and kind a Muslim is to his woman whether wife, daughter or sister the more perfect in faith he is' he declared.

In his farewell pilgrimage he delivered a famous speech *(Khutba)* on the Mount of Mercy at Arafat in which he reminded his followers of their duty towards women and ordered them to be kind and respectful to them. He said 'Fear Allah regarding women. Verily you have married them with the trust of Allah, and made their bodies lawful with the word of Allah. You have got (rights) over them, and they have got (rights) over you'. So, from the authentic Islamic perspective, a woman is 'an individual worthy of dignity and respect, an independent human being, a social person, a legal person, a responsible agent, a free citizen, a servant of God, and a talented person, endowed, like a male person, with heart, soul and intellect; and has a fundamental equal right to exercise her abilities in all areas of human activities'.

Within the context of family ties, the legal status of Muslim women can be considered at different stages: as a daughter, as a mother and as a sister. Before the advent of Islam, daughters were very disfavoured and considered to be social and economic liabilities. Boys, on the other hand were favoured and sought after (one may add that even today in some Muslim countries boys are considered preferable to girls). Islam stopped such cruelties and insisted on equal treatment between the two sexes. The Prophet asserted the right of a female child to be treated on an equal footing with her brother. He urged parents not to make any differences between the children and to be kind to them, particularly young girls.

Here are a few *Hadiths* in which he encouraged Muslims to be gentle and caring to their daughters: 'If a daughter is born to a man and he brings her up affectionately, shows her no disrespect and treats her in the same manner as he treats his sons, the Lord will reward him with paradise'. 'Girls are models of affection and sympathy and a blessing to the family. If a person has one daughter, God will screen him from the fire of the hell owing to his daughter; if he has two daughters, God will admit him to paradise; if he has three daughters, God will exempt him from the obligations of charity and Jihad'. 'If a person has three daughters whom he provides for and brings up, God will surely reward him with paradise'. 'If a daughter is born to a person and he brings her up, gives her a good education and trains her in the arts of life, I shall myself stand between him and hell fire'. Not content with moral exhortations which aimed at ensuring the equal rights of young girls, the prophet himself set an example for Muslims to follow. He treated his four daughters with parental love and compassion. He played with them, looked after them and carried them when they were young.

When they were grown up and got married, he continued to care for their well-being. Fatima, the youngest, and the only one who survived her father, was very close to him, and often he used to visit her, invite her with her family to a meal with him, and would take her warmly between his arms and offer her his seat.

Women as mothers enjoy great respect and affection. The Quran advises Muslims to show love, gratitude and consideration for parents, particularly mothers. It says 'And We enjoined man (to show kindness) to his parents, for weakness after weakness his mother bears him and he is not weaned before he is two years of age. We said: Give thanks to Me and to your parents. To Me shall all things return'. 'Your Lord has enjoined you to worship none but Him, and to show kindness to your parents. If either or both of them attain old age with you, show them no sign of impatience, nor rebuke them; but speak to them kind words. Treat them with humility and tenderness and say: Lord be merciful to them. They nursed me when I was an infant'. The prophet taught his followers how to look after their mothers and obey them. Disobeying parents, especially mothers, is one of the greatest of all sins. The Prophet is reported to have said the following *Hadiths* regarding mothers: 'Do not leave your mother unless she gives you permission or death takes her, because that is the greatest (deed) for your reward'.

A Muslim is required to have a close relationship with relatives, especially the immediate members of the family such as sisters, cousins, aunts, and so on. The Prophet instructed his followers to visit them, be kind to them and to help them if they needed help. He said 'He is not of me who severs or breaks the ties of kinship'.

Within this context, the sister occupies a special position. She is to be treated with care, respect and due consideration.

The Prophet did not have a sister but he did have female cousins and relatives whom he used to welcome properly and treat tenderly and kindly. Once he stated, 'whoever is... taking charge of two sisters, and treats them well and patiently, he and I shall be in paradise'.

Good treatment of wives is strongly emphasised both in the Quran and the Sunnah. The Quran describes the relationship between the husband and wife as follows: 'they (your wives) are an apparel to you and you are an apparel to them'. The Prophet laid great stress upon good treatment of a wife. He said 'The best of you are they who behave best to their wives'. 'A Muslim must not hate his wife, and if he be displeased with one bad quality in her, let him be pleased with one that is good'.

Apart from these recommendations, the Prophet set a good example as the model husband who treated his wives with loving compassion and due consideration. He dealt with them on an equal footing, devoted a night to each in turn, helped them with the housework, mended his own clothes, shared with them the ups and downs of life, listened to their opinions and gave them the chance to develop their own individuality, independence and talents. For example, Sauda developed her skill in fine leather work and earned a good income therefrom; Zaynab was very much active in charitable works to the extent that she was renowned as the mother of the poor'; Umm Salama, bright and clever, acted as a political adviser to the Prophet, while Aisha, the youngest and wittiest, was regarded as a judge, and was very often consulted on religious affairs in the absence of her husband. The Prophet's example was followed by the early generations who were very much impressed by his attitude toward his wives.

In a nutshell, then, Islam came to grant woman her rightful place in the society of man, raising her above the position of goods and chattels and a respectful entity and a personality unto herself. She was considered an independent social and economic unit functioning in her own individual right, if she so desired. For the first time she was given the right to education, the right to hold property in her own name, the right of inheritance, and above all, the fight to vote and pray'. Under this bill of rights women, under the leadership of Muhammad, enjoyed full freedom to develop their individuality and personality and to take part in shaping their own society.

Moreover, women took advantage of the liberty offered to them: they participated effectively in public life; took part in prayers at the mosque together with the men; acted as *imams* for women (and sometimes for both sexes in their household); joined their colleagues in military expeditions; granted protection in war and asylum to fugitives; devoted themselves to the study of theology, the Quran and the traditions; travelled widely, and moved freely and mixed with men with self-respect and dignity. However, this situation did not last long; with the death of Muhammad and the transformation of the early Islamic community into an empire, women's rights steadily underwent erosion.

Slowly but surely the rights granted them and enjoyed during the time of Muhammad were taken away. They were discouraged from participating in public affairs; prevented from visiting the mosques; denied any opportunity to express their opinions; barred from developing their intellectual abilities; restricted in their movements and confined to their four walls at home.

Gradually the bright picture of the free, courageous, independent, self-respecting and respected Muslim woman was replaced with that of secluded, lazy, ignorant and passive woman who had no role or impact on her own affairs let alone on society as a whole. The situation became worse with the political disintegration and the subsequent social demoralisation and the penetration of foreign ideas and customs. This depressed situation has persisted more or less until the present day in various shapes and forms throughout the Muslim world. It is, therefore, hardly untrue to state that women in much of the Muslim world have long been subjected to both cultural and political oppression.

While men have equally suffered from the latter, women generally have had to pay a double price: culturally as well as politically. It has long been argued that Islam liberated Muslim women by granting them full rights as citizens. It is certainly true that Islamic precepts offer women a full and positive role in society as well as personal rights, which should, in theory, leave little to be desired. The question arises, however, as to whether the reality of Muslim women's lives reflects the theory. To what extent have Muslim women been able to enjoy the fights the *Sharia* (Islamic Law) grants them without being subjected to strong countervailing social pressure? In the contemporary Muslim world, everything has been taken out of its context. Women's rights are no exception.

Women have in many cases been deprived even of the basic human rights advocated by Islam itself. Forced marriages, arbitrary divorces, female mutilations and other abuses are sadly common in the Muslim world, as are restrictions on women's education and on their role in the labour force. In order to better their position as dignified human beings we need to address these and other issues in the light of the contemporary situation.

8
The Inheritance

The chapter of the Qur'an called 'The Woman' (*al-Nisa*) details in a just manner the share of inheritance that is due to each individual, male and female. According to this chapter, women are not only no longer allowed to be inherited like chattels but, as individuals, they have a legal fight to inheritance. 'Men shall have a share in what their parents and kinsmen leave; and women shall have a share in what their parents and kinsmen leave; whether it be little or much, it is legally theirs'.

This verse was revealed when an Ansari lady came to the Prophet and complained that after her husband's death she and her daughter were prevented from inheriting any of his property. Her husband's brother justified the action by stating that, 'Women do not mount horses, do not endanger themselves and go into battle', therefore they could not be allowed to inherit.

Before Islam, women were not only deprived of their fight to inheritance, but also had no impact over their own destiny, which was a matter between the men of the husband's clan or her own relatives. During the *Jahiliyya*, when a man lost his father, brother, or son, and that person left a widow, the heir, taking advantage of the fact that her dowry was paid by the dead man, rushed to the widow, covered her with his cloak, thus claiming (unjustly) to himself the sole fight to marry her. When he married her, he denied her of her right to the part of the inheritance constituted by the dowry. But if he decided, for one reason or another, not to have her as a wife, he could then ask another person to marry her. In return he would take (for himself) her dowry. However, if the widow (at the time of her husband's death) managed to get to her own clan before the arrival of the heir, he would lose his rights over her in favour of the males of her own clan. New laws regarding women challenged the social structure of a society that had given males the upper hand over females in matters related to inheritance. Therefore, it was inevitable that it would create an uproar among sections of the male population who felt threatened by them and questioned the validity of granting women a share in the inheritance. So, they decided to ignore these laws and continued to apply the customs of the *Jahiliyya*, hoping that as time went by the Prophet would change them. But the matter was brought to the surface by women them selves who continued to suffer from the *Jahiliyya* mentality.

For pre-Islamic Arabian society, it was outrageous to allow fatherless children who could not fight or earn a living to have shares in the inheritance. Therefore, they were denied any rights to inheritance. Moreover, they were mistreated and not looked after well, especially young girls who were also the object of sexual abuse. For example the guardian very often decided to marry the prettiest ones thus securing two things for himself. (1) controlling their share of inheritance; (2) setting away from or escaping: paying a dowry for them. If a fatherless girl happened to be ugly or not pretty enough to persuade him to marry her he would use her ugliness, to oppose any marriage for her. In doing so, he did not have to pay her share of inheritance. If a fatherless girl was ugly, her guardian did not give her her share. He forced her not to marry and waited for her to pass away so that he would assume control over her inheritance. Islam, would not tolerate such inhumane practices, with its egalitarian message which aimed at redressing the injustice of society. It began by affirming the legal right of fatherless children to have a share in their own inheritance and ended by cautioning against depriving them of their due.

Rights to Muslim Women by Quran

Although Islam granted woman the right to inheritance, her share is by no means fair and equal to that given to man. The critics refer to the verse that allows the brother to take twice as much as the share of their sisters. Therefore, they view this as detrimental to the dignity of women. By giving women half the share of men, they say, there is a clear implication that women are inferior to men. This argument has been used by both Muslims and non-Muslims. But it is based on a fallacy. If it happens for one reason or another that one sex receives a greater or lesser share than the other, this does not mean that the recipient of the lesser share is regarded as inferior. The whole issue of inheritance in Islam depends entirely on the social and economic context, and the role or function of a particular sex within it. If this crucial contextual factor is borne in mind, a proper understanding of the verses related to inheritance in the Qur'an would ensue.

The Qur'an has ensured that women could get their shares of inheritance not only as daughters, but also as mothers and wives. Women have been given half the share of male heirs has to be looked at within its social and economic framework. In Islam the wife is to be cared for by her husband, even if she is wealthy enough to maintain herself. By law she is entitled to claim maintenance from her husband. At the same time she is not obliged to spend any of her wealth on the household.

In addition a Muslim woman receives at the time of her marriage a considerable sum of money. This money, which the husband is obliged to pay, constitutes her dowry, or Mahr, which belongs to her alone. She is free to use, spend or invest it in any way she likes. Therefore, as a wife she adds to whatever she receives through inheritance in her capacity as daughter and that, too, without any legal commitment to support either herself or her children.

The position of women is secure as far as inheritance is concerned. Although women have been given half the share of men, their financial situation in the long term is guaranteed. This is due to the fact that the marriage contract gives her the right to ask for *Mahr* as well as claim maintenance, both of which entail no legal commitment to anybody including herself.

But it may be objected, what about women who cannot marry for one reason or another? What about the ones who cannot work and earn a living, especially in the rural areas where women have been denied the chance to gain a decent education? How would they live and maintain themselves?

The Quranic injunctions make it clear that male relatives, especially brothers, have the obligation to care for women and meet their financial needs. At the moment, in most Muslim countries this issue has been left to the individual conscience, which has led to many cases of abuse and desertion. Therefore, in order to secure and protect these women, governments need to legislate and make it legally binding on those male relatives to pay for the upkeep of their needy women.

The Qur'an makes it clear that a person is entitled to make a will. Indeed, it is highly recommended by the Prophet that a person should prepare a will as early as possible and not wait until it is too late. Contrary to the misconception held by large sections of the Muslim public that a person has no right to make a will, both the Qur'an and the Sunnah encourage people to do so. There are even some misguided jurists who argue, contrary to clear principles in the Qur'an, that Islam does not recommend the making of wills. This negative attitude advocated by a small band of jurists has confused ordinary Muslim people and has led many to abandon the idea of making wills.

The Qur'an, on the other hand, has specifically asked for the distant relatives, the needy people and the orphans to be treated kindly and to be helped if they are present at the time of the division of inheritance:

> If relatives, orphans, or needy men are present at the division of an inheritance, give them, too, a share of it, and speak to them in kind words.

So, if the Qur'an is so kind even to distant relatives and needy people by virtue of the fact that it encourage people to give them some share of the inheritance, we see no problem, in keeping with this spirit of Divine Justice, that a bequest be made in favour of a needy person, particularly if this person is a close member of the family. The point here is emphasised that if parents think that their daughter is unable to get married for whatever reason and she is in a disadvantaged position, they can write a will in her favour in order to secure her future. This accords with the spirit of the Qur'an and the Sunnah.

The position of Muslim women as far as inheritance is concerned is secure and guaranteed by the Islamic Law. But in practice this is not the case. Constantly, the Divine instructions concerning women's rights to inheritance are violated and overlooked by Muslim societies. Social, political, economic and cultural factors play a major role in determining who does and who does not take a share. In such situations the weak have always been kept at bay when it comes to their fight to inheritance. This takes place in both the cities as well as the rural areas.

Very often, strong social pressure is applied on women to renounce their shares for the benefit of the immediate male members of the family. This is particularly the case when women are well off or married to wealthy men. Their due is automatically written off and transferred to their male relatives. Whether they like it or not they are all too often forced to accept the loss of their shares; if they refuse, they are accused of being selfish, greedy, inconsiderate and irresponsible.

Often this has led to tension, friction and conflict of interests among the members of the family, shattering the whole concept of caring and sharing which lies at the heart of the Islamic faith. Here are a few examples which illustrate the evident disregard for the Divine decrees regarding women's fight to inheritance.

The Islamic concept of broad and equitable shares which take into consideration the interests of all persons concerned has been transferred into a prerogative for males, outrageously disregarding the Divine Will. There is no doubt about the fact that in most parts of the Muslim world the Islamic Law concerning women's rights to inheritance is not in operation; instead it is social and cultural rules which dominate. It is crucial that something has to be done to rectify this situation, and women themselves have an essential role to play in the process of any such change.

9
Modesty and Veiling

Seclusion by veiling is not synonymous with social and political segregation, it rather resolves the problem of interaction across gender boundaries. Veiling denotes the Afghani man's and woman's cultural pride, his or her self image, and allows for free social mobility across social spheres. Anderson, Wikan and Altorki all suggest that the veil may define a cultural definition of sexual seclusion, without necessarily implying segregation and oppression of Muslim women in everyday reality. The discourse to be assessed here is composed of a variety of situations, with social, religious and political as well as sexual connotations.

We use the term discourse not in a strictly linguistic sense, but rather in the broader meaning of Foucault's terminology. We seek to understand the metaphors and cultural idioms associated with religious modesty and veiling, by studying them within the more extensive political, social and religious context. A decade after the Iranian revolution, the discourse of veiling is not a question of to veil or not to veil; nor is it a question of being secular or religious, as was the case during the 1978 revolution and the following years. Rather, it is a question of how and where to veil and which veil to adopt

The social and economic modernity in several Middle Eastern countries in the 1970s became synonymous with the unveiling of women. In the context of the social and economic modernity under the Pahlavi Iranian state, unveiling has often been associated with revolutionary acts, bravery, liberation, emancipation, and empowerment in the women's political and social movement. Two historical acts may illustrate such an image. (1) Upon the death of the famous mystic Mansur Hallaj in AD 922 his sister appeared in public unveiled to challenge men. (2) The story that a famous woman of the Bahai religion, Qurratu'l Ayn, in 1949 removed her veil to signal the equality of women and men. In Iran, the veil was negatively identified in the course of the economic modernity and social reforms that started with the Pahlavi regime and extended under the former Shah's regime in the early 1970s. This led to a compulsory unveiling law in 1936 and the importing of French-style clothes and hats for both men and women. The 1936 law meant a prohibition of wearing the veil at public places such as schools, the workplace, and outside on the street.

Kashfeh-hejab was one of the important socio-political reforms of the Reza-Shah (the father of the former king), who attacked whatever he considered to be the vestiges of backwardness, i.e. the *chador. Chadori* women of that period told they had to hide in corners when they were in the street, or their *chador* would be forcefully removed by the police. The Iranian tradition of wearing a *chador* (full-length veil) is customarily understood by the average people to symbolise cultural authenticity.

Recent historical studies of the veiling of Middle Eastern women support the idea that Islam did not invent the full-length veil and instead identify it with the urban lifestyle phenomenon of pre-Islamic Iran. However, the emergence of veiling as a 'true' tradition and a central aspect of the Muslim identity during the revolutionary movement, was associated with Islamic tradition. During the revolution, the wearing of a full-length veil by women became a symbolic weapon against the Shah's regime and his Western alliances. The full-length veil in post-revolutionary time-represents the victory of the Islamic state and the repression of other secular political ideologies.

The *chador* (full-length veil) covers the wearer from the top of her head to her wrists and ankles. During the Iranian revolution it has been correctly explained by many writers as a response to pre-revolutionary secular life experiences. As a revival of their identity many educated women, who previously only occasionally wore the full-length veil when visiting shrines, mosques or attending a funeral, began to wear a full-length veil in order to express solidarity with religious and lower-class women.

A full-length veil signals a cumulative identity of religious and social integrity and the authenticity of women's political protest. The practice of veiling in the ideology of the Islamic state and its local conservative agencies pertains to head and full-body cover, gender interaction and a range of bodily boundaries. The political ideology of the Islamic state views men as the weaker partner and in need of protection to control their sexual desire.

In other words, women tempt men, and thus endanger the social order and national political stability. The sexual danger of the woman in its invisible and visible forms is believed to be so powerful and impulsive that it can lead to the moral corruption of men and society. Hence, Muslim society such as Iran can remain socially ordered, harmonious, and healthy only if the women control themselves and avoid acts of exhibitionism. Many public notices put on the walls of shops, state offices and buildings warn women who do not comply with the ideal that they will not be served as proper customers. To receive proper service, women have to cover their heads completely, exhibiting no part of their forehead and wearing no make-up. Women's covering garment metaphorically produces political meaning, and failure to comply was often identified as an act of political protest and therefore a reason for punishment.

In post-revolutionary Iran, the full-length veil is not the only Islamic dress to receive public recognition. The common legitimate Islamic dress worn by the average urban woman consists of a long-sleeved, high-necked dress that stretches below the knees, a large head-scarf, trousers (not jeans) and thick dark-coloured stockings. Public control of women is dominated by *hezbullahi* men and women. There are new jobs for controllers in airports, offices, academic institutions and public places, and recruitment is on the basis of positive attitudes to the new social rules and Islamic knowledge. They function effectively and restrictively.

Wimple Head-scarf

The wimple head-scarf was traditionally worn as a praying cloth by elderly religious women in private prayers, and represented a private marginalised code of piety. Since the revolution it has been transformed from being a private sign of piety into an ideal Islamic dress that must be worn by women in nurseries, schools, universities, workplaces and government buildings. It is recognised by the Islamic experts and the educational authorities as the ideal form of veiling and an 'appropriate' public Islamic symbol.

The wimple head-scarf should cover most of the hair on a woman's head, as well as the forehead, shoulders, neck and breast. Only an opening the size of the face should remain. At school trousers like American Lee jeans were prohibited, as being symbolic of the political and cultural influences of American Imperialism. At the age of 9 girls are expected to start complying with a series of religious norms, and to make the transition from childhood to adult.

Transforming the former secular educational system by means of religious knowledge, political consciousness and ideological forces has been one of the prime concerns of the Islamic Republic since the political turmoil in 1979. Today schoolgirls, university students and state employees are expected to practise full veiling and participate in the regular and obligatory prayers and fasts. Workplaces enforce the new restrictive head and body cover for women employees under the supervision of the Islamic association. In schools and at the workplace this control has sometimes developed into violation in the name of religious duty in directing others to what is lawful and to what is not lawful. In fulfilling this duty one is considered to be constructing the personal identity of a dutiful Muslim.

The familiar religious and cultural terms *amre-be-m'aruf* and *nahi-az-monker* have served as a platform for the process of censorship and social control in the post-revolutionary period. The new Islamic control at workplaces, universities and schools is part of the state administrative policy based on the new Islamic teachings and practices, and the enforcement system. The mode of regulation is through the religio-political reforms in workplaces and the recruitment criteria set up for government positions. Religious training and the acquisition of 'correct' prayer and correct Islamic appearance at school and at the workplace have become important elements in the Islamic education of girls and boys.

Educational institutions were threatened with prosecution and closure if they did not enforce full veiling on their female students and employees, and female teachers, school administrators and female students were threatened by the Minister of Education with dismissal if they did not oblige. The Islamic state mandate on veiling at schools and workplaces has created stress and feelings of distrust. For some, not to have a proper veiling involved dramatic consequences, such as physical attacks or a few hours in detention. This strict control of the full veil in particular led to violence against women during the period of war between Iran and Iraq. At that time women were defined as the vehicle of social disorder and political instability.

The less colourful and decorative appearance of women in public represented a strong image of solidarity, an expression of sorrow to families with casualties, and community solidarity. Public control of people's behaviour in the name of Islamic authority was not an uncommon practice in day-to-day interaction, particularly in 1989. The women's Islamic police could, for example, order a woman to fully cover her head and pull the scarf down to her forehead, and a religious oriented man passing by might remind you of your religious duty of being fully covered.

Conservative Muslim men and women have redefined the veil as 'true' Islamic norms that should be observed both in public and in private family gatherings. The family of *hezbullahi's* may adopt a stricter sexual segregation than the average urban family.

According to the conservative Islamic category a single hair may be as sinful as exposing all the hair. Strict religious women wear a full-length veil only exposing their eyes. Every single sexual interaction is considered important in itself for the record of one's behaviour on the day of judgment. The preacher Mostafi further discouraged women from shaking hands and instead encouraged them to call each other a religious 'sister' or 'brother'.

The preacher Zaki insisted that the youth were full of passion since economic conditions prevented them from getting married and having legitimate sexual relations. Hence, modest behaviour is considered desirable even in relations with male relatives, despite the fact that they are traditionally classified as *mahram* (legitimate kin). As such the idea of being a 'true' Muslim woman, as instructed by conservative religious authorities, went beyond the common practice. The religious conservative men believe that the religious status of their women increases if they wear the traditional full-length veil.

There are different degrees of veiling, not only among women, but also among different Islamic categories. Both of the above cases reflect typical sources and patterns of family conflicts and the control of women for male Islamic ideological purposes. However, for some conservative Islamic authorities the public definition of what is a proper Islamic covering is more than simply wearing a full-length veil. Wearing trousers is also required.

In the post-revolutionary period, the Islamic political authorities encouraged the masses to watch over their family members, neighbours and relatives, in order to discourage them from committing non-Islamic acts. There are stories of the effects this had on the emotional relations and authoritative roles between family members. One party in a conflict could always claim the other was committing acts socially and politically endangering the stability of Islamic state. According to the view of the religious authorities, what constituted immodest behaviour of women refers not only to the public display of the female body, but uncontrolled social interactions. Religious modesty and veiling in its broader social context remain a pertinent ideology of Muslim women's femininity.

In 1989 the controversy surrounding the practice of women modesty and veiling was of concern for at least five categories of organisations. On the institutional level the following organisations were involved: the Islamic police, who seek to eliminate and punish 'incorrect' Islamic acts; the agencies of the moderate Rafsanjani government, who seek to moderate public rules by recognising different forms of covering garments; an the Islamic elite women's organisation, which is powerful in educational and work establishments, controlling behaviour in accordance with the new images of male and female roles as prescribed in the school text books.

The fourth group is represented in general by the female Islamic experts in the local area. The final category is the *hezbullahi* women, who like the Islamic elite utilise the wimple head-scarf, but in addition insist on the Iranian tradition of a full-length veil. The *hezbullahi* women's demonstration against poorly-veiled women was used by the Islamic police authority to tighten up the veiling rules. The pro-veiling slogans continued to be supportive of the revolutionary police in 1989. The street slogans in the post Iran-Iraq war period addressed whether *bi-hejab* (non-veiled) and *bad-hejab* (poorly-veiled) women should feel ashamed in the presence of mothers of martyrs.

By wearing dark colours and not wearing jewellery, particularly gold bracelets and necklaces that signify a higher socio-economic status, women express sympathy and solidarity towards the mothers of martyrs, both in the neighbourhood and the community at large. On one side of this controversy are the relatives of the martyrs who identify themselves as first-class Muslim citizens of the postwar Iran period, on the grounds of having sacrificed family members on behalf of the Islamic state and community.

On the other side of the controversy are the average urban middle- and higher-class women with very few martyrs in their families. They challenge the enforced Islamic dress by changing it to fashionable Islamic suits. In contrast, during the post-war period, the emphasis on the full-length veil has been maintained and manipulated locally by the *hezbullahis,* their argument being that it is the only 'true' form of veiling. This kind of development strengthens the existing opinion between those directly or indirectly related to martyrs and those who are not. This duality has caused considerable confusion.

The term *bi-hejabi,* with its negative implications, has been applied by the local preacher to women wearing the *manto,* although this is officially recognised by the state and is a dominant veil among upper- and middle-class urban women. Housewives busy with extra-domestic tasks such as purchasing household goods and attending to family matters associated with public life also find the Islamic suit more convenient than the full length veil. They are, for example, able to hold shopping bags in one hand and children in the other, something which is difficult when wearing the full-length veil.

Among the middle-class women the tradition of veiling is impractical in their modem social and economic lifestyle, which includes a wide range of extra household activities. The fact that middle-class women distance themselves from the traditional religious garment of the full-length veil has given rise to numerous demonstrations in Tehran, where conservative forces demand a greater control over the implementation of the Islamic suit and scarf. For example, when president Rafsanjani recognized the loose fitting suit, the *hezbullahi* and the family of martyrs reacted immediately with a demonstration, condemning any act of bad veiling.

The participants in the July 1989 demonstrations opposed the wearing of colourful scarves and stylish Islamic suits, arguing that it dishonoured martyrs and undermined the attempts to sustain a revolutionary ideology against Western influences and the search for an Islamic authenticity. Hence, to the mothers of martyrs, the *manto* and the new style of thin stockings represent a pre-revolutionary women's clothing that indicates a lack of solidarity with their suffering. An example of a more liberal attitude of the post-war period in June 1989 was the resumption of the traditional marriage ceremony, characterised by public music and the custom of driving the bride and groom around the town while blowing the car horn. This custom had, like many other communal celebrations, been strictly forbidden during the war between Iran and Iraq, when the emphasis was on communal mourning and national expressions of grief and solidarity to families of martyrs.

Another sign of the return to normal life was the increased presence of tribal women in towns, the latter traditionally being less veiled than their urban counterparts. They come to town to sell their handiwork and crafts, including local musical instruments, at the market in Shiraz. Their colourful shirts strongly contrast with the dark colours and veils worn by the *hezbullahi* women.

The religious conservatives' aim is to prohibit acts which they consider sexually provocative and socially destructive. Mary Douglas made a link between the rational behaviour of primitives and taboo-thinking. In her view taboo turns out not to be incomprehensible, but is an intelligible concern to protect society from behaviour that threatens its order. When conservative Islamists demand that both Muslim men and women should uphold community values through a series of restricted modesty and bodily boundaries, the aim is not only to moralise, but also to politicise Iranian society.

The official veiling on bodily boundaries includes both men and women, women often are most blamed for jeopardising revolutionary society. To look into the eyes, or touch the hand of a member of the opposite sex, whatever the relationship may be, is thought to lead to sexual temptation, and is therefore—outside of marriage considered a provocative act. The idea of having 'pure' eyes, a modest gaze and a plain voice, even in encounters between an adult brother and sister, is identical with *hezbullahi's* moralisation plan for Iranian society.

Preacher Mostafi, who is considered a *hezbullahi* and supporter of the Islamic regime, repeatedly warned her listeners at the fast month meetings against seductive body movement. She argued that not only would such behaviour devalue their prayers, but severe punishment would wait them on the day of judgment: 'One's body might be hanged by the breast, or by the single hair that has been displayed vulgarly in this world, and the offending part of the body might be burned.' She described the uncovered head and open-necked shirt as immodest and contradictory to 'true' Muslim morality.

The female breast and buttocks, the neck, foot and particularly the ankle, as well as the heel and arms are among the taboo parts of the body. They are often referred to with feelings of passion, and therefore are deemed seductive and detrimental to the maintenance of morality and political stability High-heel shoes are blamed as a metaphor for seductive sexual behaviour. Such a negative view of women's clothing developed publicly and was adopted by the university Islamic 'sisters', who issued a long list of clothing rules for female students and private and state employees. Such an ideology is adopted by various categories such as schoolgirls, university students, religiously oriented women, ritual experts, students of religious schools, certified religious leaders, etc. They commonly moralise and politicise women's bodily movements in religious vocabulary and request official control.

Male Modesty

Recognising male modesty as an important aspect of Muslim men's identity, it seems that the consequences of lack of modesty are more serious for women than for men. The Islamic state policy of sexual control of all its citizens does place some sanctions on male behaviour. Offensive remarks made by youths to women on the street have been discouraged by the Islamic police as being an insult to an Islamic sister. A man wearing a short-sleeved shirt with an open collar in public is also considered sinful.

In the post-revolutionary period there were several cases where youths were arrested if dressed in a Western teenage style, i.e. tight trousers and colourful patterned shirts. The fear of political repercussions, and of being arrested, has led many parents to increase their sanctions on the social activities of their children, and especially their daughters. The Islamic Republic was determined to moralise public social appearances by replacing whatever they believed to be an influence of Western culture. Hence, a T-shirt displaying a picture of a film star signified a careless identity of stereotyped manners, contrasting with the devoted Islamic youths, who were sent to fight against the Iraqi troops on the front line during 1981-8.

According to the conservative ideology men are considered the weaker part when it comes to controlling their sexual passion. Thus when enforcing social rules, some of the forbidden acts of men may be easily forgiven, as these are believed to be caused by the sexual powers of women.

Despite a conservative ideological view on veiling, the veiling practice among women is far from uniform. Women have become more creative and fashion-conscious, constantly attempting to subvert the blandness of the conventional veil. They have adopted various Islamic covering garments that play with colours, fabrics and design. Although a person's Muslim identity is defined according to the correct performance of daily prayers, veiling and modesty, women in everyday practice largely adopt a complex cultural and religious repertoire of behaviour, where a pure state of intention takes a priority over rigid appearance. To the majority, having faith is not necessarily a matter of adhering to the static norms, but a pure state of intention.

Using different forms of veil to fit different social situations is an important aspect of one's identity among middle-class women. Shazdeh's strategic veiling was once observed by the preacher Mumeni. Shazdeh replaced her full-length veil with a scarf while sitting in her car on her way back from a religious meeting. Seeing this, Mumeni warned her against this forbidden act, arguing that her fast would be broken due to her face and the backs of her hands being visible.

Shazdeh replied that the full-length veil disturbed her when driving and that it was too warm. These reasons were not accepted by Mumeni, who continued to warn her of the flames of hell and the day of judgment. This disappointed Shazdeh, and she told that she would no longer attend any of Mumeni's meetings. She did, however, continue to attend religious seminaries led by recent Islamic graduate preachers on the grounds that they were more liberal.

Despite being a devoted Muslim, the norms demanded by the preacher Mumeni were not compatible with everyday life. After all, she argued, on her two pilgrimages to Mecca, when the contact with God is especially strong, and when the seven times ritual walk between the holy places Safa and Marvah is performed by both men and women, it is not forbidden to display the oval face and the backs of the hands.

In the opinion of Shazdeh the norms advocated by Mumeni on the 'true' veil make religion static and difficult to practise on a daily basis, even for women like herself who strongly believe in women's modesty, the ritual of vow-making and the obligatory prayers, as well as in the importance of religious meetings. The decision of what veil to choose for a specific occasion is situational and reflects the realisation of a broader social and political relation. Some middle-class women use the full-length veil only at religious meetings as a shared code, and remove it once they are in the street and out of sight of other religious friends.

Ideally, a woman wearing a black full-length veil of heavy-quality cloth is identified by other religious friends as a woman deserving strong respect. The use of a thick-quality full-length veil during religious gatherings reflects religious prestige and a strong moral identity. The religiously oriented middle class, in contrast to the religiously conservative women, may at smaller gatherings of friends from a Quranic course or at wedding parties, change from a thick-quality full-length veil to one thinner and fighter in colour. Such a change can often be explained as a matter of personal comfort, informality and pressure from other relatives.

The type of full-length veil worn may signify the degree of one's religious affiliation, personal strength and the religious occasion. For example, a full-length veil may be used at annual religious meetings by the more well-educated, modem working women, and a lighter, flowery one for happy occasions, such as the votive meal services where religious meetings develop into a feast. While women may dress elegantly at family visits and parties, the opposite may be the case at religious meetings where it is important to signify a pious identity. Thus a woman's good character is not only defined in terms of her relations with her male partner encountered in the public sphere, but also in terms of the moral identity sought in relations with other women.

The privacy of religious meetings does not mean that participants are less reserved in their veiling, and women are seldom poorly-veiled in the presence of each other at religious meetings, the possible exception being religious meal feasts such as *eftari* (the meal ending a fast), or when attending a less popular Quranic course with very close co-seminary friends.

Some women may use the dress as a religious device to signal special events by changing the colour and style of veil. For example, to mark celebrations such as the birth of the Prophet, or the death of the 'Umar," women may wear dresses that are more colourful and elegant under their full-length veil. Having a head-scarf under their full-length veil, women are more willing to lower their veil to their shoulders at the religious meetings since the wimple was officially defined as a proper and fully acceptable veil as it hung down to the shoulders, covering neck and chest.

Women who remove their head cover and/or display a golden necklace or bracelet may be criticised by others as exhibitionists. Such a display of a new style of dress or jewellery is often believed by female preachers to lead to jealousy and competition. The preacher Mostafi usually raised the theme of the veil in her speeches, whether in public religious halls or at private homes. Through story-telling she sought to illustrate the Islamic ideals and frameworks of meaning.

Mostafi repeatedly suggested that the importance of modesty today was connected to judgment in the after-life, and she asked if the women were taking seriously the responsibility of their own behaviour and that of others. She warned the women present of the possibility of committing a sinful act of incorrect prayers without being aware of it, despite being a religiously learned person. Furthermore, she listed the most sinful acts often committed by women, two of which were appearing poorly veiled and gossiping. Similar moral lessons were followed up by the preacher Zaki in another Ramazan meeting a few days later. She pointed out that some participants had been seen wearing the full-length veil at religious meetings, while dressing elegantly with colourful scarves on other occasions. Then she told the participants that to obtain the world of *akhirat* they must act with piety in spite of all the counter-forces.

The preacher Mumeni, like others in her rank, remained conventional when implementing the rules of Islamic modesty and veiling to her audience. A woman who has made the obligatory pilgrimage to Mecca is expected to display greater modesty and adopt a more restricted veil than before going to pilgrimage. *Hajji* women from middle-class families who have made the obligatory pilgrimage to Mecca do not always wear the full-length veil. In their eyes those who observe a restricted Islamic garment are old fashioned.

A full-length veil is seldom removed in the presence of a female preacher unless the women are wearing head-scarves and are fully covered underneath- This indicates the women's expectations towards each other, their identity of piety. A 'pious' veiling is valued as a means of ensuring merit in the life hereafter, and it symbolises the individual's strong belief and personality As a religiously oriented woman put it to me, 'strict dress over worldly attraction'. Thus she wears both head-scarf and a full-length veil, a double-Islamic dress for religious conservatism.

Changing one's traditional full-length veil to an Islamic suit has become a common practical solution among the old and the lower middle-class women. This has distorted the rigid ideology of the conservative *hezbullahi* Muslims, who argue that a full-length veil is important to one's cultural and religious authenticity. Being aware of the distorted practice and untraditional changes among women, the preacher Mostafi repeatedly warned her audience not to follow suit. Her remarks were directed at the strategic behaviour of the participants who changed their veil according to place and occasion. Such inconsistency in veiling is considered worldly *(donyavi)* and is associated with a kind of behaviour classified as 'dolly' *(arosaki);* i.e. behaviour considered artificial and Westernised, and that should be avoided even in the private sphere of family and friends.

According to the preacher Mostafi women wearing a full-length veil, despite the heat and discomfort, display the firmness of their faith and their superiority in worldly matters. Although wearing a full veil might not seem attractive in the present, it will give rewards in the afterlife. Nezhat was among the elderly women who used to wear the new Islamic suit *(manto)* outside on the street, while carrying a full-length veil in her bag in case she wanted to enter a religious place. She was an active religious participant and played a conservative role vis-a-vis other religious friends, who identified her as a woman of strong faith. She was seen without a full-length veil several times by her Quranic colleagues and this left her with a feeling of embarrassment. In an attempt to avoid standardisation some girls change the wimple head-scarves of the school uniform, sewing an additional chin or forehead piece to make it resemble a hat. This is considered to be more attractive and makes the mandatory veil more tolerable.

Some prefer a black wimple head-scarf on the grounds that it matches their black eyes, which they accentuate slightly with make-up. A fringe of curled or dyed hair displayed on the forehead was adopted along with the Islamic suit by middle-class urban women, who insisted on looking fashionable in their adopted Islamic suits. This signified opposition and seemed to be a form of resistance and political protest, since the women risked being stopped in the street and warned by Islamic police, and even fired from their jobs or arrested. These examples illustrate that the veil is not uniform and in practice it remains subject to identity management.

10
Role in Politics

The Muslim woman, like her counterpart—the man—has a broad political responsibility and an important role to play in public life, a role that was put at the service of the nascent Islamic community in Medina and for a while thereafter in the early period of Islam. For women, especially during the Prophet's time, were very active socially and politically. They were allowed and even encouraged to participate in the process of building up the Medinan society and they proved to be up to the task.

With the establishment of the Islamic state, the role of women in the political affairs of the new society gained momentum. They became part of the nation and effective members of the community, fully involved in public affairs. For instance, right from the beginning, women, like men, gave support and allegiance to the political system which was set up under the leadership of Muhammad. This was done through the so-called *bay'a. Bay'a* in Islam is an important political institution by which the nation or the Umma grants or ensures legitimacy for the political system. It includes a pledge by the nation to be loyal to the system and its leader as long as this leader upholds Islamic principles. Hence it is a covenant *(mithaq)* entered into by three parties: the leader (who is to be given the pledge or recognition; the nation or Umma (which is to give its allegiance and loyalty); and the Sharia (which is to be respected and upheld by both the leader as well as the nation). *Bay'a* moreover, is divided into *bay'a 'ayniya,* related to the political commitment *(iltizam)* to the system, and is compulsory on every Muslim man and woman, and *bay'a kayfiyya* related to particular duties and is obligatory on a particular group of men and women.

During Muhammad's leadership, allegiance and loyalty" were given to him by both men and women without any difference in content or responsibility. For he took a pledge from women, as from men, to support the state and obey him in enjoining good and forbidding evil *(bay'a 'ayniya).* Also, he received *bay'a kayfiyya* from some prominent women; among them was Nusaiba bint Kab, who gave her word to participate in Jihad and indeed she did take part in many battles alongside men. This illustrates her determination to fulfil the *bay'a* despite the fact that it was *bay~? kayfiyya;* for this kind of *bay'a is* mandatory on those men and women with special talents. As she thought herself to be one of them, she decided to go ahead and fulfil it. This indicates that women (like men) are under an obligation to realise their individual capabilities to the full, and thus to take up the specific duties related to these capabilities, whether these duties be individual or collective.

In addition to *bay'a,* women also participated in *Shura* (mutual consultation) which is one of the foundations of the Islamic political system. The practice of Shura is obligatory on both the leader as well as the Umma. The Quran says, 'Take counsel with them in the conduct of affairs; and when you are resolved, put your trust in Allah'. We also have the verse which praises those 'who obey their Lord, attend to their prayers and conduct their affairs by mutual consent'. In these verses, it is clear that the ruler is required to consult with the ruled, while the Umma is bound in its turn to offer counsel to the ruler. Shura or mutual consultation is a tool by which the nation can achieve the objectives of the *Sharia.* Therefore, it is the responsibility of the nation to uphold it, protect it and under no circumstances allow it to be abandoned.

The exercise of Shura can take place at different levels; hence the commitment to practise it by the individual members of the community varies according to the subject under consultation on the one hand, and on individual ability, on the other. For example, regarding legislative matters concerning *Sharia,* consultation is required with scholars or the *Ulama;* regarding technical issues, consultation is mandatory with experts in these fields; for general issues concerning the whole nation, some form of consultation with every member of the community would be ideal. This could take the shape of a referendum or general elections. Within this context, women can take part in consultation at various levels depending on the subject matter and on individual capability.

For instance, they can participate in consultation at the legislative level, experts' level, or at the general public level as ordinary members of the community. Women were consulted at all-levels during the period of the Prophet's rule and that of his companions. They used to seek their advice *(mashwara)* before most important decisions were made. For example, the Prophet used to receive delegations of women presenting their cases to him. Among them was Asma bint Yazid al-Ansari, who was an outspoken woman. She used to speak and argue on behalf of her fellow Muslim women, and the Prophet used to encourage her and expressed his admiration for her strong personality. His wives, especially Umm.

Salama and Aisha, never hesitated to ask searching questions and speak their minds when they felt it necessary; and the Prophet admired this questioning attitude. In fact.-on one occasion, he had to rely on the advice (mashwara) of one of his wives, Umm Salama, to solve a problem that bewildered the Muslims at a crucial time of the Islamic history. Umm Salama with her wisdom, prudence and good judgement helped the Prophet to solve the predicament, thus avoiding a situation that could have divided the community and weakened Muhammad's mission.

Aisha : Scholar and Regional Judge

Aisha, renowned for her wit and intelligence, was trained by the Prophet to question, discuss, argue and correct, to the extent that he recommended that the Muslims should learn from her knowledge and wisdom, especially in religious matters: take half of your religion from Aisha he said. By the time the Prophet passed away she had already become a great scholar and attained the position of a religious judge. She was accepted as a religious authority during the caliphate of Abu Bakr, Umar and Uthman. Very often they used to consult her and seek her advice if they were faced with difficult issues If they disagreed with her, the judgement she recommended turned out to be the correct one and then it was gladly accepted. Also, she gave a verdict in favour of one companion against another and at a certain stage she criticised and corrected them.

Hafsa, the daughter of the second caliph Umar, and one of the wives of the Prophet, was also active in public affairs. Her insight and guidance were very often sought by the companions. For example, on one occasion her father had to consult her before he could take a decision regarding the time limit for a husband to be away from his wife. (Also, based on his consultation with other women, he either amended or cancelled decisions, which he thought would run contrary to the interests of women.) Hafsa, moreover, expressed her concern about the political situation following the assassination of her father. While he was on his death bed she urged her brother Abdullah to discuss the issue with her father and ensure a smooth and peaceful transition of power. Also, she played a crucial role in persuading her brother, who was unwilling to get involved in the conflict that erupted between Ali and Muawiyah, to attend the arbitration which was set up to discuss the conflict and solve the problem peacefully and amicably.

Contrary to the traditional image of women being secluded and suppressed, women in early Islam participated in armed conflict either by organising food and water and taking care of the wounded or through playing a crucial part in the actual fighting when it was needed. Among the many examples of women who took active part in the battles was Safiyya, an aunt of the Prophet, who defended a fortress in Medina at the time of the Battle of the Trench. She noticed an intruder who had penetrated the defences of the fortress; she managed to manoeuvre and kill him before he was able to do any harm to the women and children.

Women also reached positions of high responsibility as was the case with al-Shafa' who was appointed by the second Caliph Umar as a market inspector in Medina. Their involvement in politics, furthermore, manifested itself by the fact that they were alert and actively opposed to any rulers who they thought were deviating from implementing Islamic principles and maintaining a just society. Two examples can be cited in this context. First, there is the case of the woman who publicly opposed Umar for passing a law restricting the dowries of women. He was forced, after admitting his mistake to repeal his decision. The second case was that of Aisha who genuinely believed that it was within her right to oppose the fourth caliph Ali and fight him for failing to find the murderers of Uthman. She led an army which included prominent companions such as Talha and Zubayr and fought a battle that was to be named the Battle of the Camel, because of the camel she was riding.

Women's influence in public affairs reached its climax when their action to protect or give immunity from punishment were sanctioned by the Prophet. He approved and accepted all the *Ijara* (protection) cases licensed by women, this being a clear indication by the Prophet and the early community, of the ability and capacity of women to judge wisely and act responsibly even in matters of great concern to the stability and security of the Islamic state. There are many examples in which women accorded protection or asylum (Ijara) and the Prophet gladly supported them. It has been reported that the Prophet never opposed or rejected any Ijara extended to enemies by women. It must be stressed that the high level of political (as well as social) activities performed by women in early Islam could not have been achieved without the realisation of three important and interrelated factors: first, the recognition of the political ability or competence of women.

Women were regarded as fully-fledged citizens capable of participating in all political activities (including bay'a, shura, granting asylums, taking part in Jihad and holding prominent positions) and indeed they were allowed to do so; second, this recognition or acknowledgement gained momentum when women became politically conscious or aware of their responsibilities in society. An awareness which Muhammad undertook to raise and promote among all women. This was accomplished through instructing women to gain knowledge and education and encouraging them to attend public gatherings (especially

Eid celebrations, which often took place in mosques) even when they were menstruating this being an illustration that although women were at certain times relieved from the obligations of their daily worshipping, this did not lead to an automatic reduction in their duty to participate in annual public meetings. On the contrary, they were urged to attend Eid festivals and the congregational Jumah (i.e. Friday) prayers, which were regarded as general political meetings during which important issues concerning the whole nation were discussed and debated. This provided the minimum level of political (as well as social) awareness needed for the majority of them, especially those whose domestic responsibilities prevented them from attending congregational prayers such as Friday prayers. To achieve maximum benefit for them, the Prophet, moreover, used to give them advice and guidance, especially when he learnt that they could not hear him properly during one of his Eid sermons.

The Prophet actively supported those women with special abilities and a higher level of awareness and whose circumstances allowed them to attend the regular congregational prayers. In fact, he instructed men (their husbands or relatives) not to prevent them from doing so even if they wanted to attend the dawn and night prayers," during which time the Quran used to be recited, explained and interpreted. Such sessions formed the basis for their religious education as well as their social and political awareness.

In order to satisfy their intellectual needs, the Prophet designated a special day for this group of women in which he used to teach them the principles of Islam and other related issues. This raised the self awareness of Muslim women and increased their understanding of their responsibility in society, leading, consequently, to greater public participation; and third, the broad political participation of women which was conditioned by their abilities and their degree of self-awareness was practised in a favourable social setting that gave it its stimulus and momentum. This supportive environment was the result of determined efforts, by the Prophet, to eradicate any practices and habits that would hinder or resist the progress towards wider political engagement of women in society.

Hence, he pushed ahead the process of social change and ensured that the community would accept and regard women's activity in the political sphere as an asset and a valuable contribution to a healthy society. This was fulfilled: firstly, through the Quranic injunctions and *Hadith* regulations, both of which encourage women to be energetic and creative, while at the same time, exhort men to help them fulfil their roles as active and equal members of the community; secondly, the example set by the Prophet in dealing with his family in particular and the companions (women) in general. He constantly encouraged them to take part in all aspects of life: social, political, economic and religious. This support found its echo when women, especially the Ansari women, demonstrated their interest and eagerness to participate in all activities, thus, setting a role model for other women to follow. In doing so, they pioneered the way for radical social change that allowed more space and greater mobility for women in society.

Despite the clear-cut Quranic and *Hadith* instructions encouraging women to play an effective role in public life (alongside their private one), the general tendency, among Muslims, has been one which opposes women's involvement in politics. Most scholars prefer an interpretation that enjoins women to stay at home and not to 'interfere' in public life. They argue that women are incapable of handling public affairs; therefore, it is better for them to perform the work they are good at that is, to be mothers an wives only. According to them, women never participated in the politics of the Muslims throughout their history. And, it is argued that despite the fact that Islam gave women rights equal to those of men, Islam deems it necessary that women should stay at home and concentrate on their domestic affairs, in the interest both of women themselves and of society as a whole.

The scholars then respond by insisting that those were mere individual cases which cannot be cited to legitimise the participation of women in political affairs. Anyone who thinks to the contrary is mistaken, they say, and does not comprehend history. As for Aisha who played a prominent role in politics, they argue that although she fought a famous battle, in the end she regretted her act (for she should not have left her home and taken part in that battle) and asked for forgiveness.

Consequently, it cannot be claimed that her act is a proof for the participation of Muslim women in politics, for it was an individual act which proved to be a complete failure. It is important to stress that those who oppose women's involvement in politics differ among themselves regarding the level or degree of women's exercise of power. For example, while some are prepared to tolerate the idea that women can have limited access to politics (such as the right to vote and nominate persons for certain public offices), others deny them any political rights. However, they all agree that women cannot be allowed to hold ministerial positions or become prime minister or president of a state. They base their prohibition on the following:

Quran: They maintain that Chapter 4, verse 34 of the Quran which reads thus: 'Men have authority over women because Allah has made the one superior to the other, and because they spend their wealth to maintain them', has virtually closed the door to women's advancement to higher positions. For them, this verse has sanctioned men's authority over women and made the domain of politics or power an exclusively male preserve. This is because men have strong leadership characteristics which entitle them to rule over women who tend to be weak and more emotional. According to them, the verse is clear in entrusting men (not women) with the *Qiwama* or guardianship. It follows that since men are the caretakers (*Qawwamun*) of women, it is not possible for them to hold positions of authority which would allow them to exercise power over men.

Moreover, they argue that even if they have to accept the view which states that this verse deals specifically with family affairs and cannot be generalised to include male-female relations in public life, the proof *(hujja)* still stands: women cannot rule over men. For if they are unqualified to manage their family undertakings, by the same token, they are unfit to handle public matters. However, we are of the strong opinion that this verse (4: 34) deals exclusively with family affairs and has nothing to do with the relationships between men and women in public life. This is because the verse is mentioned solely within the context of married life, in which one party—the husband—is charged with the responsibility of being the head and caretaker of the family—bearing in mind that relieving the wife from such a responsibility is by no means an indication of her inability to do the job properly; on the contrary, she can easily replace him if he is absent (for whatever reason) or unfit to fulfil his duty. Therefore, it is not right to generalise the ruling of this verse (which handles only marital matters) to encompass the relationships between men and women in society, so as to deny women the opportunity to hold public offices.

Hadith: Two Hadiths are of particular importance in this issue. The Prophet is reported to have said 'O women! Give alms, as I have seen that the majority of the dwellers of Hell-fire were you (women). They asked, why is it so, O Allah's Messenger? He replied, you curse frequently and are ungrateful to your husbands. I have not seen anyone more deficient in intelligence and religion than you. A cautious, sensible man could be led astray by some of you. The women asked, O Allah's Messenger! what is deficient in our intelligence and religion? He said, is not the evidence of two women equal to the witness of one man? They replied in the affirmative. He said, this is the deficiency in her intelligence. Isn't it true that a woman can neither pray nor fast during her menses? The women replied in the affirmative. He said, this is the deficiency in her religion' This *Hadith* is used, by the opponents of women's rights in politics, to prove their point in saying that women cannot be trusted with handling public matters.

They stress that the above *Hadith* makes it clear that women cannot have power over men because they are spiritually as well as cognitively deficient. They thus associate deficiency with womanhood and insist that women, by nature, are less prepared (rationally and emotionally) than men to cope with the pressure of public life. Therefore, God, according to them, has relieved them from certain duties (such as attending Jumah prayers and participating in Jihad) which are compulsory for men. However, there are those who see the *Hadith* differently: some do not accept it and consider it as fabricated or at best a weak *Hadith,* which ought to be abandoned because weak *Hadiths* usually do not carry any legal effects; others acknowledge the *Hadith* as authentic, but stress that it has been grossly misinterpreted.

They argue that the deficiency mentioned in the *Hadith* does not refer to natural but rather specific deficiency. In other words, there are two forms of deficiencies: (a) natural or innate deficiency *(naqs fitri),* a form of natural defect which hampers the human intellect at various levels, the extreme one being madness. This does not include women categorically because they are regarded (from the Quranic viewpoint) as accountable and responsible human beings capable of fulfilling their duties; (b) specific deficiency *(naqs naw'i)* of two types: (i) casual defect *(aradi),* which can temporarily upset the natural disposition of a person, especially during menstruation and pregnancy. This form of frailty does not weaken or impair women's natural abilities; (ii) incidental defect of long-term effects which results usually from living in special conditions (such as confinement to four walls, constant engagement in pregnancy and childbirth, etc.) that are not conducive to contacts and interactions with outside world. This, in time, lessens women's social, political and economic awareness of their surroundings and reduces them to their private circle-of ladies, with devastating consequences on their potential for playing an active role in public life. It must be stressed, however, that this form of deficiency can be remedied by altering the circumstances that lead to its existence.

As for the link made in the *Hadith* between women's intellectual deficiency and their testimony in law, we might point out that the connection occurs only in one case, namely, the evidence which requires the testimony of one man and two women. This testimony is mentioned in the Quran in Chapter *2,* verse 282, which deals solely with financial matters. And this is the only testimony in which the issue of gender is a dominant factor; in other testimonies the Quran stipulates justice rather than gender.

Therefore, it is not right to use this verse in order to accuse women of being intellectually deficient. For it is no more than a guiding verse aiming at promoting justice when dealing with complicated financial issues. In other words, the verse is meant to give advice that if, under certain circumstances, men are not available to testify, the alternative is to accept the testimony of two women (who could be ordinary members of the public, having little or no experience with financial matters, or who could be undergoing temporary disturbances resulting from menstruation or postnatal conditions) as being equal to that of man; the aim here being to ensure that precautionary measures are in place when dealing with an area where women are less likely to be experts.

The deficiency referred to in the *Hadith,* therefore, is not natural but rather contingent or casual and does not necessarily contradict the fact that there are women who possess high qualities and enjoy special capacities in comparison with ordinary men and women. Indeed, in some cases there are those who are wiser, well-advised, and more intelligent than men. The second *Hadith* which is reported in Bukhari and reads as thus: Abu Bakra said 'when Allah's Messenger was informed that the Persians had crowned the daughter of Kisra (Khosrau) as their ruler, he said, such people as ruled by a lady will never be successful. This *Hadith* has been widely cited to block any attempts to give women the opportunity to wield power in society.

The opponents argue that the Prophet in this *Hadith* advises Muslims not to follow in the footsteps of the Persians who appointed a woman as their leader and consequently led them to a disastrous end. For them, the *Hadith* contains a clear-cut warning (for Muslims) to be vigilant and not to allow women to overstep the line and enter into politics; otherwise, their fate would be the same as that of Persia before Islam: defeat and humiliation. However, one has to disagree with this view for two reasons: first, the *Hadith* deals mainly with a specific case, namely, the situation of Persia at the time of the Prophet. Indeed, it is no more than a prophesy *(bishara)* in which the Prophet predicted the fate of the Persian empire. As such, it has no legal ruling and therefore it cannot be generalised to include all women at all times; second, if the *Hadith* is to be accepted as general, it would surely contradict the Quran, and this cannot happen.

The Quran, in chapter 27, speaks highly of the Queen of Sheba, Bilqis, who ruled over her people with wisdom and insight and led them to success and prosperity 'I found a woman reigning over the people. She is possessed of every virtue and has a splendid throne'. The only fault found with her, was not her position and authority as a woman, but her false faith 'she and her subjects worship the sun instead of Allah'. Later, the wise woman met Solomon, admitted her sin (for not worshipping God) and, along with her people, accepted Islam: 'Lord', she said, 'I have wronged my own soul. Now I submit with Sulayman to Allah, Lord of the creation'." From the above, we can deduce that the Hadith is not general, but rather specific and is related to the episode of the people of Persia.

The opponents point out that there is no precedent in early Islam which indicates that women were appointed to high positions, despite the fact that there were ample opportunities for such appointments. Neither the Prophet nor any of his companions invited women to take part in the administration of the state. Moreover, women themselves, and although there were many who excelled men in their abilities, did not show any interest in holding public office. In response, one can mention the example of the second Caliph Umar, who appointed a woman (al-Shafa') as superintendent in a market in

Medina. This position was, at the time, more of a political than a business office, as the market was not only a centre for trading but also a focal point for political activities.

The fact that few women were at the top of the administration does not reflect badly on the abilities of women to run public offices. Moreover, one has to bear in mind the nature of the social setting prevailing at the time, in which pre-Islamic customs were still competing and resisting any changes brought about by Islam." So, although the social environment was favourable (due to the changes brought about by Islam) and allowed women greater mobility in society; yet it was still less willing and less amenable to the idea of entrusting women with governmental positions.

Social practices *('Adat)* should not be allowed to take precedence over Divine instructions. Most importantly, they should not be used as a pretext to continue to neglect or even (in some cases) abandon the Islamic principles, which oblige women to have their shares in public life and be active and effective in society. For social customs are subject to change; they change with time and place, while Divine principles are meant for all times and all places. As such, the emphasis should be on the Divine tenets not social customs.

The Consensus (ijma) there are those who stress that there is an agreement among scholars on the so-called 'unsuitability" of women to hold public office. However, invoking the issue of consensus is no more than a fallacy since there is hardly any unity among them on this subject. For example, the position of Judge is regarded by some to be suitable for men only; Abu Hanifa, however, disagrees and allows a woman to be appointed as Judge and gives her the right to deal with all matters except those under the penal code. Ibn Jarir al-Tabari, on the other hand, qualifies a woman for the post of judge without any restrictions. This renders the whole issue of the existing consensus among scholars suspicious and, in fact, a mere sham. Moreover, it is essential to bear in mind whether the *ijma* (on a particular question, and, in this case, the issue of women) takes into consideration the overall interest of the community. For if it runs counter to the social interest, then there is no use in accepting it in the first place.

The opponents argue that permitting women to occupy public positions would be detrimental to both society as well as family. According to them, top jobs require courage, wisdom and strength, and women, in general, lack these characteristics; they are feeble and can be easily misled. As such, they cannot be trusted with executive roles, especially leadership roles. For instance, a president or a ruler in an Islamic state needs to perform important and not merely ceremonial duties such as: conducting war, signing peace treaties, defending the country, delivering sermons, and leading people in prayers—all of which women cannot cope with, because of their fragilities and emotional vulnerabilities.

Furthermore, they state that woman's advancement to executive power goes against her social function: that is to be a good wife and mother. They argue that if she is to assume an executive role—which is a full-time commitment—this would inevitably force her to neglect her household duties, with devastating consequences on the stability of the family in society. They point out that even if there are some women who can handle both roles, they are, in reality, exceptions; therefore, it is unwise to set up and accept rules on rare cases. It must be stressed, however, that those who think that female leadership would damage state-interest base their view on the assumption that women are, by nature, incapable of coping with public responsibilities. But this is not the case as we explained earlier; women, like men, are qualified to run state affairs.

The opponents view public positions, especially state leadership as a one-person responsibility, thus neglecting the *shura* principle, which makes state affairs a collective responsibility. Moreover, they regard the state system as more or less similar to that of the Medinan or tribal system with limited scope and structure, hence, confining the Islamic concept of state within a particular historical context. In doing so, they contradict the universal vision of the Islamic state. As for the welfare of the family, the assumption is that only those women whose domestic responsibilities permit them to engage in public duties should do so. Having said that, domestic responsibility should not be taken as pretext (by both men and women) to discourage or prevent women, especially able ones, from involvement in public activities.

In other words, women should strike a balance between their domestic and public commitments and try and avoid a situation whereby one commitment overshadows the other. This means that, in essence, only a few women would be able to qualify in terms of this criterion. Hence, the standard of judgement should be based on the few not on the majority as the opponents claim. This is because prominent jobs are usually based on ability and merit rather than on gender."

The opponents stress that leadership positions require public display and constant contacts with people. This would inevitably facilitate mingling between the two sexes; an issue which is clearly prohibited in Islam. According to them, the Quran explicitly orders women to stay at home and avoid any public exposure; therefore, it is not appropriate for them to take on public duties, because this would expose them to all forms of public immorality. In response, we can say that this view is certainly out of context with both the Quran as well as the practical Sunnah of the Prophet. For instance, the Quran in Chapter 33, verse 32 ordered (solely) the Prophet's wives to stay at home and not to display any public appearance, because they were regarded as the mothers of the believers; other women were not included. For they used to take part in public worship, seek knowledge and education, participate in Jihad, enjoy wider social interactions, and attend vocational training.

So, the verse deals with a specific case, namely, the status of the Prophet's wives, and therefore, it is not right to generalise it to include other Muslim women; in doing so, they reject the practical Sunnah of the Prophet, and this cannot be right. It must be made clear, moreover, that of all social interactions only *Khulwa* (seclusion), promiscuity, lustfulness, and extravagance or excessiveness are prohibited in Islam. Other societal activities, which are needed for the conduct of normal and respectable social life are allowed and encouraged.

So, to use *fitna* (temptation) as an excuse in order to change a religious ruling is indeed unjustifiable. For women, especially nowadays, cannot perform their duties without meeting men. Also, it must be remembered that God, who is the legislator, knows better what the state of his creatures is in terms of their piety or corruption. When Islam encouraged women to take part in public life, it did so by laying down certain rules of conduct, so as to curb any tendency towards *fitna* or corruption. It did not show any inclination to restrict or prevent women from mixing with men under the pretext of *fitna.* This is despite the fact that many unpleasant incidents occurred, especially during the Prophet's time, as a result of the wide social contacts that prevailed between the two sexes. Nevertheless, those incidents were regarded as exceptions, and they did not disturb or stop the normal course of social life.

11
The Scenario in Arab World

All the changes which are taking place in the position of Moslem women are phases of a fundamental renaissance in the East to-day-the rethinking of religion. Educational opportunity, social equality, economic independence, the widening of the find of women's interest beyond the four walls of the home are all different manifestations of a vital reorganization of Eastern life. The transformation in the position of Moslem women is to a certain degree, both the cause and the effect of this change in religion. Any variation in the status of women challenges the customs of Islam; on the other hand, until these customs are challenged, little or no change in the life of Moslem women will occur.

As one talks with young Moslems of the rising generation, one realizes that they are beginning to question the authority of Islam, which has been held inviolable through the centuries, and that they are discarding customs which have held the Islamic social system static for centuries. Hence the far-reaching changes in the life of the Moslem woman.

"Islam," to quote a Moslem leader in Egypt, "has set its seal to inferiority upon her, and given the sanction of religion to social customs which have deprived her of the full opportunity for self-expression and development of personality."

Justice to Womanhood

Although the Islamic world has often failed to do justice to womanhood, there is little doubt that the Prophet was inspired by the ideal of elevating the position of women of his day and improving social conditions, without, however, violating the prevailing concept of masculine superiority, that was characteristic of a primitive people, dominated by the ideal of physical strength. His teachings. Represent a social reform movement against existing practices which was very significant for that day, and included such measures as the abolition of infanticide, limitation of polygamy, protection of widows and orphans, marriage contract, the granting of marriage dowry and inheritance rights to women. Mohammed himself took advantage of the limit of four wives, prescribed by the Koran and caused his wives to veil and avoid public contact; that is, all except his first wife Khadija, the elderly widow who is said to have attended all the meetings.' Customs rather than the actual teaching of the Koran resulted later in the veiling and seclusion of women. For example, in regard to the veil, according to the Koran, a woman should not show her ornaments (Zinet). This was subsequently interpreted to mean that a woman's ornament is her hair-an interesting parallel to the Biblical idea of a woman's hair as her crowning glory-and therefore the hair must be covered. From this the latter customs of the veil developed. Personal example rather than literal teachings regarding women as a whole were included by the commentators of the Koran in the Islamic social system.

By incorporating the various social reforms such as the restriction of polygamy and inheritance rights directly into his religions teachings, Mohammed proved himself to be a practical idealist. Religion has always been an effective instrument for social action, but was especially so in Arabia, because the Arabs, naturally religious by temperament, were more interested in religion than in social reform. In claiming for his social teachings the authority of divine revelation, Mohammed therefore made an irresistible appeal to the Arabs of his time. Unfortunately for Moslem women, however, these socio-religious reforms designed for the seventh century have not furnished a basis for continuous progress and reform.

Too often the identification of religion with social custom has precluded any idea of change for orthodox Islam. Every utterance and act of the Prophet, since supposed to be divinely inspired, have been given permanence and finality. The social habits of early Islam have persisted in spite of changing conditions, since the interpreters of the Canon Law were not imbued with the spirit of social reform and the ideal of elevating womanhood, that would have made change possible as the situation changed. They have remained reactionary in their thinking, basing the teaching regarding women literally on the customs of the seventh century, and even making a more rigid interpretation than the actual customs of Mohammed's day required. Thus the teaching regarding women which may have represented an actual advance in the status of women for the seventh century, when applied literally to the nineteenth and twentieth centuries has discouraged change and kept Moslem women from being affected by the new conditions of the modern world.

Regardless of any change in conditions, the orthodox Moslem position in reference to women, as in everything else, has remained unchanged. This point of view is illustrated by the reply of a desert chief in Trans-jordan who when asked whether there was any change in religion, answered, "We don't need to talk of religion, we are all Moslem. There can be no change." His physical environment of the far-sweeping desert has remained the same since the days of the Prophet, and his concept of life is no less unchanged.

To maintain this traditional conception of women was possible as long as the Moslem world was a world apart. But the force of the twentieth century has broken with tremendous strength against the bulwarks of medieval Islam. Powerful influences outside the realm of religion-political, economic and social-have engendered widespread dissatisfaction with a social system that sanctions polygamy and is typified by the veil. Hence although reactionary authorities may be antagonistic to modern social ideals, the impulsion of progress is irresistible. The reality of change therefore is affecting the practices of Islam, and the very bases of the religion itself

Social changes due to the impact of modern civilization have involved inevitable changes in religious thought. At the same time, by a strange interaction of cause and effect, changing attitudes toward religion, which have come in modern Islam through world contact, are making possible and motivating social progress. This interaction of social and religious change is a subject of vital significance in the study of the changing status of Moslem women, since the emancipation of women is at the very heart of social reform and also the acid test of difference between the ancient and modern points of view. The twentieth century has invoked a new relationship between religion and society in the Islamic world, since the old, completely integrated religious social system with all its details prescribed has been trees passed upon by a modern world.

A careful study of the religious phases of this interrelated social and religious problem would present the intricacies of ajigsaw puzzle. But viewed in broad outline, the problem seems to be resolving itself along two main lines. In the first place certain radicals are deliberately trying to disestablish the authoritative socio-religious system of Islam. In so doing, however, they do not attempt to discredit it as a personal belief. In the second place, a less radical group is reinterpreting Islam in order to bring it into harmony with modern life, while still maintaining its authority as a religious system. Since the most debated point in orthodox Islam in the twentieth century is its social system, based on the seventh century, and since the central fact of this social system, as has been shown, is the position assigned to women, the reinterpretation of religion seeks to harmonize the emancipation of women with the spirit of the Koran. The modern conception of Islam is concerned with its teachings concerning the veil, polygamy, divorce and other social questions affecting women.'

Confronted with the conflict between religious tradition and modern life, Turkey has chosen the first of the two solutions-the repudiation of the inviolable authority of religion over the State and Society and the pursuit of progress as a single goal. The rest of the Moslem world has followed the second course and attempted to keep all social reform within the spirit of the Law. Of this approach to the problem Egypt is perhaps the best example. The coun tries that are trying to adapt themselves to the new soci - al order by seeking to harmonize the spirit of Islam with modern thought differ widely and represent various stages of advance. Their difference, however, is one of degree rather than of kind, as they all recognize the authority of Islam to determine the bounds of social progress. It is interesting to consider the dominant religious attitudes in the different countries of the Moslem world toward their common problem of the relationship between religion and modern civilization. Although Egypt seems to be distinctly European, judging by the general atmosphere in Cairo, the dominant official attitude toward religion is distinctly that of Asia. There is no idea of repudiating the power of Islam, but rather a definite united policy of the forces of Church and State to make Egypt the bulwark of religion, the defender of the faith. Egypt occupies without question a position of religious pre-eminence in Islam as a result of the prestige of A] Azhar, the great Moslem University, which has for over a thousand years radiated its influence through the Moslem world; also because of the influence of a Moslem sovereign committed to upholding Islamic traditions. This is a very powerful combination of forces.

The reasons for the close co-ordination of Church and State in Egypt are largely political rather than religious. The maintenance of the strength of the monarchy is served by upholding the power of established religion, which is represented by Al Azhar. Both represent a status quo. The fact that Egypt as a whole adheres to a conservative religious attitude is not interpreted by careful observers of Egypt as indicative of an especially religious temperament of the people, but may be considered rather as the natural result of the alliance of the influence for religious conservatism with the established policy of the State.

Because of the powerful vested interests of Islam in Egypt and the official support given to Islam, all progress in Egypt must meet the primary condition of being in harmony with Islam. Social reform receives at the present time a good deal of attention in Fgypt and modernizing tendencies are very much in evidence. A reformer like Kasim Amin, who at the beginning of the century advocated the emancipation of women on the basis of a modern interpretation of the Koran, and paid the usual price of pioneers, public censure and condemnation, to-day would not be considered an extremist or opposed to religion. But all advance must be carefully justified on the grounds of its being in harmony with the spirit of the Koran. Although the increasing latitude in interpretation is one of the hopeful signs of change in Egypt, the transition naturally takes place slowly. There is no evidence there of abolishing the Shari'a, the Moslem religious law, and adopting a modern civil code based on a united social system for Christians and Moslems alike.

Although no legal reform which runs counter to Islam has as yet been successful in Egypt, there are distinct evidences of new elements in the religious thinking of Egypt. The installation of electric lights in Al Azhar is a significant trend toward the modernization and improvement of Islamic institutions. The establishment of a new system of primary and secondary instruction in religious education, the change of old forms of instruction and the introduction of a modern curriculum, modern languages, sciences, and comparative religion, the transfer of students from the old mosque into modern buildings-all these changes in Al Azhar are motivated by the desire to strengthen Islam. In these reforms there is no idea of social change, but it seems probable that the exposure of thirteen thousand Moslem men students to the study of modern science and comparative religions may have some effect on the social system.

Religion and Politics

Because of the relationship of religion to politics, religion is a subject of much discussion and general interest in Egypt. The majority of the educated class follows the prevailing current of conventional religious thought for reasons of expediency, if not from belief. A certain number of Egyptian intellectuals, however, represent an articulate opposition to the authority of religion to determine social reform. Between this group, which has its centre in the Egyptian University, and Al Azhar, the centre of the conservatives, there is a constant struggle. In spite of the fact that the religious forces in Egypt prevent any drastic reforms which would run counter to the Koran, social evolution is inevitable in a country where modern ideas are assimilated as easily as the air one breathes. Furthermore, since the dominant motivation for action in Egypt tends to be political rather than religious, the compromise method of social reform through a modern interpretation of Islam is gaining in influence. The periphery of Islamic privilege for women as sanctioned by the Koran is therefore steadily widening.

There is little question of the influence of Egypt across the Pan-Islamic world. Through a very active Press and a vigorous literature current Egyptian thought is being broadcasted from North Africa to the Indian Ocean, and is reshaping the thinking of the rising generation. Egypt offers the outstanding example of social advance through the modernization of religion, which is being followed with profound interest by other Islamic countries, especially by the intelligent conservative elements in Islam that arc conscious of the need for change but antagonized by the extreme reforms of Turkey, which they regard as progress at too great a price.

A night's journey from Cairo to Jerusalem gives one the impression of having travelled back in point of time several decades when one compares the religious atmosphere of Egypt and Palestine. Jerusalem is not the advance guard of modern Islam as is Cairo, but a stronghold of religious conservatism rooted in the past. Islam in Egypt represents the co-ordination of Church and

State, both united under a foreign Power. Islam in Palestine represents the separation .of the Moslem Arab community from other racial and religious elements in a highly divided world under foreign control. Cairo is an expanding modern city, a Paris of the East, vibrant with intellectual activity and modem life. Jerusalem is an Eastern city of narrow streets within historic walls, with a heterogeneous modem city expanding on the outside, a mixture of foreign elements unrelated to the life within the old city. The physical difference between Cairo and Jerusalem typifies the difference between the religious attitude of Egypt and that of Palestine.

The reasons for the Orthodox position of Palestine are not difficult to understand. Jerusalem is a sacred city of Islam and all sacred cities tend to intensify the religious feeling of their devotees. In Jerusalem, moreover, as the shrine city for three great world religions, the followers of all three faiths are more deeply imbued with religious intensity than are the devotees at other holy cities. The competition of these different religions, each claiming the same city as sacred, has tended to crystallize religious feeling into an extreme conservatism. Hence the Moslem religious current in Jerusalem flows into an orthodox channel. The political situation, moreover, tends to cause Moslems in Palestine to cling tenaciously to their religion. They find themselves on the defensive against a twofold influence-a foreign political power and an aggressive, competitive, racial and religious element, which is protected by the foreign Government and rapidly growing. Both of these alien forces are feared because it is felt they prevent Arab development; a protective attitude toward Islam is the result. This expresses itself in a careful safeguarding of Moslem social customs.

Religion and culture are inseparable ideas in Jerusalem since Islam is the product of the Arab's mind and temperament. The voice from the minaret speaks the language of the Arab and appeals to his soul. His religion and institutions, language and culture are all an inseparable composite which makes up the idea of Arab personality. Adherence to religion and safeguarding its institutions from any modernizing influence is therefore an assertion of Arab individuality and a defence against a dual aggression. This fear of losing personality, if religion and customs are changed, is voiced by a young Arab intellectual of Western education, "If a nation loses its religion, its social institutions, customs and traditions, it loses its personality." The common instinct of defences of'Arab personality is expressed in an orthodox attitude toward Islam which unites the conservatives and many liberals who, because of education and modern influence, might follow a different course under other circumstances.

This common impulse of conservatives and progressives to safeguard Islam and its institutions prevents rapid social change which would affect Moslem customs. Any aggressive movement toward a reinterpretation of Islam, or an intellectual analysis of the social religious problem, such as one finds in Cairo, is also lacking. A few individuals may express the opinion that the veil and religion have no relationship, but there is no open effort to promote the idea. The attitude toward social reform bv law is illustrated by the answer to the question which I ~ad the temerity to ask in a conversation with three learned and worthy Moslem sheikhs in Jerusalem steeped in Islamic lore, as to their opinion of the legal reforms in Turkey, "Turkey knows no more about the Moslem law than you do," was the reply uttered by the oldest and most learned of the three, in a tone of utter firiality and scorn.

As to the effect of other Moslem countries on Palestine, one has the feeling that Palestine is rather segregated from outside influence. There seems to be little interest or sympathy with the religious and social reform in Turkey; with the process of change in Egypt, Palestine is more sympathetic. But the Grand Mufti occupying the Citadel in Jerusalem, which overlooks the spacious area of the Dome of the Rock, is firmly maintaining, at the present time, the authority of Islam in Palestine.

In Trans-jordan also orthodox Islam holds sway. Inspired in an environment not unlike that of Trans-jordan to-day, the 'religion of' the desert is not as yet challenged by any modern ideas. Education has only just begun in Transjordan, the social urge is as yet scarcely perceptible; hence the conflict has been until now hardly evident between the old and the new, and religion is not a subject for discussion in Trans-jordan. According to a sheikh with fairly modern ideas attached to the private staff of His Highness, Emir Abdullah, Trans-jordan, however, represents a greater degree of fi-ecdom than Mecca or 'Medina, where the Wahhabis wage their Puritan warfare against a man's special liberty; for example forbidding him to smoke or shave his beard. But Islam in Trans-jordan has riot modificd its control over women. Orthodox religion in this new frontier State is as yet uncontaminated by any higher criticism.

In Syria as in Palestine the prevailing Moslem trend seems toward the orthodox point of view. Although one is conscious of more cross-currents in Moslem thought in Syria, the dominant impression, if one judges by the a ttitud(! toward social reform, is that ancient tradition is still very generally upheld. There are, of course, as we have shown in preceding chapters, abundant signs of a social evolution in Syria, but this is due to general forces rather than to an active programme of social reform. There are individual Moslems of advanced religious views but the collective impact tends to strengthen Islam along orthodox lines.

This dominant conservative religious trend in Syria may be due, as in Palestine, to the interplay of religious and political influences. The French Mandate has had something of the same effect as the British Mandate in building up a general protective attitude toward Islam as a line of defence against foreign power. "Whatever our belief or however modern our ideas may be, we become more Moslem. under foreign pressure, since we feel ourselves a minority," was the frank explanation of a progressive Moslem doctor of Beirut as to why he did not actively promote social change.

As a modern young Turkish woman, commenting on the difference between Turkey and Syria, said, "If Turkey were in the same situation, I would probably wear two veils instead of one and pray regularly at the mosque." Also contrasting Syria with Turkey, a thoughtful Moslem woman in Beirut expressed this feeling of need for protection against foreign influence. "A sovereign Moslem State has no fear of reproducing the wrong kind of Western influence. It can choose and not have something imposed upon it. We would naturally have more confidence in Moslem leadership than in foreign."

The contrast between Beirut, and Damascus and Aleppo has already been discussed in reference to cducational developments. Out of the zone of Western influence of all kinds, with a large Moslem majority, the two latter cities and the area they include are dominated by a distinctly Moslem atmosphere. But there is also a marked difference between Damascus and Aleppo. Damascus, like Jerusalem, is an historic city of Islam, where religious enthusiasm is always a deep smouldering fire, which may be quickly fanned into flame. Moslem traditions are therefore zealously guarded against the encroachment of subversive foreign influence. Aleppo is not so steeped, as Damascus is, in Islamic culture. The focus of life in Aleppo is economic, not religious. The social influence of Turkey is more in evidence in Aleppo than elsewhere in Syria, a fact which naturally affects the religious point of view. The political situation has had some effect in retarding social change, but one is certainly less conscious in Aleppo than in other parts of Syria of the Moslem defence attitude induced by the political situation.

In Syria as a whole, there is a certain amount of rethinking of religion but the subject calls forth much less discussion in the Press in Syria than in Egypt. Beirut is not an intellectual centre of modern Islam. There are very few individual leaders trying to interpret the Koranic laws so as to make modern social practices permissible. Some of the educated class, however, are promoting the idea that social conventions are not identified with Islam. There is probably a fairly large number of liberally minded Moslems who are only conservative from reasons of expediency. There are also many in Syria, as elsewhere, who have a definitely secular point of view, believing that there is an unsolved conflict between Islam and progress. Two expressions of opinion from young Syrians show this: "As people become educated they grow more open-minded, leave their beliefs and accept the truth," and "No educated person can have religious conviction. He may keep religion as a cultural legacy but not as a conscious belief." Naturally this group has no interest in reinterpreting Islam in order to clear the path for social progress.

As to outside influences from other Moslem countries which are affecting religious trends in Syria, Egypt plays a greater role than Turkey. The Arabic language gives the literary activity of Egypt a Syrian public and the general contact of Syria~ with Egypt, moreover, is far closer than with Turkey. The influence of Turkey on Syria in religious reform is negligible, although the fearless method by which Turkey has accomplished the social and religious revolution makes an appeal to a certain number of the younger generation. But as a whole religious thought in Syria is not affected to any marked degree by other Moslem countries.

The varied foreign influences from the West, especially evident in Beirut and the Lebanon, are undoubtedly having an effect on religious thought. But any change in religious attitudes of Moslems that may be taking place is an unconscious process. As long as the political situation claims the centre of attention, Moslems and Christians alike will probably view everything from that angle. "Like a horse with blinders" as a Syrian nationalist expressed it, Syria looks straight ahead along the way of political interests; other problems are viewed entirely in that perspective. Nationalism, which in Syria means political independence, is the ruling passion and religion is not the major determinant of action.

Baghdad to-day forms a striking contrast with Baghdad, the proud city of the Abbasids of the Middle Ages. Once the treasure-house of Islamic art and learning, Baghdad is to-day a centre of vigorous nationalism with less interest in religion. Orthodox Islam is still ostensibly in command but the centre of interest in Baghdad since the World. War has shifted from religion to politics.

In King Feisal's support of Islam there was probably no idea of any aspirations to the Caliphate; his concern was to keep firm the bonds of relationship with Arabia. King Ghazi, in following this same principle-strict adherence to Islam-is doubtless actuated by political considerations, as well as by loyalty to his racial heritage and family ties. Whatever may be the reason for the official policy, Iraq admits less elasticity of interpretation of the Koran than does Egypt. Conditions do not encourage the development of a higher criticism of Islam in the interest of social reform. Furthermore, there are no religious leaders in Baghdad of the type of those in Cairo, who are interested in a modern apologetics of religion, nor is there much evidence of any urge to make such an interpretation.

Many of the younger generation, however, feel that religion is a social drag. "Religion has clamped the lid on the freedom of men as well as women. We have only the coffee-houses for social amusements" is the spirit of protest uttered by educated young Moslems returning from university life in Syria, or England or America. For them the conflict between religion and progress urgently demands a solution. These educated young leaders in Baghdad are not inhibited from social reform by any cultural defence of Islam due to the political situation as in Beirut and Jerusalem. In Baghdad the spirit of nationalism is aggressive, and antagonistic to the restraint of religion. "Islam is a retrogressive force, not only blocking progress, but opposing nationalism, since it still emphasizes too much of the old idea of Pan-Islam, an impossible ideal to-day," said a Baghdad teacher just returned from study abroad. "It seems hopeless to try to do anything with Islam. The only solution is to cut loose," was the opinion expressed by another Iraqi student. In such a mood the young Moslem leaders of Iraq make no attempt to reinterpret the Koran and to compromise between social reform and religion as in Cairo. Their approach to the social-religious problem is not intellectual but pragmatic.

Forces other than Islam arc determining the flow of life in Baghdad to-day. Modernism presses hard against orthodox religion. Ramadhan is loosely observed; the coffee-houses during this month of fasting are no longer closed; mosques are scantily attended. The shrine cities of Najaf and Kerbela are no longer richly endowed and filled with pilgrims. Islam in Iraq to-day has ceased to be the sole power which controls all national development. But although a secondary interest, religion still plays an important role.

Turkey's successful nationalism has inspired widespread admiration in Iraq and would inspire more direct imitation if conditions were more favourable. The fearless drastic methods of Turkey, taking tucks in the decades, as it were, to make up for lost time, makes a tremendous appeal and awakens the hope of a similar solution for the retarded civilization of Iraq. "Turkey proves the possibility of the successful a&ptation of a Moslem country to modem civilization in breaking with traditions and the rigid teaching of the Koran, while still remaining a Moslem power," said a Cambridge graduate, one of the influential young Iraqi leaders. Discarding, the hindrances of Islam but retaining the Moslem affiliation, seem to many in Iraq the only way out. The influence of Egypt although vigorously exerted through the Arabic Press, makes less of a direct impression on Iraq than does the example of Turkey. The intellectual force from Egypt does not give the dynamic urge to action, such as that which comes from Turkey. It is true, that the change of letters from Arabic to Latin in Turkey may eventually affect the sense of relationship of Iraq with Turkey, since it cuts off the influence of the Turkish Press. However, Baghdad, although in the heart of the desert, eagerly faces Westward and will doubtless continue to feel a close relationship to Istanbul.

Specifically with reference to Moslem women in Iraq, the most direct outside influence has come from Syria through the Syrian teachers and through the Iraqi girls studying on scholarship in the schools of Beirut. We have already discussed the educational and social significance for Iraq of this contact with Syria. Unquestionably this relationship with Syria has had also an influence on religious attitudes. The continuous injection of modern ideals into the stream of Iraq life through the students and teachers who have been educated in Syria has had the effect of liberalizing the whole atmosphere. All of the undercurrents of religious reaction in Iraq against the controlling spirit of conservatism, will find freer outlets eventually in definite religious and social changes. "Wait till the old beards di6," the remark of an elderly Baghdad woman in sympathy with modern thought, is full of Eastern wisdom.

12
Scenario in India

The women of the minority communities suffer from the dual handicap of being women and belonging to minority communities. They form a large group in the lowest economic categories. Demanding equitable treatment for these women does not amount to asking for doles or undue favours for an indolent, lazy section of our society, rather it is to recognize that they form a very vital force whose potential it fully utilized, could transform this nation. Harnessing the full potential of this section is challenging, and requires an integrated approach. There is a need to improve their employment quantitatively and qualitatively to ensure the balanced development of human resources.

The developmental effort for women of the minority communities, has so far been too meagre to make any significant impact on their condition. The government of India has accepted the fact that the 'trickling down effect' has not worked as expected. So target-oriented programmes have been given importance specially from the Sixth Plan onwards. The 'Approach to the Eighth Five Year Plan' document has acknowledged the fact that the economic development of women, the first step is the recognition of the dignity of women's work and a proper understanding of its dimensions and contribution in the Indian context.

The basic approach in the upliftment of women would be to empower women by raising their status and bringing them into the mainstream of national development, not as mere beneficiaries but as contributors and partakers along with men. The emphasis would be on encouraging women to mobilize themselves to join cooperatives and other democratic organizations with a view to realizing their full potential for development.

The government must make an effort to understand the changing profile of the work-force with the entry of women and to provide an appropriate environment for their advancement and growth. At the same time, initiatives have also to come frorn the women themselves to meet job challenges and sustain their growth.

The government should evolve and implement human resource development policies that would facilitate women's development and in that process the development of the economy in general. Women would be a critical factor for realizing the goals of the Eighth Plan. Therefore, the government is required It formulate policies of optimum utilization of human resources which are gender-sensitive and nondiscriminatory. Even though the Constitution guarantees equal treatment, equal opportunities, equal status for women, in actual fact. Discrimination on the grounds of sex is rampant and practised with impunity.

Many studies by anthropologists, social scientists and economists have established this as a fact. Between men and women, women always take the cellar—health, nutrition, wages, status or in any socioeconomic activity. Even systematized and regular data on women in general and women of minority communities in particular has been unavailable so tar.

Voluntary organizations is seen as a great source of moral and managerial strength in supplementing the efforts of the government. A substantial contribution will have to come from social action groups and organizations that are in constant touch with the people, particularly with the marginalized and deprived sections. Voluntary organizations can also act as pressure groups on their behalf and help in increasing the effectiveness of various programmes aimed at women and at the minorities.

Governments, at the central as well as local level, have earmarked quotas for women. For example, it has been stipulated that 30 and per cent of the beneficiaries of' the Integrated Rural Development Programme should be from the weaker sections of women. However, during 1986-87, as against this target, only 5.67 lakh women (15.23 per cent) received benefits under the IRDP. Even financial institutions like the commercial and cooperative banks have decided to allocate 30 per cent to 40 per cent of credit flow to women.

The Reserve Bank of India and National Bank of Rural Development have also issued directives to various categories of credit institutions for direct finance as well as refinance facilities to serve the interests of the weaker sections of the women population.

Industrial Development Bank of India has been implementing a special scheme [Development of Women & Children in Rural Areas (DWCRA)] for the betterment of women. It is a group finance scheme which is channelized through lead banks. The twin objectives of this scheme are providing training and extension services to women entrepreneurs through a comprehensive package suited to their skills and socioeconomic status, and extending financial assistance on concessional terms to enable them to set up industrial units in the small-scale sector.

It has been proved by many research studies that the effect of these various poverty alleviation programmes on the target group of women has not been encouraging and the betterment has been only marginal. The minorities coming under this study are the religious minorities. They are Muslims, Christians, Sikhs, Parsecs and Neo-Buddhists.

According to the 1981 census, minorities form 11.4 per cent of the total population out of which 49 per cent are women, i.e., nearly 5.5 per cent of the total population. If this considerable chunk of our country's human resources is left untapped, it is bound to result in the slowing down of the process of economic development of the country itself. On the other hand, if this large segment of the labour force is harnessed in the production process, it is bound to have a positive impact on our economic development.

The government of India has acknowledged that a concerted effort should be made to see that the fruits of economic development reach the minority communities in a fair and adequate measure. The programme for alleviation of poverty should thus have a strong focus on the development of women of these communities. In recognition of this fact the Janata Government in 1977 established the All India Minorities Commission. Then again, Mrs. Indira Gandhi emphasized the need for the flow of development benefits to reach the minority communities; the Prime Minister's 15-point programme was proclaimed. Since then governments have reiterated the importance of women's development and resolved to implement the 15-point programme more efficiently. Special mention should be made of the 5th and 13th points of the 15-point programme wherein the credit flow to the minorities is stressed. The 5th point states that victims of communal riots should be given immediate relief and provided prompt and adequate financial assistance for rehabilitation, and the 13th point declares that in various development programmes, including the 20-point programme, care should be taken to see that minorities secure in a fair and adequate measure the benefits flowing therefrom.

According to the area-wise concentration of minorities, the government of India had identified forty-one districts in the nation to monitor the economic development of the minorities closely. This has been done under the 15-point programme to improve the lot of the minority communities.

The Industries Ministry has also asked the authorities of the minority districts to choose at least one hundred persons under the Special Employment for Educated Unemployed Youth scheme and give them the necessary benefits. Through the 15-point programme, some select schemes were to be devised speciality for the minorities. The Government proposes to develop the skills of these people so that they can start their own enterprises.

But while the government schemes for the poor, including the poorer sections, belonging to minority religious groups are highly commendable their implementation leaves much to be desired. The deserving among the poor are not identified properly.

A good deal of 'pull' and corruption at all levels frustrate the schemes in every detail. Most of the officials who are interviewed, confirmed the fact that no special schemes were formulated for the minorities as such, and that very few officers were specifically entrusted with the task of implementing the schemes and monitoring credit flow to minorities. The commercial banks or cooperative banks do not segregate or disclose in their annual reports the quantum of credit sanctioned or disbursed to the minority communities in general and women of these communities in particular. Even in the forty-one notified minority districts, no clear strategy for their economic development has emerged either through District Annual Action Plans or by way of specific schemes from District Industries Centres. Under these circumstances, any benefit accruing to the women of the minority communities is a distant dream. It is here that voluntary organizations can act as catalysts in their development.

Women of the minority communities, of whom a majority are Muslim women, are illiterate, poor and backward. Left to themselves these women are not in a position to benefit from all these poverty alleviation programmes. Though there are a number of schemes to benefit them, most of these women are not even aware of these schemes.

Illiteracy, poverty and the presence of the patriarchal system makes it very difficult for these hapless women to benefit from the economic development that is taking place around them. The absence of any link between the emerging demands of the national economy and the educational inputs and technical skills of these women has resulted in most of the opportunities being out of their reach.

A Statewise Survey on Muslim Women's Condition (West Bengal)

Therefore, the quickening pace of economic development in the country has accentuated the difference between the levels of development of the women of the minority communities and specially Muslim women, and the better off section of women in general. It will not be remiss to mention the observation made by Dr. Gopal Singh's Commission in one specific area, viz., handicrafts.

Dr. Gopal Singh's Report on Minorities contains data collected by its research team regarding the benefits which have accrued to the Muslims from the schemes implemented in the handicrafts sector frorn thirty-one districts spread over twelve states including West Bengal, Andhra Pradesh and Maharashtra.

In 1983, 1.68 lakh artisans were Muslims, accounting for 51.09 per cent of all the minorities. A study of the ownership pattern of these units showed that out of 0.22 lakh units, 995 units were owned by Muslims accounting for 4.4 per cent of the total.

In the cooperative sector, only two units belonged to the Muslims accounting for about 1 per cent of the total. Thus, it is found that Muslims, despite their expertise in handicrafts, have hardly derived any benefits from cooperative or financial institutions. The benefit received from beneficiary-oriented schemes was a pittance as compared to their overall requirements.

The Muslim artisans are poor, illiterate and live in remote villages or in the congested pockets of urban areas. 'Their enterprises can succeed only if all services involving the supply of raw material and inputs, as well as marketing support and then credit, are given to them at their doorsteps. An integrated administrative infrastructure to ensure the flow of adequate credit and other inputs is required if these artisans are to succeed in their economic ventures.

A decade after the Dr. Gopal Singh Report on Minorities was presented, the plight of Muslims in general and the women of this community in particular has not changed for the better. For example, the conditions of the Muslims of West Bengal is most alarming in the socioeconomic field. Constituting about a quarter of the total population of the state, and having a numerical strength of about 13 million, Muslims have lagged far behind the other communities and figure insignificantly in educational and economic fields. Suffice it to say that Muslim students appearing in Madhyamic (school final) examination in the year 1990 were only 1 per cent of the total, i.e., 4,500 out of 4,50,000. Likewise in the sixty-three postgraduate departments of the Calcutta University only one department is headed by a Muslim. There is a conspicuous absence of Muslim employees in educational institutions and commercial establishments in West Bengal. Their representation in government institutions is nominal. A recent survey conducted by the cultural anthropologist, M. K. A. Siddiqi, published in the book, Educating a Backward Minority gives an alarming picture of the state of education as well as the economic conditions of the Muslims in the state.

In primary education, the enrolment figures for Muslim children in Calcutta is 2.3 per cent. It is still less at the secondary level and in higher education, they constitute only 0.5 per cent of the total, in the city of Calcutta where Muslims form over 15 per cent of the total population. In the districts, the position is still worse as was brought out by a case study of a village in the Notified Minority District of South 24-Parganas in West Bengal. This case study was conducted in the village of Chandpur, Thana and Bishnupur, in the district of South 24-Parganas, roughly a one-hourdfive from Calcutta. It has an equal share of Hindus and Muslims, with three predominantly Muslim localities called Shaik para (having 83 houses), Mullick para (110 houses) and Tarafdar para (25 houses). There are 218 houses in all. The predominantly Hindu locality has 173 houses, with a total population consisting of around 3,000 people. The survey schedule was designed with the intention of seeking information on various socioeconomic para-meters. Sixty houses were selected, on the basis of simple random sampling. A door-to-door survey was conducted. From each household one working woman was interviewed with the help of an interview guide, and secondary data were collected from the lead bank of the area. This survey was confined to the minority Muslim community, placing special emphasis on the women of this community. The information thus collected clearly revealed that the emerging general scenario is one of poverty and deprivation.

In this study it was found that illiteracy was widely prevalent, with 87.6 per cent of the women in the age group of 25 years and above being illiterate—a proportion that is well below the national average and also that of the average literacy rate of West Bengal. The literacy rate amongst the female members is less than half that of males. As far as school education is concerned, the percentages are extremely low compared to those for West Bengal as a whole. Female children around ten years of age are promptly made to work at bidi binding. The major occupation of the Muslim women is bidi making. The standard of living of the households is extremely low. There is hardly any luxury item available. Even items like bicycles, transistors, chairs, sewing machines, etc., were rarely found. All were using traditional chuthas for cooking. A few households had stoves that were utilized at times, with the kerosene obtained from the Public Distribution System. None of them possessed any milch cattle, although eighteen of the fifty-eight families had animal assets like goats and poultry. It was observed that almost all families lived in small kuchcha huts. Eight out of fifty-eight families possessed an insignificant area of agricultural land failing under dry agricultural fanning conditions. Since most of the people were engaged in bidi making, which is a very ill-paid economic activity, their economic condition was very poor. This was reflected in the per capita monthly income of the families belonging to the minority community.

As per the government of India's criteria for poverty alleviation, a family of five is stated to be below the vert line if the annual family income is below Rs. 6,400, i.e., below Rs. 1110 per month. Going by this criteria it was observed that almost 85.4 per cent of the population belonging to this minority community lived well below the poverty line and under conditions of abject poverty. In particular, the condition of the women of this community was shocking. Illiteracy, lack of any productive skill and the unorganized character of their economic activity (*bidi binding*) renders them helpless and makes them an easy prey to the unscrupulous and exploitative practices of the middlemen.

The Directive Principles of State Policies under Article 39 of the Indian Constitution provide for equal pay for equal work irrespective of sex. Even the Equal Remuneration Act of 1976 provides for payment of equal wages to male and female workers for the same work, and prohibits any type of gender discrimination in the matter of either employment or wages. In the present case study it was found that not only were the wages paid to the women workers low, but women were also discriminated against vis-a-vis the male workers. Binding 1000 bidis fetches them Rs. 10 usually and occasionally Rs. 12 whereas in Calcutta city the going rate is Rs. 30 to Rs. 35 per thousand bidis. And again, compared to men, women get less remuneration for the same work. These (Muslim) women of the village are dependent on the *dalal* (middleman) for both the supply of the raw material as well as the sale of the end product.

Most of the women respondents were aware of the fact that they are being discriminated against and exploited by these middlemen, i.e., were allowing themselves to be exploited simply because of a lack of any alternative. They are caught in a vicious circle. They are illiterate, all they can sell is their labour, which is unskilled and hence of low productivity resulting in low remuneration. These poverty stricken, illiterate (Muslim) women of this village eke out a bare subsistence after putting in ten to twelve hours of hard labour everyday. They find neither the time nor the resources to approach various programme-implementing agencies, governmental or financial, to derive any benefit from them. They are so preoccupied in coping with the problems of day-to-day survival that the future does not enter into their calculations.

There are in fact many programmes exclusively meant for the upliftment of women, including some specific programmes for the minorities. But none of them have had any impact on the weaker sections of these Mush ' in women as has been revealed by this study. It is here that voluntary organizations can catalyse their development. They can bring these schemes and the deserving beneficiaries together. In Calcutta, there are a few voluntary organizations which are doing pioneering work for the economic upliftment of Muslims in general and Muslim women in particular. Mention must be made of the All Bengal Muslim Association, All India Council of Muslim Economic Upliftment (AICMEU) and Minority Upliftment Society (MUS), and the Muslim Welfare and Educational Trust. But they are urban-based, catering to educational advancement rather than economic development of the community.

For instance, the All Bengali Muslim Women's Association which is based in a typical Muslim dominated locality in Calcutta serves the needs of the local Muslim women. The objectives of this Association are to uplift the Muslim women educationally and economically, to organize its own craft and training-cum-production centres for poor women and to help them to attain self-sufficiency in daily necessities.

The role of Voluntary Organizations

This voluntary organization is able to provide subsidiary earnings to some deserving Muslim women through various economic activities. Sewing training is given free of cost. This voluntary agency is creating, albeit to a limited extent, the much needed awareness among women regarding the availability of channels for self-improvement. Many more such voluntary organizations should be established in Muslim concentrated areas.

The government of India should also provide support to voluntary agencies to strengthen the organizational side technically, by providing financial assistance for appointed technical personnel for programme planning and supervision. Therefore, minorities should be allowed to start their own cooperative urban banks. Such banks will also emotionally satisfy the various minorities, they will encourage thrift and self-help among them and induce them to take to industry and commerce rather than make them dependent on government jobs and other odd ad hoc assignments. Cottage industries should be esta-blished to provide gainful employment to this target group, i.e., the economically viable schemes should be brought to the door step of these people.

Voluntary organizations should strive to pressurize the authorities concerned to provide the necessary infrastructure like hastening the electrification of these villages, establishing training-cum-production centres, arranging for finance, etc., till their economic ventures become viable and self-sustaining. Voluntary organizations of all India character, which are engaged in the work of economic upliftment of women of the minority communities, should procure grants-in-aid. It is necessary to create sound voluntary organizations so that through their organizational pressure they can counteract the inadequacies of administration and opposition of the vested interests. They should help these women to make themselves eligible to claim as their fight the benefits that should accrue to them.

Zakat money can be tapped by these voluntary organizations. This money can be channelized for the financing of anti-poverty and self-employment schemes. The concept of paying *zakat* in a collective system should be encouraged. Since the receipt of interest is prohibited in Islam, interest free loans can be utilized for the economic development of the weaker sections of Muslim women.

Dissemination of information regarding various schemes available to them to improve their skills and eligibility should be provided. Sales and marketing centres should be established to provide outlets for the goods produced. These centres can be organized and run by Muslim women themselves on cooperative lines. Such centres will help in connecting the artisans with the consumers, retailers and wholesalers on more favourable terms.

The Muslim community, and especially its women, should realize that the economic development that is taking place in the country will not automatically result in their betterment. The community as such should make a concerted attempt at not only creating an awareness among its women but equipping them with better education and skills to make them eligible to grab the opportunities that are emerging as a result of the rapid economic development that is taking place in the country. There is a common belief that Muslims in India have not only remained largely unaffected by the economic development of the country but also that their general economic condition is becoming worse than before. The explanation may be that they are the victims of the discriminatory implementation of various schemes, resulting in the deprivation of the benefits to them. It may also be due to their conservative, social and cultural ethos and their tendency to remain aloof from the mainstream of national progress. The social attitude to work is one of the major reasons for their economic misery. In this regard it is interesting to note the response of the women covered by the village survey, to a question as to whether they would like to receive training in handicrafts.

On examining the sociopolitical reality today we see a dismal picture of communal tension and political aggregation in terms of narrow sectarian interests. The present Muslim Personal Laws are playing havoc in the lives of the Muslim women.

Divorce and the Qur'an

According to a precept of the Prophet, divorce is condemned as the most reprehensible of all things permitted. There is nothing more displeasing to God than divorce. The fight to absolve a marriage is given to the husband as well as the wife. Women have to observe *adat* for three months to ascertain paternity.

The Qur'an does not permit any outsider to separate a couple who want to live together even if one of them has a physical defect, though this can be a legitimate cause for divorce.

The Qur'an emphasizes that divorce should not be a hasty impulsive act but should be finalized only after a period of waiting during which time the couple is counselled and given a chance to rethink on the decision. They would either reconcile or separate after *iddah.* The procedure for the dissolution of marriage is entirely different for men and women. Husbands use *talaq,* wives take recourse to *Khula'.*

Talaq

It is a procedure that can be initiated by the husband alone without the consent of his wife. Besides, the exercise of *talaq* is extrajudicial and in no way subject to external check. Technically, therefore, the power of the husband to divorce is absolute.

Talaq may be pronounced in a number of ways, e.g., (1) *Ahsan* (2) *Hasan* (3) *Bid' ah.*

The *Ahsan* form of *talaq* is *Talaq*-i-*Sunna.* The repudiation does not take place at a single sitting nor can it take place during menstruation. *Iddah* is observed during the period following menstruation that is *tuhr* or the purity period. Two arbitrators from both sides are appointed to bring about reconciliation. During the *iddah* period the marriage is not dissolved. If reconciliation takes place, and the husband and wife have intercourse, the marriage is saved and no *nikah* is needed.

In *Ahsan talaq* even after the third pronouncement of *talaq,* after the *iddah* period, the marriage is revocable. The man can remarry his divorced wife. This practice is in accordance with the teaching of the Qur'an and according to *Sunna* rules. Both the Sunni and Shia schools approve of *talaq-a-ahsan.*

The *Hasan* form is *talaq-a-Sunna* but is not as commonly accepted as *talaq-a-ahsan.* The man is supposed to pronounce *talaq* during the successive periods of purity or *tuhr*. A couple can live together as husband and wife if the husband so desires before he pronounces the third *talaq*.

On the third *talaq* the marriage is dissolved and the *talaq* is irrevocable. Therefore, he cannot remarry her. If she wants to she has to perform *Halala*, i.e., marry another man, consummate the marriage and consequently validly dissolve it and only then remarry her divorced husband. This process of *Halala* is condemned by prophets and Caliph Ali. They narrate the message of Allah cursing the man who committed *Halala* and the one for whom *Halala* was committed.

There is some controversy over *Hasan Talaq*. One school of thought says, *Talaq* should be pronounced in three consecutive *tuhrs*, i.e., when the wife is not menstruating. This dissolves the marriage. Another school says, 'If a man pronounces *talaq* and reconciles and cohabits with his wife the *talaq* continues.' After two years if he pronounces *talaq* and again cohabits, this becomes the second *talaq*. If he pronounces *talaq* a third time this will be the final *talaq*. The wife loses her rights of inheritance with the pronouncement of *talaq*.

Talaq-a-Hasan has been approved of by all Shia and Sunni schools of thought. Since it is not irrevocable it is not very popular; yet, the Hanbali Sunni school gives it more importance than to other types of *talaq*

Talaq-a-Bid' ah is a form of divorce which is severely criticized since it goes against the rules laid down by the Qur'an. However, it is approved of by the *Sunna*. In this form of *talaq* the husband unilaterally, without the consent or knowledge of the wife, pronounces *talaq*.

Talaq is pronounced once or three times simultaneously whether the wife is in a state of *tuhr* or not. This form of divorce was clearly not approved of by the Prophet. It was Caliph Umar who legitimized this. Caliph Umar seemed to be rather than permissive about this type of *talaq.* Yet, he held it permissible to impose certain restrictions on loose tendencies relating to divorce which had crept in during his regime. 'Umar's object in making three pronouncements of *talaq,* on one occasion effective, was to warn the man that he would have to take the evil consequences of following an un-Islamic practice, but the result was contrary to what Umar intended. It became a general practice to pronounce divorce thrice on one occasion. Thus, a revocable divorce was transformed into an irrevocable one. If a man wanted to remarry his wife, she had to perform a *Halala* marriage.

A rule, originally meant to punish a man, is today used against women. This *bid'ah* form of *talaq* is not accepted by the Shia schools. It is sanctioned by the *Hanafi* Sunni school. It is authentically reported by Ibn Qayyim that Caliph Umar regretted having allowed it even as an emergency measure. Today this form of *talaq* is used in India and only in some of the Arab countries.

Khula

The Qur'an, however, was the first to allow women the privilege of seeking divorce earlier denied by the primitive society of the Arabs. When *Khula'* is sought by a woman, her husband is given compensation to release her from the marriage tie. *Khula'* is irrevocable. There are indications that wives have enjoyed the right to *Khula'* even when their husbands did not agree to it. Many stories during the Prophet's lifetime revealed that marriages were dissolved because of incompatibility or any other reason and the men did not object since *Khula'* did not displease God. In *talaq* a man has to give mehr.

In *Khula'* a woman has to forgo her mehr and sometimes pay for her freedom. If the husband agrees to a divorce, then no school permits the Qazi to give women the right to *Khula'*. According to Islam separation by *Khula'* is not the worst form of divorce since great importance is placed on the happiness of a couple living together and it does not approve of two people living together merely to keep up the facade of marriage.

The newly enacted laws in several Muslim countries enforce this Quranic recommendation, contradicting what is prevalent in Pakistan and other countries where the freedom to divorce is not given equally to both the sexes. According to *Hanafi* law, no single word is necessary to effectuate *Khula'*.

Mubarat

Mubarat may be initiated by either the husband or the wife, but once it is accepted the dissolution is complete. Where the desire for separation is mutual, the law requires a woman to offer her husband compensation, after which the *Mubarat* is effective.

Dissolution of marriage by the couple jointly can be extrajudicial on terms that may be mutually agreed upon. Unlike *Khula'* or *talaq* which does not require the consent of either husband or wife, *Mubarat* is a divorce which both the husband and wife may equally agree upon. *Mubarat* is accepted by both the Sunni and Shia schools and neither objects to court injunction.

Talaq-a-tafwiz

Tafwiz is when a woman has a right to pronounce *talaq* if her husband has delegated that right to her. In Islam, marriage is a contract between two parties. The husband in the *nikahama* gives it in writing that if he commits polygamy or if his wife cannot get along with him, she has the right to *Khula*'. This is accepted by both the Shia and Sunni schools.

Faskh

Dissolution by judicial decree can be sought by either the husband or the wife. In practice, where unilateral *talaq* is permitted, it is only the wife who seeks this judicial decree. The grievances of a woman seeking separation by judicial decree may be considered:

1. *Than* or charging the wife with adultery.
2. *Ila* or taking a vow of abstinence for four months.
3. *Zihar* or comparing the wife to any of die-female relations within the prohibited degree.
4. Defect in her spouse.
5. Failure to observe marital obligation.

All the schools of thought sanction *Faskh*, except that minor details regarding each charge vary,

The Muslim divorce law in India

The existing divorce laws in India are:

1) Dissolution of the Muslim Marriage Act, 1939
2) The Muslim *Shari'a* Application Act 1939
3) Various customs and usages indicated by the *Shari 'a* which are not wholly divine and uniform —jurists used their own judgement for the compilation of the *Shari 'a* in the light of varying geographical, social and temporal conditions.

Thus, all schools of Islamic law do approve of *talaq-a-bid'ah*. The *Shari' a* laws existing in India are not totally divine. What exists in India as Muslim Personal Law is Anglo-British Law. These uncodified practices were unconsciously justified by the Maulavis to suit the interests of the British. After Independence, several books on Muslim law have misinterpreted this, permitting the practice of extrajudicial divorce in Islam. They have failed to distinguish between the general guidelines for spouses in the matter of divorce and the legal requirements for a divorce. This has complicated and to a certain extent also distorted the Muslim divorce law. This complicated, and partially distorted law, has unfortunately been recognized by the Indian judiciary. Now the husband does not have to go to court to get a divorce and the divorced wife cannot challenge the unilateral divorce which is accepted by the law. Thus, the male sex is favoured.

1. Among the *Hanafis*, who constitute nearly eighty per cent of the Indian Muslims, *talaq*-a-*ahsan*, *talaq*-a- *hasan* and *talaq-a-bid'ah* are the most favoured. But among twenty per cent Ishna Asheris, Bohras, Khojas, etc., *talaq-a-bid'ah* is not permitted. Here, too, it is not necessary to go to court to obtain a divorce. The dissolution of marriage takes place only when the 3 months of *iddah* in the respective Jamats, is over.
2. Among the Sunni and Shia schools a man, who is not insane or problems of Muslim Women in India below the age of puberty, is free to divorce his wife whenever he wants to without giving any reason.
3. A man need not pronounce *talaq* in the presence of his wife and need not give her notice. After pronouncing *talaq* (if he has more than one wife) he is expected to name her. Unlike the Ishna Asheris, the Bohras and Ismaili Jamats have set up councils to attempt to bring both husband and wife together before the final decision is made. However, if she refuses to come, the man can give her *talaq*
4. *Talaq*-a-*ahsan* is *talaq* accepted by orthodox Sunni and Shia schools. The Hali Memon Jamat of Bombay discourage their members from observing *Talaq-a-bid' ah.*

5. If a woman has not gone through her menopause, *talaq* should not be pronounced during her menstruation. However, the *Hanafi* school which accepts *talaq-a-bid'ah* does not attribute any importance to menstruation.
6. Among the *Hanafi*, *talaq* pronounced in anger in one sitting is valid and irrevocable.
7. The presence of two witnesses is an essential prerequisite for a Shia divorce to take place whereas for *Sunnis* it is not so.
8. *Talaq* can be pronounced by the husband by either uttering the word *talaq* or by saying words which by implication mean *talaq*
9. In the case of *talaq* which is revocable by law (raji), no revocation is possible after the expiry of *iddah.*
10. Among *Sunnis* and Shias *talaq* is valid even when pronounced while a man is intoxicated.
11. Shias insist on a written *talaq*nama in Arabic though this is not absolutely necessary among *Sunnis.*
12. Among the Shias, if a man writes a *talaq*nama and sends it to his wife during the period of *iddah* and also dies within the *iddah* period, the woman remains his lawful wife since the *talaq*nama is merely a record of the first *talaq* and therefore the marriage is not dissolved.

Though women enjoy the right to *Khula*, there is no such legal sanction in India. In Pakistan and Bangladesh the law of *Khula* has been enforced as a result of Supreme Court decisions. *Khula* is not permitted among the Sunni nor the Ishna Asheris without court interference. The Bohras and the Ismailis try and intervene in order to keep control over their Jamat members. If the woman wants a separation she has to obtain the consent of her husband and pay him compensation to set herself fire. If he disagrees she has to wait till he agrees. Indian courts do recognize the woman's right to *talaq*-a-*tafwiz.* Here the right to dissolve the marriage is handed over in writing by a man to his wife at the time of the *nikah* ceremony. This fight is enjoyed by a few Sulemani Bohras (Khandaris) who follow the *nikahanama* drafted by Danial Latifi.

Among Muslims in India, divorce by mutual consent is possible but a woman has to give her husband something to free herself. This practice is generally encouraged by Dawoodi Bohras. For Muslim women in India there is no way of dissolving a marriage other than by getting legal permission from court. According to the Dissolution of Muslim Marriage Act of 1939, the judicial decree of *Faskh* permits Muslim women to obtain a divorce on seven grounds.

1) The whereabouts of the husband are not known for a period of four years. In a suit filed on this ground, the husband's immediate relatives have to be given notice, and they have a fight to be heard. A decree passed on this ground will not come into effect for a period of six months. If the husband appears within this period the decree will not be valid.
2) The husband's neglect or failure to provide the basic necessities to his wife.
3) The husband being sentenced to imprisonment for a period of seven years or more.
4) The husband's failure, without reasonable cause, to perform his marital obligations for a period of three or more years.
5) The husband being impotent at the time of marriage and continuing to be so when the suit was filed.
6) The husband's insanity for at least two years or his

suffering from leprosy or some virulent venereal disease.

7) The exercise of the right of 'repudiation' of a marriage by the wife.

Besides these rights, the court is also empowered to dissolve a marriage on any other ground recognized as valid for the dissolution of marriage under the Muslim Law. It is significant to note, however, that before partition, in Lahore, the court refused *Faskh* to a wife if she was incompatible with her husband. Prophet Mohammed had permitted the women to divorce. It is clear from the above study of the divorce laws in India that women who are given the privilege of seeking divorce are at every stage at the mercy of their husbands. The existing law is an Indo-Anglican judicial parody which is unfair to women and needs to be altered drastically. India is the only country in the world which has not brought about changes in the existing Muslim Personal Law.

Divorce Laws Practised in Other Countries

In Egypt, Sudan, Jordan, Syria, Lebanon, Morocco and Iraq the laws are the same as those followed in India. *Talaq-a-bid'ah* is permitted, but restrictions have been put upon *talaq* pronounced while a man is intoxicated. Other Muslim countries such as Pakistan, Bangladesh, Malaysia, etc., have imposed a court injunction against the husband pronouncing *talaq*. Thus, *talaq-a-bid'ah* is not permitted.

In Turkey, all cases of divorce are resolved by the Family Marriage Divorce Act of 1951, and in Cyprus by the Cyprus Civil Code of 1926. In both countries unilateral divorce is disapproved of and court intervention is necessary.

In Tunisia where the Iranian Family Protection Law of 1967 is in force, both the husband and wife are given the right to approach the court of law. In Tunisia and Algeria, divorce on grounds of mutual agreement (*Mubarat*) is allowed. 16 In Algeria the Marriage Ordinance of 1959 does not dissolve a marriage by unilateral divorce. A court decree is necessary.

In Jordan, according to the law of family rights of 1951, unilateral divorce is permissible, giving a women the right to *Khula'*. When a woman applies for *Khula'* the court a, joints arbitrators to attempt to bring about a reconciliation. If the court fails to succeed in reuniting the couple then it permits *Khula'* to the wife.

The Syrian Law of Personal Status of 1950 authorized a woman to stipulate the right to unilateral divorce at the time of her marriage. Thus, the divorce form, *talaq*-a-*tafwiz*, which prevents bigamy, is allowed.

The Iranian Family Protection Law of 1967, does not grant a man the right to unilateral divorce or to repudiate his wife without judicial intervention. The court appoints arbitrators to bring about reconciliation, failing which a certificate of impossible reconciliation is issued by the court and then divorce takes place.

According to the Iraqi Law of Personal Status of 1959, an arbitrator is appointed by the court for reconciliation. However, if arbitration fails, divorce is finalized.'

In Pakistan, the Family Law Ordinance of 1961, does not permit unilateral divorce. A man wanting to dissolve his marriage has to issue notice. The divorce is only effective after ninety days, if the arbitration by the council fails to bring about reconciliation. *Khula'* is permissible even if the husband does not give his consent.

The Family Law Ordinance of 1961 curtails the right to unilateral divorce in Bangladesh. According to the Dissolution of Marriage Act of 1939, women are permitted *Khula'* depending on the decision of the court." Recently the Marriage and Divorce Registration Act of 1979 was introduced.

In Sri Lanka according to the Muslim Marriage and Divorce Act of 1951, the husband is still permitted to pronounce unilateral divorce. Divorce is effective only after a lapse of three lunar months. Within this period the Qazi, residing in the wife's natal family area, tries to bring about reconciliation. *Khula'* is permitted to a woman when she is able to prove the fault of her husband in the presence of two witnesses. Grounds such as insanity, impotency, leprosy and inability to maintain the wife financially are accepted. Incompatibility and polygamy are not accepted as adequate grounds for *Khula'*.

In Malaysia, Borneo and Singapore according to the Family Law of 1955 when a man or a woman wants a divorce, the court appoints two arbitrators, one from either side, to bring about reconciliation. If the arbitrators fail to reunite the couple, divorce follows. In Singapore, the Muslim Ordinance of 1957 insists on registration of divorce by the *Shari'a* court and the couple has to attend counselling sessions before divorce.

Unilateral divorce is not permitted to the husband in Indonesia. A man and woman have the same right to apply for divorce in the court of law.

Islam claimed to be a universal religion, intended for all times. It emerged as a practical religion and must continue to aid each of its followers, irrespective of race, nationality, language and gender. If we study the social, political, cultural and economic life of the early followers of Islam, we find that Islam adopted various customs, traditions and laws of the people of Hijaz and Najd. It tried to refine those laws and customs without disrupting the sociopolitical organization of the community.

Thus, for instance, the limitation of four wives for a man was a revolutionary step in the days when it was common to take hundreds of women and concubines. Several other customs and practices adopted by Islam were also common to the semitic races and even African tribes.

In a male-dominated society, where women were thought of as chattel, and female infanticide was normal, it was but natural that the rights of divorce were given to men alone. The Prophet had to adapt to the moods of the patriarchal society around him. But, He proclaimed two basic tenets of His religion to be the unit of God and the finality of His Prophet hood. He announced to the world that the religion that he was bringing was not a rigid, unchanging and inflexible one.

Apart from the fundamental beliefs, every Islamic custom or law has to march with the times. And that is what Islam means—peace. If a society is to remain peaceful, law-abiding and nonviolent, then the law it formulates has got to fulfil the needs, and aspirations of every generation. In the last fourteen hundred years of 'Islam, wherever Muslims have marched with the times, they have progressed.

On the other hand, static societies, whether Muslim or non Muslim, have remained backward. It is evident from fundamentalist societies like those of Saudi Arabia and Iran, where women are cloistered behind their veils, that progress has been slow despite the outward facades of modernity.

In contrast, progress has been phenomenal in Turkey, Malaysia, Indonesia, Syria, Egypt and the nations of the Arab 'Maghrab'. Women in each of these countries are no longer the victims of tradition. Therefore, the denial of complete equality to the women of Islam, in all spheres and in all matters, cannot be Islamic.

The subject of Divorce, Marriage and Charity is dealt with in the second *Sipara* (*Saiquool*) of the Quran. The great detail in which this topic is dealt with clearly underlines the divine intention.

The commandment in the 231st *Aaydt,* continues the discourse on *iddah* and enjoins men to offer equitable terms to women. 'Do not treat God's signs in jest, but solemnly rehearse God's favours on you and the fact that He sent down to you the Book of Wisdom for your instruction. Then again, important topics such as Women's and Orphans' Rights, Inheritance, Marriage and Dower are dealt with in *Surat-un-Nisa*'.

One must remember that the *inzal* of this *Aayat* is post-*Uhad.* The unrestricted number of wives of pre-Islamic times is now restricted strictly to a maximum of four, provided each wife is treated with perfect equality in every way. This strict and almost unrealistic condition prevents a man from having more than one wife. Principles of equality, justice, fair play and good conscience in the distribution of intestate properly are propounded in the *Aayats* in great detail. This makes it imperative that the dictates and ordinances of the Quran are not misinterpreted. The Quran admits of the widest possible interpretations as to what is just and proper at a particular period of time.

The Quran says that the Jews, Sabians, Christians, and all those who believe in God and the Last Day and lead a righteous life should have no fear, nor shall they grieve. This *Aayat* occurs after the Muslims are repeatedly admonished for making alliances with the nonbelievers and after the Jews and Christians are imprecated for their rebellions against God and the ill-treatment and crucifixion of their apostles and holy men. Significantly, in the subsequent *Aayats* the blasphemy of the Jews and Christians is mentioned again—the Jews for calling their apostles impostors, and the Christians for calling Christ God—instead of Son of Mary, and also including God as one of the Trinity.

Therefore the notion that is assiduously sought to be inculcated in the minds of the Bohras, that we are the only chosen people entitled to ascend to heaven, is contrary to the injunctions of the Quran. On interpreting and reinterpreting Islam in the light of Quranic injunctions, one cannot but arrive at the conclusion that the hardships suffered by Muslim women, particularly in the matter of divorce, have no basis whatsoever in Islamic theology, jurisprudence or secular law. With due respect, we disagree with the views of the learned judges in 209 IC 248, that the Act VIII of 1939, i.e., The Dissolution of Muslim Marriages Act merely codified in Section 2, the Principles of Mohammedan law pertaining to divorce. The law contained in Section 2 of the Act merely states the grounds under which a Muslim woman can obtain a decree for divorce. It leaves untouched the right given to the husband only to dissolve the contract of marriage at his will, without the intervention of a court and without assigning any reason whatsoever.

The sufferings of Muslim women, particularly the poorer sections, on account of this Draconian Law is well known. Moreover, litigation is so expensive and justice in our courts of law so dilatory, that it is almost impossible for over sixty million Muslim women of India to get any redressal on account of cruelty, or neglect. In our opinion the simplest way to remedy the,situation will be to enact a law whereby a Muslim contract of marriage, performed by any *Qazi* or *Mulla*, should be made compulsorily registrable. And in the marriage contract itself a *talaq* should be made operative, contingent upon cruelty or neglect by the husband. In addition, the divorce must be made effective by the wife giving a registered notice in writing to her husband that he is guilty of cruelty or neglect and that she wants to have the marriage dissolved. Court intervention should not be necessary, as is the case when the husband pronounces *talaq*.

All growth and progress is achieved by creative elite minorities which bring about a new way of life, either by the masses of people undergoing the actual experiences of the creative elite or by Mimesis which has been the only alternative route for progress for an overwhelming majority of the world's population. The inspirational idols of one age invariably become the tokens of liability in another.

During the last several decades the proportion of Muslims in India's population has been steadily increasing while the proportion of Hindus has been steadily failing. Taking the subcontinent as a whole the Muslim share increased from 20 per cent in 1881 to 24 per cent. The growth rate has also been consistently higher for Muslims in all intercensal decades.

The average annual geometric growth fate for Muslims in undivided India showed no consistent trend but it was always higher than for 'all religions' or Hindus. In the post-partition period, although the growth rate for Muslims was higher than that for all religions or Hindus, it showed a declining trend over time.

Higher growth rate of Muslims in the past might probably have been due to conversion but since the conversion of non-Muslims to Islam has been rare in recent times, the observed difference between Muslims and other religious groups must be sought in terms of differences in the components of population growth, viz., fertility, mortality and migration.

In modem India, the volume of international migration is not significant, although illegal migration across the border may affect the population growth rates in some selected states. So the observed differences in growth rates between Muslims and Hindus are to be explained in terms of differences in mortality and fertility. The available evidence seems to suggest that whatever may be the differences in mortality between Muslims and Hindus, they are not so great as to account for the differential growth rate between them. Therefore, one must explain the difference in growth rate in terms of differences in fertility between Muslims and Hindus.

Davis examined Hindu-Muslim fertility differentials for the period 1891-1941 using child-woman ratio as an index of fertility based on census data. This study revealed that Muslims had shown higher fertility than Hindus. Davis attributed this to higher widow remarriage, higher marital fertility and a slightly lower infant mortality among Muslims. No information on fertility was obtained from the 1951 and 1961 censuses. From the 1971 census onwards, fertility data were obtained from all currently married women.

The fertility data obtained from the 1971 and 1981 censuses suffer from various types of reporting errors and the quality of data is far from satisfactory. However, assuming that the quality of data in reporting births is the same for all religious groups, the census data of 1971 and 1981 showed that Muslims exhibited higher fertility than other religious groups. In 1971 Muslim fertility exceeded Hindu fertility by 11 per cent in rural areas total marital fertility rate (TMFR for Muslims 6.26 and for Hindus 5.63] and by 20 percent in urban areas (TMFR for Muslims 5.63 and for Hindus 4.70). The 1981 census also showed that Muslims exhibited higher fertility than Hindus and other minority religious groups.

In rural areas, TMFR was higher for Muslims by 16 per cent (Muslims 5. 1; Hindus 4.4). In urban areas TMFR was higher by 25 per cent (Muslims 4.5; Hindus

3.6) (RG, 1983). It is important to note that although Muslim fertility was higher as compared to Hindus, a decline in fertility of Muslims has been noticed during 1971-81.

A number of fertility surveys were conducted in different parts of the country from 1950. A review of these studies reveals that the religious differences in fertility were found to be rather weak in the 1950s and early 1960s and that Muslims' fertility was not significantly different from that of other religious groups. In fact these studies showed that socioeconomic differentials in fertility were rather weak and that none of the socioeconomic variables had a significant effect on fertility.

Emergence of socioeconomic differentials including religious differentials in fertility in recent periods is a consequence of the decline in fertility that occurred in India from the 1970s. The pace of fertility decline seems to be relatively slow among Muslims as compared to Hindus. Among several proximate variables of fertility, nuptiality and contraception are most important. Contraception has an impact on the fertility of married women whereas nuptiality has impact on the fertility of all women.Socioeconomic factors such as education, income and the status of woman affect fertility via such proximate factors as nuptiality and contraception.

The age at which women many, and the cultural factors governing marriage patterns are important factors affecting reproductive behaviour. The practice of polygyny is rare among Muslims and there is no evidence to show that the percentage of polygynous marriages is significantly higher among Muslims than among other religious groups. Available evidence indicates that during the intercensal periods 1931-41, 1941-51 and 1951-61, the percentages of polygynous marriages among Hindus were 6.79, 7.15 and 5.06 and the corresponding figures for

Muslims were 7.29, 7.06, 4.31 respectively. Among tribals the percentages were 9.53, 17.53 and 17.98. The incidence of polygynous marriages had been declining among Muslims and Hindus. A survey was conducted by the census authorities in 1961 on a sample of nearly one lakh marriages. Among these 5,911 marriages were found to be polygynous.

The incidence of polygynous marriages was found to be the highest among the tribal communities (15.25 per cent) followed by Buddhists (7.97 per cent), Jains (6.72 per cent), Hindus (5.8 per cent) and Muslims (5.7 per cent). It should, however, be kept in mind that these figures have to be interpreted cautiously in view of the fact that census data are subject to reporting errors. In the selection of second wives, Muslim men preferred relatively older women; this would have its due effect on reproductive achievements of their second wives.

On the other hand, Hindu polygynists were noted to prefer very young wives below 15 years in age in both first and second marriages, relatively more strongly than the Muslims. In comparison to the Hindu polygynists the Muslim males with first wives only maintained the highest average of children born alive, but with second wives, they yielded the lower average.

The Hindu, polygynists produced through their second wives distinctly more live births on the average than their Muslim counterparts. Polygynous form of mating does not appear to be an essential prerequisite to invest the distinction of 'superior fertility' with Muslims of India. Child and adolescent marriages are prevalent among Muslims but less so than among Hindus. Divorce, and remarriage of widows and divorcees, do take place, but the extent is not known.

The marriage patterns of Muslims and Hindus are similar except for polyandry and sororate. The similarity arises because the majority of Indian Muslims are descendants of converts to Islam and their ethnicity is mainly Indian. In the past, converted Indian Muslims adopted many of the social customs and nuptiality practices of the Hindus.

According to the census data of 1971 and 1981 the age at marriage did' not differ much between Muslim and Hindu women. So also the proportion of currently married women in reproductive ages did not differ much between Muslim and Hindu women. Contraceptive practice is an important intermediate variable affecting fertility. It is found that the observed variation in fertility levels in human populations is largely explained by the level of contraceptive practice.

It is often alleged that Islam does not approve of the use of modem methods of contraception. But it is necessary to examine Islam's position on family planning and Muslims' attitudes to family planning on the basis of available empirical evidence, before making any general statements regarding Islam and family planning. A review of Islamic literature reveals that Islam is not against family planning. The opinion of different scholars supports this position. Islam is a rational religion.

In all matters it adopts the middle course which we may call the golden mean. In matters of procreation also, there appears to be no objection in Islam to adopt the middle course without going into the extremes of unrestricted multiplication of children or nullification of procreation.

The spacing of child birth as mentioned under birth control in family planning programmes appears to be quite justified and according to the spirit of Islam. To increase population is no religious service at all if material resources are few. To produce children who cannot be trained in the temporal and religious sciences is an unforgivable crime in the eyes of religion, morality and common sense.

A review of empirical studies to find out the contemporary Muslim attitudes, knowledge and practice of family planning reveals the following: Data from the NSS 16th round on urban couples reveal that attitudes were slightly less favourable, knowledge and practice of family planning were slightly lower among Muslims.

The Operations Research Group (ORG) conducted three national surveys on family planning practices in India, first in 1970-71, then in 1980-81, and later, in 1988. Data on the practice of family planning and attitudes towards it, among different religion groups were also collected in these surveys. These data reveal that attitudes of Muslims to family planning were less favourable and family planning practice was lower than for Hindus. Over time, disapproval has declined and family planning practice too has increased, among both communities. But this decrease in disapproval and increase in family planing practice has been less for Muslims.

It is observed that, compared to Hindus, Muslims favour spacing methods rather than sterilization. Data on sterilization and the use of intrauterine device (IUD) for India, taken from official sources from 1968-69 to 1979-80, show that the use of family planning methods was less among Muslims.

Terminal methods have been less popular and spacing methods more popular among Muslims. The acceptance rates per 1000 currently married women show that for India and all the major states, the acceptance rates of sterilization are lower and in a few states rates of IUD use are higher for Muslims. In those states where sterilization rates are higher for Hindus, they are also higher for Muslims. The difference in acceptance rates between Muslims and Hindus is lower for IUD use than for sterilization.

Findings from local surveys regarding knowledge awareness and practice of family planning are in general consistent with these observations at the national level. A substantial percentage of Muslims in India seem to undergo abortion.

Compared to Muslims in most other countries, Muslims in India have relatively higher sterilization and abortion rates. Interspouse communication, education and socioeconomic status are some of the factors that account for differences in family planning practices between Muslims and Hindus. It seems that interspouse communication is weaker and male dominance greater among Muslims.

Though overall contraceptive practice is lower, it increases with the level of education. Socioeconomic status and the use of family planning are found to be positively correlated. Low educational level, low socioeconomic status and low status of women, besides some degree of opposition on the grounds of religion, are the main factors that account for lower acceptance of family planning by Muslims in India.

Therefore some of the studies have suggested that the cooperation of Muslim religious leaders should be sought in propagating the family planning message, spacing methods should be popularized and general welfare programmes to raise the socioeconomic status of Muslims, should be undertaken. Though the acceptance of family planning is low among Muslims, the resistance to family planning on grounds of religion is declining among the younger generation of Muslims. With the increase in education of women and improvement in the socioeconomic status, contraceptive practice among Muslims is expected to increase.

The characteristic hypothesis maintains that the differences in fertility between religious groups are explained in terms of differences in socioeconomic conditions among religious groups. According to this view, the socioeconomic backwardness of Muslims is one of the main factors accounting for their higher fertility. We do not have sufficient data at the national level to examine the relative socioeconomic conditions of Muslims as compared to other religious groups.

Even the census of India do not give any information on religious differences in literacy and educational attainment. But there, is fragmentary evidence to support the contention that Muslims are relatively more socially and economically backward than other communities. 'There is no denying that they have been at the lowest rung of the ladder in terms of the basic categories of the socioeconomic indicators of development'.

About two-thirds of the Muslims in India live in the rural areas and are small/marginal farmers or self-employed artisans. Of the remaining one-third who live in the towns, roughly 80 to 85 per cent are skilled workers, tailors, retailers, petty businessmen, small manufacturers or are engaged in traditional industries like bidi-making, perfumery, block-making, etc.

Thus, more than 90 per cent of Muslims are small and marginal farmers, artisans and workers. The occupational structure of Muslims makes them poor. Their educational backwardness and lack of modem skills do not allow them to enter high-income occupations.

In modem industry and trade, except for rare instances, Muslims have not owned large-scale industry or business and generally lack high entrepreneurial traits. There is not a single Muslim house among the top fifty industrial groups in the country, while at the lower end of the scale, most Muslims are poor and backward. To a large extent Muslims lag behind other religious communities in education.

In an all-India survey of Muslim managed schools (430) and degree colleges (44) undertaken by Hamdard Education Society in the early 1980s, it was observed that the percentage of Muslim students decreased while that of non-Muslim students increased with the level of education. A widening gap in the proportion of Muslim male and female students was also observed.

In a national survey on socioeconomic conditions of Muslims in India, it was found that in all categories from non-literate upto university and higher and technical levels, Muslims lagged much behind non-Muslims. The dropout rate of Muslim students is significantly higher than that of non-Muslims with the result that the number of Muslim students as a percentage of the total number of students keeps on declining as the level of education goes up. At the high school and intermediate level the percentage of Muslim students is roughly one-third to one fourth of what it should be according to their population.

In the year 1981, only 3 per cent of IAS officers were Muslims. In the same year, only 2.9 per cent of all the UPS officers in the country were Muslims. About 3.1 per cent of income-tax officers recruited during the period 1971-80 were Muslims. For the same period, of the officers recruited to Railway Traffic and Accounts Service, only 2.7 per cent were Muslims. In banks, the Muslim officers formed only 2.2 per cent of the work force. In central and state government offices, the percentages of Muslim employees were 4.4 and 6.0 respectively which is slightly higher than the figures given above. The percentage of Muslims in public sector undertakings is still higher at 10.8. Compared to the rest of the population, these figures reveal that Muslim representation in government jobs is poor and it is only in public sector undertakings that their share comes nearer to their proportion in the population of the country.

Data on income by religious groups at national level are not available. But some surveys have found that compared to non-Muslims, poverty levels are higher among Muslims. The benefits of various government schemes, aimed at improving the lot of the weaker sections, have not accrued to Muslims. Of the houses allotted by state governments to lower and middle income groups only 2.9 per cent were allotted to them. Of the licences issued for fair price shops, only 6.9 per cent were awarded to them. Finally, Muslims received only 0.2 per cent of the tangible benefits extended to artisans by the Khadi and Village Industries Commission. In the cooperative sector too, Muslims do not fare well. Of the loans advanced by financial institutions only 3 per cent of those between Rs. 50,000 and Rs. one lakh was given to Muslims. Of loans between Rs. one lakh and Rs. two lakh, less than 2 per cent was received by Muslims. For loans between two lakh and 10 lakh the figure was under 1 per cent. Thus, economically too, Muslims seem to be more backward.

The status of women is an important determinant of fertility level. Worldwide data reveal that high fertility prevails in areas where the status of women is low and low fertility exists in areas where the status of women is high. Revisions of the theory of the demographic transition have taken into account the fact that the rising status of women can generally be an effective spur to economic development and growth, partly by generating motivation for smaller families.

Women tend to gain status by engaging in activities formerly reserved for men—especially obtaining an education, engaging in non-agricultural labour force activities, and becoming involved in social and political organizations. These activities generally compete with child bearing and child rearing, and the motivation to limit family size becomes well entrenched, even though pronatalist pressures continue everywhere to encourage having children.

An improvement in the status of women does not depend upon economic development, though that often helps; nor is it typically an individual option in the absence of a broad-based social consensus. It comes about as a result of concerted collective effort within a community. The status of Muslim women has at least in theory been superior to that of women belonging to other communities. However, in practice, due to assimilation of Hindu thought and practices, her status has been similar to that of a Hindu woman. The assimilation is due to two factors: first, most of the Indian Muslims are descendants of converts from Hinduism, and secondly, they live amongst a large society of Hindus.

Among Indian Muslim women, divorce is a rarity. 'Evidence provided... indicates that divorce is disapproved of socially among most groups and results in loss of social prestige not only for the parties involved, but for the families as well and is consequently an occurrence of considerable rarity.'

Indian Muslim women are not in favour of exercising the freedom given to them fourteen centuries ago. The Hindu high caste concept of endurance as the highest virtue of a woman has so completely overtaken the minds of the Muslim women that they would rather die than obtain a divorce. They have also imbibed the Hindu ideal of lifelong association with one man only. So even if the husband is incompatible or marries for the second time, and the wife has the right to seek a divorce, she will normally not do so.

Often, Muslim women in India are not allowed to enjoy their right to inheritance, and even when they receive a share, only a pittiance is given to them. For instance, Kokni women do not inherit landed property. Gujar Bakarwal women too do not inherit pastoral lands in Uttar Pradesh too, sisters are forced to surrender their right to inherit in favour of their brothers. Under the influence of Hinduism the practice of claiming mehr (dower) from the husband, has become an act of disgrace and when a claim is made it is restricted to a paltry amount.

Ironically, Indian Muslims have incorporated the pernicious Hindu custom of dowry in their marriages. Today, the Muslim woman has a low status mainly due to her low educational level, consequent low participation in economic and social activities, and observance of purdah. In a stratified survey of Muslim women conducted in nine major cities, Muslim women invariably reported that education and employment were their major problems.

Index